GROUP RELATIONS CONFERENCES

GROUP RELATIONS CONFERENCES

Tradition, Creativity, and Succession in the Global Group Relations Network

Volume III

Edited by

Eliat Aram, Robert Baxter, and Avi Nutkevitch

Routledge
Taylor & Francis Group
LONDON AND NEW YORK

First published 2012 by Karnac Books Ltd.

Published 2018 by Routledge
2 Park Square, Milton Park, Abingdon, Oxon OX14 4RN
711 Third Avenue, New York, NY 10017, USA

Routledge is an imprint of the Taylor & Francis Group, an informa business

British Library Cataloguing in Publication Data

A C.I.P. for this book is available from the British Library

ISBN-13: 9781780490014 (pbk)

Typeset by V Publishing Solutions Pvt. Ltd., Chennai, India

This book is dedicated in loving memory to Anne-Marie Kirkpatrick

CONTENTS

ABOUT THE EDITORS AND CONTRIBUTORS

Editors

Eliat Aram, PhD, is the CEO of the Tavistock Institute of Human Relations. She is a Chartered Scientist psychologist (BPS) and a UKCP registered gestalt psychotherapist and supervisor. She is a member of the Royal Society of Medicine in the UK and of OFEK in Israel. When she is not busy overseeing the daily activities of the Institute, thinking about its future, strategising, and nurturing its cutting-edge profile, she works with other "agents of learning". She is informed by concepts of emergence and self-organisation as well as power dynamics and dialogue including developing skills and attitudes for working in conditions of uncertainty and ambiguity. She helps, supports, and challenges change and learning agents through their journey of growth by inviting them to think about and reflect upon their flow of experience as leaders in their organisations. She is regularly on staff of group relations conferences nationally and internationally. Since 2007 she has directed and made innovations to the TIHR's Leicester conference—*Authority, Role, Organisation*—the Institute's annual two-week group relations experiential learning conference.

Robert Baxter, MD, is a retired professor of psychiatry at the University of Louisville where he was Director of the Division of Child and Adolescent Psychiatry and Executive Director of the Bingham Child Guidance Center. He is a fellow of the American Psychiatric Association and the A. K. Rice Institute for the Study of Social Systems. He formerly served on AKRI's board of directors and was its president for eight years. He also directed AKRI's national conference for four years and chaired AKRI's training and certification committee for several years. He now divides his time between Bonita Springs, Florida, and Santa Fe, New Mexico.

Avi Nutkevitch, PhD, is a clinical psychologist, training analyst, and organisational consultant. He is a full member of the Israel Psychoanalytic Society and teaches at the Israel Psychoanalytic Institute and other postgraduate programmes for psychotherapy. He is a founding member and former chair of OFEK, the Israel Association for the Study of Group and Organizational Processes. He is currently co-director and faculty of the Programme in Organizational Consultation and Development: a Psychoanalytic-Systemic Approach. He holds a senior teaching position on the MBA programme of the College of Management in Rishon Le'Tzion.

Contributors

Daphna Bahat, MA, is a senior clinical psychologist, supervisor, and organisational consultant. She works with groups and individuals for the empowerment of women through belly dancing. She is a member and former board member of OFEK, the Israeli Association for the Study of Group and Organizational Processes, where her roles included treasurer of the organisation and head of the marketing committee.

Siv Boalt Boëthius, PhD, is professor (emerita) at Stockholm University, a psychoanalyst, and an organisational consultant. She is a founding member and former chair of AGSLO, the Swedish Foundation for the Study of Leadership and Organization. She is a member of the Swedish Psychoanalytic Association (IPA), ISPSO, and OPUS. She has been a visiting professor at Copenhagen University. She is currently director of an advanced level two-year training programme at Stockholm University in Organizational Psychology: a Psychodynamic and Systemic Approach. Her main areas of research are group and organisational development and group supervision, and she has published a number of articles and books within these areas of interest. She is a member of the international editorial board of *Small Group Research* and the *Journal of Social Dynamics*.

Louisa Diana Brunner, MSc, is an organisational and leadership development consultant. She is founder of BeYOU Group—Career and Executive Coaching. Her main areas of intervention and interest are family business, generational transitions, leadership, organisational culture, group relations, team-building, and crisis management. She does selection and career coaching to the Executive MBA Courses at Bocconi School of Management, Milan (Italy). She is a board member-treasurer PCCA (Parteners in Confronting Collective Atrocities); an honorary member Il Nodo Group; and a member: CSGSS—the Boston Affiliate of AKRI, Family Firm Institute, ISPSO, OFEK, and OPUS.

Gouranga P. Chattopadhyay, PhD, initially trained as a social anthropologist in the mid-1950s. In the early 1960s he re-invented himself as a behavioural scientist and joined the faculty of the premier business school in India—Indian Institute of Management Calcutta. In the early 1970s he met and worked with Eric Miller in Manchester Business School where he was a visiting senior lecturer while Miller was a visiting professorial fellow. This experience led him to further change his area of work to unconscious group processes. Since then his focus has remained on socio-analysis. Apart from teaching, consulting, offering workshops and seminars in five continents, he has also directed, co-directed, and worked as associate director and consulting staff in group relations programmes in India, Australia, England, Israel, the Netherlands, and Trinidad. His publications include five books in his area of work, five volumes of poems, 108 articles, an English translation of a Bengali novel and a selection of Rabindranath Tagore's poems (in press). He is an honorary fellow of acknowledged institutions in India, Australia, and England, and Karma Sannyasin Tattwaratna of Bihar School of Yoga, initiated by Paramahamsa Niranjanananda Saraswati.

Frans Cilliers, DPhil, is a professor in industrial and organisational psychology at the University of South Africa in Pretoria. He teaches in the masters and doctorate programmes, supervises student research projects, and does research in systems psychodynamics and positive psychology. He is an organisational psychologist and consultant.

He is an honorary life member of SIOPSA (Society for Industrial & Organizational Psychology in South Africa) and a member of PsySSA, APA, SIOP, ISPSO, and OPUS.

M. Fakhry Davids, MSc (Clin Psych) F Inst Psychoanal, is a psychoanalyst, adult psychotherapist, and clinical psychologist who practices full-time in London. He is training and supervising analyst of the British Psychoanalytic Society, a member of the Tavistock Society of Psychotherapists, and a founding board member of PCCA (Partners in Confronting Collective Atrocities). He has held academic and clinical positions in South Africa and the UK and is a visiting lecturer at the Tavistock Clinic. He has written on a number of psychoanalytic topics, and his book, *Internal Racism: A Psychoanalytic Approach to Race and Difference*, was published by Palgrave Macmillan in 2011.

Angela Eden works as an organisational consultant in organisations across the public, commercial, and third sector. She has her own consultancy practice, "Eden Evolution", and is a visiting lecturer at the Tavistock and Portman NHS Trust on the "Consulting to Organizations" and "Group Dynamics" courses and a principal is an Associate consultant at Cass Business School's Centre for Charity Effectiveness. Her focus is to influence policy, culture, and performance through customised interventions in structured workshops, communications, and culture change programmes. Her work is with individuals, teams, and groups. She designs and runs workshops and publishes papers around her special interest with leadership, organisational power, conflict resolution, and diversity.

Vivian Gold, PhD, is a clinical and consulting psychologist in Los Angeles, California. She is an associate clinical professor at the University of California at Los Angeles in the Department of Psychiatry and Biobehavioral Medicine. She is on the attending medical staff of the Veterans Affairs Greater Los Angeles Healthcare System. She is a fellow of the A. K. Rice Institute for the Study of Social Systems and has twice served on its board of directors. She has served as pesident of Grex, the West Coast affiliate of AKRI. She also was a founding board member of OFEK, the Israel Association for the Study of Group and Organizational Processes. She is currently teaching in the UCLA School of Medicine's doctoring programme, teaching young medical students to listen to patients. She is also involved in interfaith work, involving intergroup processes of social change.

Doris Gottlieb, MSc, in mass communication, is an organisational consultant, coach, and facilitator based in Amsterdam and a founding partner of Contorno Consulting. She served on the board of Group Relations Nederland from 2003–2010. Originally from the United States, Doris has lived and worked in Europe since 1989. She has worked as an educator and consultant to higher education in the Netherlands, including in programmes at the Rotterdam School of Management and the Haagse Hogeschool and the Hogeschool Utrecht. As a consultant and coach she works with a wide diversity of clients throughout Europe.

Yermi Harel, MD, is a senior psychiatrist at Lewenstein Rehabilitatin Hospital in Raanana, Israel. He is a lecturer in Sackler Faculty of Medicine, Tel-Aviv University, Israel. He is a board member of OFEK, the Israel Association for the Study of Group and Organisational Processes. He is a psychiatric consultant at ALUT, the Israeli Organization for Autistic Children. He works in a private practice as psychiatrist and psychotherapist in Bet-Halevi, Israel.

Britta Högberg, PhD, is a clinical psychologist. She is working as a research leader in the Stockholm County Council and as a researcher at the Department of Education, Stockholm University. Her field of research is social pedagogy, focusing on participation and social processes. Her latest publications have been on cultural and organisational processes in relation to the UN Convention on the Rights of the Child. She is presently working with a project on supervision in a social pedagogical perspective. She was a founding member and former board member of AGSLO (the Swedish association for group relations).

Lilian A. J. Hupkens, CMC, MPC, has a broad background both in organisational sciences and psychoanalysis. She holds academic degrees in experimental physics, industrial Engineering, and management, as well as psychodynamic counselling. She worked both as a management consultant and executive director. In her work she integrates both approaches—psychoanalytic theory and organisational sciences. To enhance her understanding of unconscious processes in organisations, she went on to train as a group therapist. In 2011 she started doing research for a PhD. Her doctorate subject is around certain aspects of group relations conferences.

Oren Kaplan, PhD, MBA, is an associate professor, clinical psychologist, associate dean, and academic director of the MBA Management &

Business Psychology Programme, the School of Business Administration, The College of Management, Rishon Le-Zion. He is a member of OFEK, Israel.

Rachel Kelly, BA, MSTAT, is the professional development coordinator, The Tavistock Institute of Human Relations. She also is a teacher of the Alexander Technique and a member of the British Wheel of Yoga. Previous roles include administration at Thames and Hudson Ltd, book publishers, and at University College London and the School of Oriental and African Studies, both part of the University of London. Currently she coordinates and manages the courses, programmes, and conferences at the Tavistock Institute, including the Leicester conference.

Magnus Larsson, PhD, is an associate professor in organisation development at the Department of Organization, Copenhagen Business School, Denmark, where he teaches organisational psychology, organisational development and consultation, and leadership. He is a licensed psychologist in Sweden and board member of the group relations organisation, AGSLO, in Sweden, and he has participated as a staff member in a number of group relations conferences in Sweden and Denmark. His research focus is mainly on leadership, leadership development, and organising processes, with recent publications in *Leadership* and *Leadership and Organization Studies*.

Mónica Velarde Lazarte, Lic.Psy, is a senior consultant and researcher at the Tavistock Institute of Human Relations. She is a social and organisational psychologist and a candidate doctorate at the Tavistock and Portman NHS with a postgraduate degree in psychoanalysis and management at IFSI. She is the founder and director of T-Consult, a Peruvian organisation that works with applied systems psychodynamics across the private and public sectors and native communities. She is a professional associate of the Grubb Institute. She is currently director and faculty of the group relations programme at Universidad Peruana de Ciencias Aplicada and Esan Business School in Peru.

Judith Levy, PhD, is senior teacher (retired) in the Department of English, Hebrew University of Jerusalem. She is on the faculty of the MBA programme in Management and Business Psychology at the College of Management, Rishon Le'Tzion. She is currently the chairperson of OFEK, the Israel Association for the Study of Group and Organizational Processes, and is a member of ISPSO and OPUS.

Susan Long, PhD, formerly professor of creative and sustainable organisation, supervises research students and conducts organisational research at RMIT University in Melbourne. As an organisational consultant she works with organisational change, executive coaching, board development, role analysis, team development, and management training. She is a member of Comcare's advisory board for the Center of Excellence for Research into Mental Health at Work, is currently president of the Psychoanalytic Studies Association of Australasia, was the founding president of Group Relations Australia and a past president of the International Society for the Psychoanalytic Study of Organizations. Her participative research has attracted grants through the Australian Research Council and industry. She has published five books and many journal articles. The most recent is with Prof. Burkard Sievers, *Towards a Socioanalysis of Money, Finance and Capitalism: Beneath the Surface of the Financial industry*, published by Routledge in 2011.

David Sierra Lozano, MA, in organisational and work psychology, post-graduate process consulting, University of Barcelona, is partner and organisational consultant of Innova, Association for Organizational and Social Innovation, Barcelona. He is professor of management master of arts in advertising, University Ramon Llull and has participated as an organiser and staff member of numerous group relations conferences (Argentina, Cuba, Holland, and Spain). He is a staff member of the programme "Roles, Systems and Contexts", Innova, and is currently developing programmes that integrate perspectives of soft systems methodology and viable systems.

Beverly Malone, PhD, RN, FAAN, is the chief executive officer of the National League for Nursing. Prior to joining the NLN, she served as the general secretary of the Royal College of Nursing in the UK. She was elected for two terms as president of the American Nurses Association and became deputy assistant secretary for health within the US Department of Health and Human Services in 2000. She was ranked number twenty-nine on *Modern Healthcare's* one hundred most powerful people in healthcare list for 2010.

Ajeet N. Mathur, PhD, is a professor at IIM Ahmedabad and has directed group relations conferences in India and Europe since 1994. The focus of his research is on uncertainty and risk, motives and powerbases, group relations, organisation strategies, politics of disharmony in the management of gender differences, missing markets, market barriers, governance breakdown, and the management of institutional diversity in cross-border value chains. His publications include fourteen books and over a hundred papers in scientific journals and anthologies. He has been a member of the board of directors with corporates in India and Europe and is consulted by businesses, governments, international organisations, and the policy research community. He served a term as the director, Institute of Applied Manpower Research, with the rank of secretary to the Ggvernment of India in the planning commission.

Michelle S. May, D Litt et Phil, is a senior lecturer in industrial and organisational psychology at the University of South Africa in Pretoria. She teaches in the honours, masters, and doctorate programmes, supervises student research projects and does research in systems psychodynamics and diversity management. She is currently developing an undergraduate course exploring diversity management from a systems psychodynamics perspective. She is a clinical psychologist and organisational consultant.

Brigid Nossal, PhD, is a socio-analyst and organisational consultant. She is a senior associate at Innovative Practice Consulting (www.innovativepractice.com) and a senior lecturer in the master of organisation dynamics programme at RMIT University. Brigid is a founder member of Group Relations Australia (GRA) (www.grouprelations.org.au) and the National Institute of Organization Dynamics Australia (NIODA) (www.nioda.com.au). She is also a member of ISPSO and OPUS.

Jacqueline Sirota, MSc, BACP, is a senior registered practitioner, UKRC independent psychodynamic counsellor, and organisational consultant and associate of the Tavistock Consultancy Service. She is an experienced social dreaming host and has employed this methodology in research projects. She is a member of ISPSO, the International Society for the Psychoanalytic Study of Organizations, an associate member of OPUS, Organization for the Promotion of Understanding of Society, and an associate member of the Canterbury Consortium of Psychoanalytic Psychodynamic Psychotherapists. She was, until relocating to Kent, chair of the Bridge Consultancy Group and director/trustee of Avon Psychotherapy Service. She had made a special study of the sibling/lateral dimension and dynamics of groups and organisations and continues to develop this theme in her work and writings.

Pim Stafleu, MSc, is a clinical psychologist and a consultant in organisations. He is partner and co-founder since 1998 of the consultancy company VECU Organisatiebegeleiding, Utrecht (NL), supporting nationally and internationally a wide variety of client systems. He is an associate of OPUS (UK) and co-founder and member of Worknet International. He was chair of Group Relations Nederland from 2005–2010.

Rina Tagore, MA (Psy) from Delhi University, India, currently works as a principal policy analyst with the Auckland Council, New Zealand. She has worked in the area of community and social development in India with the Swiss Agency for Development and Cooperation. She has taken up opportunities to work in group relations conferences in India and Leicester, UK. She has been an associate member with the Centre for Socio-Analysis, Melbourne, Australia.

Miri Tsadok, MA, is a clinical psychologist and organisational consultant; she practices psychoanalytic psychotherapy as well as teaching in the area of organisational and group psychodynamics. She is currently on the faculty in the management and business psychology programme at the College of Management, Rishon Le'Tzion, and faculty in the programme in organisational consultation and development: a psychoanalytic-systemic approach. She is a board member of OFEK, the Israel Association for the Study of Group and Organizational Processes.

Janine van Oosten, MPc, is chair of the board of Group Relations Nederland and a member of Opus (UK). She is currently state harbourmaster and deputy director of the Port of Amsterdam.

Gerard van Reekum is an organisation scientist and consultant from Amsterdam (NL). He is a board member of Group Relations Nederland and an associate of OPUS (UK).

Dorothee C. von Tippelskirch-Eissing, PhD, is a psychologist and psychoanalyst, working in private practice in Berlin, Germany. She is President of the Berlin Psychoanalytical Institute (Karl Abraham Institute) and a Board Member the German Psychoanalytic Association (DPV) where, previously, she chaired the committee on outreach and interdisciplinary dialogue. She is also a Protestant theologian, an ordained minister of the Church of Berlin-Brandenburg. She is a member of Partners in Confronting Collective Atrocities (PCCA) and a supervisor and teacher at the Abraham Geiger College, a college for the training of Rabbis and Cantors.

Simon Western, PhD, is Director of Privileged Conversations Ltd, offering ethical leadership, strategy, OD interventions, and coaching to c-suite leaders across all sectors. Author of *Leadership: A Critical Text* (Sage, 2008) and *Coaching and Mentoring: A Critical Text* (Sage, 2012), he offers seminars and keynote speaking, bringing innovative and critical theory to life in the practice of leadership. Previously a family therapist, nurse, and factory worker, he is interested in how work, technology, and organisational culture shape human subjects. He is an honorary teaching fellow, Lancaster University Management School, an honorary associate fellow, Department of Psychosocial Studies, Birkbeck University, and a senior associate, Birmingham University, Health Service Management Centre.

PREFACE AND ACKNOWLEDGEMENTS

This book, the third in a series based on the Belgirate conferences, reflects the thoughtful work of numerous people, without whom neither the conference nor the book would have become a reality. We are grateful to all of the conference participants, some of whom traveled great distances and each of whom added their experience and thinking to our collective exploration of the evolving theory and practice of group relations.

We are especially grateful for our experience with Anne-Marie Kirkpatrick, our beloved colleague and friend who died unexpectedly in May 2011. Anne-Marie held the administrative boundary of the 2009 conference before, during, and after the conference, and she did so with a firm but gentle hand. She also joined us in our initial work on this book. Her steady, practical presence and her genuine warmth and supportive nature are greatly missed.

Our special thanks go to our contributors; without their dedication to creating these chapters, this book would not have happened.

To Elio Vera, our Italian colleague who contributed both enthusiasm and material supplies to the conference.

To Ovidio Mugnai and his family, owners of Hotel Villa Carlotta, for their gracious hosting of the conference and for their persistence in working with us across the Italian/English language barrier.

To Mary Colton of the A. K. Rice Institute, who processed all of the conference registrations.

To our respective institutions—OFEK, The A. K. Rice Institute for the Study of Social Systems, and The Tavistock Institute of Human Relations—which authorised and supported us in this endeavor.

To our families, who frequently had to compromise for our attention.

This book includes most of the papers that were presented at the Belgirate III conference in early November 2009. They are divided into three sections according to their focus. The fourth section consists of nine post-conference reflections written by conference participants.

Avi, Bob, and Eliat

FOREWORD

What can you expect from a book of a conference?

This is in part an adaptation, a recreation of a lived experience on the printed page. If it *is* that—which is possible only to a limited extent—it has a different form, and has the advantages and disadvantages of another process of gestation and birth. Thoughts and feelings continue their merry dance.

The experiential tradition of group relations does not lend itself easily to the discipline of the written word. Even those of us who like to write—and I count myself as one—do not write easily from our experience as directors and members of staff of conferences, where we have worked. Often participants do better. It is one of the successes of the Belgirate series that it has given opportunities to struggle with that inhibition—the oppressive demand that we have to get it right.

The book is addressed primarily to the "global group relations network"—those who were at the conference and those who were not—and it is also of interest to anyone who wants to look at this network in play. A word of caution, though: generally speaking the writers assume you know what they are talking about, that you were there—or should have been there. This is an open system looking in at itself. (But those of us who were not at Woodstock can still enjoy the movie.) Rather like the management group at a conference, the work of the contributors is open to observation and, one way or another, to engagement. Actually, I think this book is worthy of serious study by those who were not there, even by those who did not want to be there but have the energy to think what all of this might represent in the rapidly evolving world of psycho-social research and practice. As the editors imply, innovation is always in process of transmuting to tradition. They ask, after three conferences, where is the Belgirate tradition to go next? This collection of essays points in a certain direction but with quite a lot of deviation, like a quivering compass.

I should declare an interest. I had a certain role in this event—working with Martha Mens to convene the early morning sessions of reflection and association. I remember the room as full, and the sessions crowded, as participants jostled for mental space. Individual need competed with communal sense-making.

The American psychoanalyst Tom Ogden has said that the reader becomes the silent co-author of the text. This is the challenge to us. This is not so much a book about group relations as a book of group relations, and we can experience for ourselves the relatedness of the different voices. It is not a reference book or a monument to past achievement, but a living document to work with, to taste the desire and look to our own thirst.

Reading the chapters of this book is at times—the bits I like best—an experience of being alongside the contributors as they work to make sense of their experience.

An effective staff group in a group relations conference brings a mix of experience, of cultural perspective, of psychodynamic and systemic orientation, of academic prowess and existential adventure. So it is with the contributors to this book. Not only is the book lightly edited—no official line has been drawn—but several chapters are jointly written, conversations begun at the conference and continued.

The keynote addresses took us back to ten thousand years' tradition of reflection and action and forward to the experience of emergent leadership in our time. The presentations that follow have some of the characteristics of a here-and-now event, their content being a description of the process of collaborative work in a context of transition and transformation. Autobiography and theoretical formulations interact and make new insights, as they do. Learning from the personal growth of the individual, you can see how history is interpreted in the cause of future development.

Reading this chapter or that, we may hear a wise interpretation of the system or simply a beating heart. The search for a critical stance may result in short-circuits and sometimes the links are momentarily breathtaking—from slavery to mentoring. Elsewhere the analysis ranges from the unimaginably unlikely creativity of the sperm and the egg to the unimaginably destructive potential of the holocaust.

We may want to escape the confines of definition, but what is it like to exist without a name or theme? How does the post-modern speak with the modern? In such contributions we see how the outsider justifies their status. I retain the image of the dance, at times like clubbing, frantic and heated, but also the more ordered social event, where it is still possible to talk, when pairings are made and closely observed, where youth and age can both have fun.

There is a pervasive theme in the book about the dynamics of succession, of dying and birth in a global context where no-one knows what is happening. Are we questioners without priests or priests without a flock? A continual spiralling around in search of authority—in ourselves, in those we have the desire to work with—sometimes moving too far away from important mundane questions about the effective organisation of work in the individual, in the community, in networks and the wider society, and sometimes moving too close to the bright sun of transcendent insight. It is risky to write about the politics of envy, but it is done well here. I suggest that other readers will have to do like me, and locate themselves in the projections of others. Are we thought of as older, younger, traditional, innovative, at the core or on the periphery, as the contributors position themselves and others in this virtual chess game without a board?

Read this book and see a community restless with itself. In this restlessness is the encouragement to new life.

Tim Dartington

INTRODUCTION

Tradition, creativity, and succession in the global group relations network

Eliat Aram, Robert Baxter, and Avi Nutkevitch

Traditionally, books such as this one begin with an introductory chapter, a chapter which attempts to present an overview of the contents to follow and, in this case, briefly describe the conference—Belgirate III—from which these chapters derive. It would seem that the writing of such a chapter would be a relatively simple task, yet we found it quite difficult to even start. Repeatedly, we found ourselves confronted with a sense of "freeze". "We're tired," we said. We couldn't agree on the primary focus for the chapter. We didn't seem to even understand the title we had chosen; why did we go with "tradition", "creativity", and "succession" in the first place? We found ourselves wondering why we put these three words together as if they are somehow polarised. Are they really? And whether polarised or not, what are the tensions among them?

Ultimately, we realised that we could not address or resolve the questions about polarity and tensions in this chapter; we, like others, were simply caught up in them. (However, aspects of those questions are addressed in many of the subsequent chapters.) Once we understood this, we were then clear that we could, in fact, speak to our original conceptualisation of Belgirate III.

As many readers who are familiar with the Belgirate series of international conferences will know, the first of these was held in 2003 for directors, consultants, and administrators in group relations conferences. As an outgrowth of this conference, which was sponsored by the Tavistock Institute of Human Relations and OFEK, participants began to consider the idea of an international network of group relations practitioners, the so-called "global group relations network". And in a sense, this network has found a kind of home in Belgirate, Italy. In 2006, the A. K. Rice Institute joined in sponsoring the second conference, and the three of us, representing our respective institutions, took responsibility for designing and managing Belgirate II.

We again agreed to take up our roles as the management team for Belgirate III, the 2009 conference on which this book is based. Planning began in earnest at a meeting in London in April 2008. During that meeting, we reviewed our experiences with the second conference, which had focused on adaptation and innovation in group relations conferences and their applications, and agreed that issues of tradition, creativity, and succession had emerged as prominent, sometimes controversial, and nearly universal themes in both of the earlier conferences. Therefore, we concluded that these themes should serve as the focus for exploration in the third Belgirate conference.

Tradition

What is tradition? Generally, it is defined as the handing down of beliefs, customs, practices, and information from generation to generation. It involves a continuing pattern of cultural practices or a customary, characteristic methodology.

With regard to group relations work, we are most likely to think of traditional culture, practices, and methodology as those which originated with the first Leicester group relations conference in 1957. (That conference, of course, was an innovation, but once established, it became the very definition of the group relations tradition.) Or at a more individual level, one might define tradition as that which was experienced in one's first group relations conference. Nonetheless, we think all would agree that the group relations tradition includes an emphasis on experiential learning, on unconscious processes, authority relationships, and concepts of primary task, roles, and boundaries.

All of us have an internal, perhaps unconscious, relationship with tradition, whether that be admiration and gratitude, envy and hate, or ambivalence. For some, tradition is represented by form, for example, the traditional conference model, and any deviation is considered suspect. Others, however, hold tradition more broadly, seeing in it highly valued concepts and purpose, while adapting the form itself to fit different times, populations, or organisational structures.

Creativity

Creativity refers to the ability to transcend traditional ideas, rules, patterns, or methods, thereby developing meaningful new ideas, forms, or interpretations. In other words, creativity, as we understand it relative to group relations work, means doing something differently but with fidelity to the traditional purpose and intentions of the work.

Doing something creative, of course, is always a risky undertaking since one cannot know the result ahead of time. Thus, there is always some tension between creativity (the unknown) and tradition (the known and proven). Yet without creativity, tradition remains stagnant, perhaps becoming old, irrelevant, even dying.

Succession

The coming of one person, or one generation, after another, whether planned or not, is referred to as succession. While this is a simple concept, its implementation rarely proves to be simple in any organisation, and group relations organisations are clearly no exceptions.

To us, succession is strongly linked to both tradition and creativity. Does one succeed into an existing tradition, or must one innovate, create something different, in order to succeed? Does one need to be the loyal follower, diligently upholding tradition, in order to succeed the leader, or should one be more creative, seeing tradition as an evolving concept? This dilemma, paired with the ambivalence of current leaders, or generations, about stepping aside (or down), often leads to disruptions, or even outright despair, in organisations.

Network

For Belgirate III, we included the term "global group relations network" in the title for the first time. This was done in recognition of the evolving, but loose, association of group relations practitioners who have chosen to come together every three years in a seaside village in Italy in order to exchange ideas and, hopefully, nourish one another's thinking about, and collaboration in, our work.

At the moment, this network has no actual authority structure and no defined, formal leadership. It is dependent, we suppose, on the Belgirate management team calling us together every three years, but it has no established mechanism to continue this new Belgirate "tradition" when that team steps down or if their respective organisations should decide not to sponsor the conference in the future. Thus, creativity and succession plans have become issues for the global group relations network itself.

Belgirate III

The conference design

As with previous Belgirate conferences, Belgirate III was designed for people who had taken staff roles—directorial, consultative, and/or administrative—in group relations conferences. Continuing with the design established in the 2003 conference, this conference wove together the traditional scientific mode of formal paper presentations with discussion and a structured here-and-now exploratory event. Not surprisingly, perhaps, notions of weaving and knitting became prominent conference themes, particularly during the exploratory event.

As stated in the conference brochure, the primary task was:

> To provide opportunities to learn about, and explore, the roles of tradition, creativity and succession in the global group relations network.

Some of the learning opportunities available during the conference came in the form of formal presentations. In addition to nine parallel presentations (given over three separate ninety-minute time periods), two keynote presentations by Eliat Aram and by Ajeet Mathur and Gouranga Chattopadhyay were featured. Both keynote addresses and most of the parallel presentations can be found in the chapters that follow.

The exploratory event provided the other major, structured opportunity for learning. With the task of exploring conscious and unconscious forces and meanings underlying the conference and its themes, this event included an opening and a closing plenary as well as four ninety-minute sessions in-between. While the exploratory event had many similarities with the familiar institutional event in group relations conferences, it differed in that the management team and administrator (referred to collectively as the management and administrative team or MAT) participated in the event like other participants. While we convened the plenaries and worked together as one group throughout the event, we made no attempt to work toward a comprehensive sense of the system. We did not collect data, develop hypotheses, or offer interpretations about unconscious processes that were taking place. Consequentially, we mostly did not know what other participants' experiences were, at least until the closing plenary. However, some of those experiences are reported in the post-conference reflections section of the book.

In addition to the above, the conference also included three early morning sessions—morning reflections and associations—which provided further opportunities for shared exploration and learning. And then there were many less-structured, informal opportunities—coffee breaks, meals, late nights in the bar—available for participants.

Once the conference was over, we invited participants to continue reflecting on their learning by writing a post-conference reflection to be included in this book. We originally anticipated publishing four or five such reflections, but we were gratified to receive a large number of interesting proposals, so we finally settled on nine, which are found in the last section of the book.

The participants

As was true of the 2006 conference, Belgirate III was over-subscribed; a waiting list was established long before the conference opened, and we scrambled to find sufficient hotel space to accommodate the ninety individuals (including ourselves and the administrator, Anne-Marie Kirkpatrick) who participated in the conference. In 2006, participants represented eleven countries, but in 2009, they represented nineteen countries (Australia, Denmark, Finland, Germany, Greece, India, Israel, Italy, the Netherlands, New Zealand, Norway, Peru, South Africa, Spain, Sweden, the United Kingdom, and the United States.) Of the participants, forty-four had previously directed one or more group relations conferences, eighty-three had served as consultants and thirty-five had administered at least one conference. Seven individuals had served exclusively as administrators.

The age distribution among participants was of interest, particularly when compared to the individuals who participated in the 2006 Belgirate conference.

Age	2006	2009
20–29	0	2
30–39	1	3
40–49	15	23
50–59	33	26
60–69	32	22
70–79	3	3
Unknown	2	11

In this conference, at least twenty-eight individuals were younger than fifty, whereas three years earlier only sixteen were. In some way, this demographic shift may speak to the issue of succession itself.

As has become a part of the Belgirate conference tradition, the meeting was created and hosted by a small group—the MAT—but it was implemented through the collective participation of colleagues. Nineteen individuals presented papers (and several others, who did not attend, participated in writing them) while eleven others chaired their presentations. Two of the other participants convened the morning reflections and associations sessions. When the MAT is included, a total of thirty-six of us held specifically authorised roles during the conference.

Summary

With the closing of Belgirate III, we have concluded that what was once (2003) an innovative experiment has now become a bit of a tradition—a triennial international meeting of colleagues with an established identity of place, time, format, and purpose. And now that that tradition has been established, we find ourselves wondering about how to creatively carry it forward into the future. We also wonder about who will succeed us in the management and administrative tasks. Who in the global group relations network is ready to sustain the Belgirate tradition now?

SECTION I

EXPLORING PERSONAL, INSTITUTIONAL, AND CULTURAL JOURNEYS IN GROUP RELATIONS CONFERENCES

This opening section includes three chapters that raise some questions to do with the historical, creative, innovative, and traditional dimensions in group relations conferences and the creative tension between those. The three chapters examine key functions of the GR conference and its core methodology. Two of those provide a contemporary overview and insight into the Leicester conferences which are seen, as Kelly points out in her paper, as the "cradle of all group relations conferences", now in their sixty-fifth incarnation. The section offers the Leicester director's point of view, moving from her personal journey as a successor into describing the dance between tradition and creativity and her work to conceptualise the Leicester conference in a contemporary context. It also offers an insightful view by Rachel Kelly into the role and function of the administration as a creative source and container for the work of the conference. The chapter by Chattopadhyay and Mathur takes the reader through a fascinating journey of the creation and development of group relations work in India and the question of innovations, tradition, and succession in this unique part of the world.

CHAPTER ONE

"Climbing fast up the ladder?!" The lived experience of directing

Eliat Aram

My chapter opens with a description of my journey in the world of group relations (GR) conferences, my journey on the ladder, with specific attention to the themes of the third Belgirate conference, namely tradition, creativity, and succession. I will also reflect on the place of the Leicester conference within the GR global network and my understanding and experience of these.

I will start with a chronological tour of the years leading up to me taking up the role of conference director and will include key themes and experiences of them. I will then attend in more depth to three specific developments I introduced into the conferences' journey.

The first has to do with the link between creativity and spirituality and their place and form in a GR conference. The second has to do with the notion of "learning" and "experience", particularly changes that I encouraged in the training group-cum-advancing praxis group. The third has to do with some thoughts I have about leadership in the GR conference context.

The journey

The title of my paper is based on a real exchange between myself and Bob, the mythological Leicester barman, that took place when I arrived to Leicester for the third time in my life, on 6 April 1998. He remembered me from the previous two years and said:

> "Hello there, you're here again … haven't you had enough yet?"
>
> "Yes ... no …" I answered—not sure to which bit of the question I was replying.
>
> "… and you're a day early too!"—he added kindly *(perhaps feeling sorry for this overly ambitious poor sod was my fantasy).*
>
> "Well, em, no," I said, tentatively, "it's because I'm on staff this time."
>
> "Oh, I see," he said, "climbing fast up the ladder, hei!"

That 1998 conference was to be my first experience on a full length GR conference staff. I was struck then how Bob, who never participated in a Leicester conference as a registered member but has been there forever as far as I could tell, has nevertheless picked up some key dynamics at work in the conference to do with prestige, status, tradition, success, and succession.

Bob was right. I was the youngest, the least experienced in conference work, the newcomer, a foreigner—themes that would inform and recur in my journey on staff to date. I was then invited to take up a staff role the following year (1999), an experience that helped consolidate an identity as an emerging GR consultant.

My staff journey since then has become more international. I did not return to the Leicester staff until 2006 in the associate director role to Mannie Sher. In the intervening years I have completed my PhD, my psychotherapy training, had two children, and been on GRC staff in Israel, The Netherlands, France, and India, where I first encountered yoga as part of a GR conference, and in the Grubb Institute's BME conference in the UK, which was broadening out its conception of working with faith and spirituality.

I have therefore become savvier, not only in the GR methodologies and ethos, but also in the international inter-institutional dynamics and politics and the underlying theoretical debates which would inform the different ways of working.

In those years, I had little direct contact with the Tavistock Institute of Human Relations (TIHR), with the exception of running the MBA

GR weekend for Hertfordshire University annually, which I did as an independent consultant with GR experience.

Most of my professional experience up to that point was in the CMC[1], which has deepened my knowledge of systemic and complexity theories, and in my developing psychotherapeutic practice which was based primarily in gestalt therapy theory but into which I integrated psychoanalytic and group analytic thought.

The TIHR in those years was also living through a period of change. Eric Miller was retiring from GR, and his successor, Mannie Sher, was appointed; later into the twenty-first century, in 2002, Eric passed away, the management of the TIHR was undergoing structural change, and a director of institute was appointed for the first time in 2004. When I joined as a member of staff in the spring of 2005, I encountered an organisation in flux, with a GR "unit" far smaller than has been held in the collective imagination globally.

The institute that I joined in 2005 was quite a split place; known internationally for two key areas—evaluation research and group relations—it was surprising to discover that, internally, people did not know or understand each other's areas nor did they necessarily have the inclination or the interest for doing so. I became aware of other professional splits at that time: colleagues of mine from the CMC and from the gestalt community were questioning my involvement with the TIHR.

For me, however, the apparent theoretical schisms were unsound; action research, gestalt therapy theory, and complexity theory, all in different as well as similar ways, are addressing work in the here-and-now, interdependency of individuals, systemic framework—all core elements of the GR methodology and thought that have ignited my passion for the values and purpose of group relations globally.

During the next three years, as well as the period preceding those years, the group relations programme was under constant challenge and pressure to generate income, not just prestige and learning. In 2006 the Leicester directorate was faced with a traumatic experience. We discovered in January, six or eight weeks before the conference was due to take place, that we were holding different dates to those of Leicester University, and we realised that for the first time in around fifty years we did not have a venue for the conference. We eventually managed to find another venue which then provided a temporary home to the conference both in 2006 and in 2007.

Following the 2006 conference I was invited by the director of the TIHR's GR programme to direct the 2007 conference. This invitation, which was endorsed by the institute's director and the chair of the board of trustees, moved me, quickly yet again, to another chapter in my GR career ladder.

The Leicester conference, 2007

The conference took place in Sundridge Park, South London, for the second year, following the loss of Leicester University as the venue the previous year. This was the first time (and later became the last time as well) that the conference was actually advertised to be taking place not in Leicester. Planning a "Leicester" conference not at Leicester was a key dynamic for the coming conference and its branding was a significant output of the identity question. It was then that we experimented for the first time with a Leicester conference logo on the brochure and flyers.

At the TIHR we associated the changed venue, as well as the shifting of the dates away from university spring holidays, to the difficulties of recruitment we faced in the months leading up to that conference. We also wondered about the impact of the change of directors and the succession process that had then begun.

As a personal reflection, I associated the displacement of the venue to the Jewish Israeli migrant director and the theme of the "wandering Jew". This theme, which was very much part of my personal experience, was only just touched upon in that conference, mainly reflected by the work done through and with the only Jewish Israeli member of that conference, who had to struggle on occasions with being cast as my mirror, and sometimes as a caricature of me. There was and probably still is ambivalence around this aspect of me as director. One piece of evidence is that in all four years that I directed the conference there were only two Israelis in the membership—one in 2007, an Israeli Jew, and one in 2008, an Israeli Arab[2]. At the same time, the configuration of the membership was very diverse. In 2007 we had forty-four members and eleven staff. Out of a total of fifty-five people, eighteen mother tongues were spoken and seventeen nationalities were present. This has continued to be so and even increased in the next three Leicester conferences.

In 2009 the theme of migration bubbled up in a beautiful moment of recognition in the staff meeting that all the staff of the emerging subconference were migrants—a deployment of staff that came about without awareness: an Australian from Greece; an American from the Netherlands; an Indian from New Zealand; a South African from the UK; and myself—an Israeli from the UK.

In my debut as director I had to deal with the painful process of "redundancies" and to disinvite nearly half of the staff I had planned to employ. Due to the fewer numbers of members, we eventually had to do away with the three-tier conference and run a working conference and an advanced praxis (AP) subconference.[3] That meant that the African-American I invited as associate director did not have the chance to take up that role until 2009, but the very fact that I invited her and that she took part in the directorate pre-conference preparations until very near the event, marked a shift in the picture-in-the-mind of the Leicester directorship, which until then had never consisted of a non-Brit or a non-Tavistock staff.

Leicester used to be co-sponsored by the Tavistock Clinic and the Tavistock Institute for many years, with some years preceding that of collaboration with the Grubb Institute. But by the 2000s the co-sponsorship became nominal, that is, Leicester had at least one staff member from the clinic but the trust has not shared any financial risk with the institute.

So, to have invited an African-American associate director was a socio-political and inter-institutional statement that provided an important theme of exploration to do with: the third, the inter-generational work, the Jews and the Blacks (one of the pictures drawn combined a striking image of Black Power with the Jewish Menorah), fertile and productive pairs, seduction and insect, and of course, succession—one of the archetypal images used was that of Zeus and Athena; the Director of the Tavi's GR programme thought me up and I was born out of his head.

There was also the beginning of working with the themes of colonisation, migration, taking over, and oppression that were explored very tentatively then but returned to with deeper exploration in subsequent conferences.

Believing in diversity as an important aspect of creativity and innovation, I have continued to pay enormous attention to my recruitment of staff by taking into account not only all the usual criteria of representation of diversity but also knowledge and experience in the Tavistock Leicester model as well as knowledge and experience in other GR ways of working through other GR organisational affiliation.

In the first three years of directing, a number of creative methods were opened that I believe have enriched the conferences' life and expressiveness. In my opening addresses I invited members to be open to the creative potentials they had within and between them, and encouraged them to find ways of working with those potentials as they developed relationships and relatedness to the staff.

I introduced music into Leicester for the first time, drawing on my experience of music being played in other conferences. The use of music opened up a conversation of a different order and worked as a kind of a barometer for the state of the conference as experienced and understood by director and staff at that time. Over time, it has become a second language in the conference experience, and members and staff alike have taken more responsibility around voicing and expressing the collective and individual dance of experience through music so that 2009 saw the creation of a song collectively produced by the membership during the world event.

Throughout the 2007 conference, staff were capturing their experiences and interpretation of events as pictures, drawn collaboratively in the staff room. These collective drawings started in a spontaneous moment when I was standing alone in the staff room, waiting for my colleagues to return from their here-and-now sessions, and feeling the urge to do something, so I drew something on the flip chart and invited them to join in. By the end of the conference we had eleven drawings, exactly the number of staff members.

Members of the AP subconference used to come to the staff group regularly every evening to report on their work with the review and application groups (RAGs), so they had access to the staff's work with the unconscious processes. Witnessing the staff's willingness to expose and work with their inner world across the member-staff boundary enabled the AP members to also move more adeptly between their member role in the large study group (LSG) and the institutional event (IE) to staff role in the RAGs.

Opening up the staff room for the daily visits of the AP members was one of the risks I took in my first year, and it was in that conference that I discovered my interest in the relationship between authority and risk, which I later introduced more explicitly into the conference and its title in 2008.

Many people, both staff and members, wrote poems, which they shared during and after the conference, reflecting on their conference experience. One of these—*Tavifox*—was later published on the conference brochure for 2008. Tavifox has since become a character in the Leicester "fairy tale" and has returned to the discourse of the large study group and other events in following years.

> Tavifox
> I met a fox on my way back here
> last night
> I'd been to dinner with my father
> and sat alongside him for a while
> before leaving
> driving through a calm night along
> smooth empty city streets evenly
> avoiding stoplights
> but along the private hotel drive I notice
> annoyance, at the halting, and acceleration
> past sleeping policemen
> when a flash of orange betrayed itself
> then retreated into learning and skill
> I stopped completely
> It was a ridiculous and free offer
> of a ride, to be alongside me
> my passenger
> I watched the fox for the time it stayed
> For the time that he did not run.
>
> Head of Strategic Commissioning (Suffolk County
> Council's Adult and Community Services);
> member at the Leicester conference 2007.

In my choice of staff I surrounded myself with eight GR experienced directors, very much mindful of the dependency I was feeling towards them to support my first directorial experience and to help me hold and contain the important Leicester tradition. But how to innovate without being perceived as attacking tradition? And how to engage with the process of succession without killing off the ancestors?

My ambivalence around these questions and my anxiety around the innovations surfaced as early as my opening plenary address where I made two interesting mistakes. First, I forgot to introduce two of my most senior colleagues. And as if that in itself wasn't enough, the further significance of the two was that they were deployed to work in the AP sub-conference.

And as if that wasn't enough, when I reached the point of closing the opening plenary, I instead announced that I was closing the conference. The message was clear: the new director couldn't wait to be out of there and for that conference to be all over.

These two significant and embarrassing moments of exposure in that opening plenary were also useful. They gave members the freedom to explore the nature of competence and incompetence in the conference and the tension between ability and disability, and how these were linked to competence and creativity and age and experience. This became pronounced through the experience of a member in a wheelchair; the fire alarm went off early one morning, leaving that member exposed in her vulnerability and neediness of others' support, which failed to arrive, bringing out the question of how we look after each other in this conference, and, more broadly, questioning mindfulness and citizenship. One of the most memorable moments in the institutional event (IE) for me was when a group of representatives of the different groups—that came out of an inter-group meeting session—came to the management with a hypothesis, which they delivered through a live human-sculpture they called "connecting dis/abilty".

Before I move from 2007, I feel I must refer to the theme of female leadership. Leicester was directed by only one woman before me, a talented and strong woman who nevertheless had to work through an interesting set of projections, having been the wife of Eric Miller.

Having me, a young non-English female as director was unusual in our circles and unusual for many of the members in their organisations back home. Some of the myths and symbols that were generated included:

> The staff room was talked about as the womb;
>
> The music experienced as holding and containing;
>
> On the other hand, long dark hair became dangerous snakes;
>
> Sexuality was by and large denied or seen as platonic (e.g., the Zeus and Athena metaphor);
>
> Motherhood was not experienced as nurturing until long into the second week; and
>
> Breast feeding mothers were "lactating sour milk".

In subsequent years, when I changed the names of all of the subconferences, people associated the new names with the female cycle of sexuality—emerging, furthering, and advancing—as opposed to other sub conferences' names made up by other conference directors, which are associated with male penetrative acts such as "entry", "access", "progression" and "application".

But it was not until 2008, 2009, and 2010 that I felt we were experiencing a different period in the GR global network, when many established, as well as new, conferences around the globe were all directed by women at the same time in different parts of the world including Israel, India, Australia, Peru, France, Denmark, Italy, and USA.

At this point I will leave the chronology and explore some of the themes that became important and evident of the direction in which I have been leading the Leicester conferences' evolution.

Location, tradition, and change

The 2008 Leicester conference saw the return of the conference to its original grounds, those of Leicester university, its student accommodation, and its botanical gardens, after two years of migration, or being dis-located. This return to "home ground", where the trees and the buildings seem to hold the history and memories of about sixty Leicester conferences over fifty years, was a significant theme running through and underlining many of the conference's events.

For me, being back at Leicester and directing the Leicester conference in Leicester for the first time, was powerful, and informed my work in many ways. Admittedly, I felt faced with tradition and history and the ghosts of the past, the awe of stepping into someone else's shoes, and the feeling of fear of the mess I could have made.

The relationship that unfolded between myself as director, the staff, and the members, had as a core issue the experienced contrast between the director being a young(er) woman, a migrant to the UK, and the Leicester tradition. The director embodied change, nearly a tear from tradition. This was commented on as early as the opening plenary by an AP member from Australia, who spoke about her surprise when I opened the conference, which very quickly turned into her surprise at her surprise—why shouldn't she expect a younger female with a foreign accent to lead the Leicester conference? And why would she feel disappointed, having travelled half the world only to not be faced with an old gentleman director?

As the conference unfolded, two key issues, related to this tension between tradition and innovation, emerged and forced the staff to deal with this in many, and creative, ways.

The first was the fact that the then-director of the Tavistock Institute came as a member to the conference. Specifically, he was a member of the furthering sub conference which is the sub conference for people with some experience in group relations work.

The furthering subconference therefore found itself holding not only the complexity of being an "experienced learner" but also a role confusion between the director of the TIHR being a conference member and the director of the conference being his employee. These two topsy-turvy hierarchies were met with periodic expressions of anger towards staff. One dream comes to mind, that of an emerging subconference member seeing a knife about to kill his director, who was me, but in the telling of the dream in the LSG it wasn't clear for a while which director he was talking about and who was killing who.

The second was an incident between two members of the emerging subconference which indirectly involved a few other members and had escalated and taken different turns throughout the second week of the conference. The key was a constant threat of one or both of these members becoming casualties, by one of them being seen as the "victim" of an alleged attempt of rape by another member who was cast as the "perpetrator". Despite the woman saying, in the LSG, that this was not the case, that they had had a debate about the nature of male-female relationships that was heated and led to them having a loud argument in the presence of a third member, this, in fact, was not heard and was re-interpreted in a way which increased the risk to their well-being for a big chunk of the second week. There was an extraordinary systemic insistence on perpetuating and invigorating the event, which puzzled members and staff alike and which challenged time and personal boundaries. I eventually dealt with it within the boundaries of the IE by calling a public meeting between the management and the "perpetrator", discussing the projections and thinking through a way forward. The meeting was open to representatives of other groups and I was struck to see that all the representatives who turned up were stake holders of the TIHR, including its director who was representing his group, as well as a number of the TIHR clients who were conference members. There was a breakthrough in that collective and unconscious process of producing a casualty after I pointed out my observation to the meeting.

I believe that this was a systemic response to the experience of a near-desperate need for tradition in that Leicester conference, which reached a perverse degree in so far as the message seemed to have been: if we cannot have any other tradition in the Leicester conference at the very least we would have the tradition of the casualty.

The emerging subconference, being directed by myself and consisting of people who had no previous experience in GR, was therefore a vulnerable subconference. There were unconscious attempts, particularly the one described above, to use its members as guinea pigs, particularly by AP members being mobilised by their back-home professions (e.g., a priest and a psychotherapist) to protect and support the "victim" and unwittingly reinforcing their victimhood and potential collapse.

This subconference, however, seemed to have the most fun in the conference; it was bubbly and creative, youthful and dynamic. They also had the highest diversity in terms of national background and languages, and members in this subconference came from vastly different societies and political structures in the world including Cuba, India, Singapore, Kuwait, Australia, South Africa, USA, eastern Europe (Romania), and western Europe. Being led by a staff group with diverse identities—a Catalan, a Dutch woman, a French/Israeli Palestinian, and two African-American consultants, as well as a Jewish Israeli director—all provided rich opportunities for exploring the meaning of freedom and participation in a globalised society (which was the sub title of that conference) and one's roles and authority within this context.

By the way, it was the first time that a subtitle had been added to the Leicester conference's familiar title—"Authority, Role (or Leadership), and Organisation". The subtitle in itself was a Leicester innovation and exploring it was taken up with a mixture of excitement and anxiety.

Spirituality, creativity, body

The 2008 conference also saw the introduction of yoga to the Leicester conference. The yoga event opened the collective work of the day with a one-hour session before breakfast.

Introducing yoga into Leicester was a next step for me in my realisation of something about myself in relation to spirituality, creativity, faith, curiosity, and the place of the body and its physical experience in a GRC; a reflective process that had begun for me a while before and was first expressed the year before, mobilised by my work with colleagues at the Grubb Institute, conversations at the TIHR and, mostly, my work in India.

I am not an observant Jew, but in my first conference opening address I had a strong desire and sense that it would be really appropriate to quote from Jonathan Sacks, the UK's Chief Rabbi. Jonathan Sacks describes in his book *The Dignity of Difference*, a particular way of understanding the notion of hard work, which I conveyed to the conference institution and would like to convey here as well:

> ... work is more than mere labour. Biblical Hebrew has two words to express the difference. Melachah is work as creation, and avodah is work as service or servitude. Melachah is the arena in which we transform the world and thus become, in the striking rabbinic phrase, "partners with God in the work of creation". God deliberately left the world unfinished so that it could be completed by the work of human beings.
>
> (Sacks, 2002)

I then invited a spirit of inquiry and work which is not about hardship ("avodah") but about joint creation ("melacha"). As a gestalt therapist, the notions of encouraging the openness to what emerges, what is, and remaining curious without pre-judging, fit very well here. Gestalt therapy is based in phenomenological philosophy and hence requires the therapist to suspend judgement and hold open their curiosity to the phenomenon in front of them as it unfolds in the here and now of the interaction. The working principles also require the gestalt therapist to bracket their beliefs and work with what is coined as a stance of "creative indifference" which is not about being indifferent—that is, not caring what happens with the patient—but holding open the numerous possibilities for the patient's next steps without prioritising or preferring one to the other on their behalf, not even the patient's well-being.

For me, this thinking articulates very well what we might mean by "a spirit of inquiry" which I think is also expressed by Bion, in *Attention and Interpretation*, that "the 'act of faith' (*F*) depends on disciplined denial of memory and desire" (Bion, 1984, p. 41). For Bion, the act of faith is based on an acceptance of the unknown, since nobody knows what will happen, and it is essentially a spiritual approach to the self, but from his point of view, the act of faith derives from a scientific state of mind and should be freed from its usual religious connotations.

His closing comments in the book are:

> what is required (for Achievement—EA) is not the decrease of inhibition but a decrease of the impulse to inhibit; the impulse to inhibit is fundamentally envy of the growth-stimulating objects. What is to be sought is an activity that is both the restoration of god (the Mother) and the evolution of god (the formless, infinite, ineffable, non-existent), which can be found only in the state in which there is NO memory, desire, understanding.
>
> (Bion, 1984, pp. 128–129)

There is a particular form of leadership that really speaks to me, which is embedded in this idea and to which I would like to return towards the end of my chapter.

Moving on from "training group" to "advancing praxis"

The 2007 Leicester conference was exactly ten years on from my own experience as a training group member where I learnt through experience about envy and rivalry and particularly about the potentially inhibiting impact of the desire to be on staff. My experience already then got me to think about how the wish to become staff on the conference had the potential of hindering people's learning in the here-and-now and how the question of "who is on staff" lingered beyond the notion of the conference as a temporary institution.

In that spirit Mannie Sher, as director of the advancing praxis (AP) subconference, and I spent much time thinking about and preparing for this new subconference configuration. In 2008 Mannie had a chance to develop further the AP task and design, and it took yet a further step with John Bazalgette in the AP director role in 2009.

One of the issues I have been studying since my PhD, is the relationship between teaching and learning and looking at a different way of understanding the process of education. Traditionally, the relationship between teacher and student, or pupil, or trainee, is hierarchical on the knowledge scale in that there is a notion of an expert and a novice, where a transactional process of active giving and passive absorbing of knowledge takes place.

Our modus operandi in the GR experiential learning conferences is that we—the staff—are not there to teach and hence are not "experts" in any academic way. The tradition of GR conferences has removed some conventional rules of engagement from its staff's behaviour, which is founded in the intention to provide learning opportunities for the exploration of fantasies and projections around figures in authority and leadership positions. We also hold that we are not, and cannot be, experts on experience and that we are all learning in that process of engagement in the temporary conference institution that we co-create.

This stance is often experienced as aggressive, but it does provide opportunities for members to grapple with finding their own authority in role, with finding their dependency on their peers and not on their staff, and with developing projections and fantasies that are then worked with and worked through. As I always say to the members in my opening plenary talks: "You are authors of your own experience".

This removal of conventions also generates anger and shame; people often report feeling embarrassed at having tried to converse with a member of staff and feeling stupid and infantile in that process. In my thinking and practice I have connected shame, panic, and learning intricately. It is my belief that shame and panic are inevitable aspects of any learning process which is challenging to one's sense of identity; it is not an emotion that one can grow out of or even aspire to mature from.

The notion of a "training group" does not fit with this complex notion of learning. What I am working with is the notion that learning processes based on GR methods are challenging one's sense of identity and are therefore paradoxical because the experience of learning is naturally felt and held in an individual's body. At the same time, however, it cannot be generated without the group and context around the individual. So what I always find interesting in the GR work is the ongoing tension of the individual-group-organisation interdependencies; it is useful to think of these as nested systems.

The change of name from "training" to "advancing praxis" indicated a move away from the expert-novice notion of training into a more collaborative effort, through different roles as staff and members, to advance and deepen practice. It also conveys my wish to move away from what I have found to be an inhibiting and limiting idea that this group's task is to prepare consultants to take up staff roles in future Leicester or other GR conferences, and to broaden the task to exploring the purpose and task of an organisational change agent (organisational development consultant, manager, and so on) as a practitioner having to reflect on actions in action. In a true Tavistockian way, I suggested that members and staff alike can be "action researchers" when they engage in GRC.

I wanted to problematise the meaning of "experience" and the assumptions around the "progression" of learning. In fact, I think that in Belgirate II the "in experience" group was grappling with something quite similar—that is, what does it mean to be experienced? Particularly in a conference dedicated to the "here-and-now", where learning in the moment can be nothing but fresh, unique, and mostly new.

It was about letting go of the idea that learning is developmental in the sense of moving from infantility to maturity; I was looking for a way to work with the notion that learning is ongoing and that whenever we experience something new, we will feel a sense of shame (for the fear of being embarrassed by a blind spot, or feeling exposed, or feeling lacking in some way) and a sense of panic (that is, an overwhelming terror when we are touched at a deep level, a challenge at our core, a process that asks of us to change something fundamental in our belief system and for which we feel potentially out of control).

This problematisation was alive for the members from the 2007 conference and thereafter. In the working, and later in the furthering subconference, there were people who could easily "qualify" for a place in the AP and chose not to do so, resulting in quite a few challenging episodes for AP members who sometimes ended up feeling more exposed for having either articulated their ambition or declared their competence by joining the AP sub-conference. But over time they found their voices to challenge back the GR consultants who were "hiding" in the other subconferences.

Either way, it was possible and beneficial in the conference as a whole to work through the question of what it really means to be a novice, what it means to further or advance learning.

In 2009 the AP subconference took a further new step. Inspired by Tim Dartington's development in the Tavi Clinic conference the previous year, we decided to offer the AP members different consulting opportunities than those they would have traditionally expected. Hence, in the first week we sought to offer the AP members opportunities to consult to larger systems where their experiences would be closer to the everyday situation of consultants and managers. They were offered opportunities to consult to the inter group event (IGE) rather than take up RAG consultant roles.

In the second week, since the 2009 conference introduced the world event (WE) instead of the IE (institutional event), the AP members were offered a range of opportunities for taking part in this event, including participating on the same basis as all other members or forming a discrete group of their own. Within this second option they were offered the chance to explore projects of interest, be these identifying issues within the event which required consultation, for which they were authorised to seek authorisation from the management of the event, or undertaking research studies of the evolution of the WE or any other research which drew their attention and passion.

The complexity introduced by the authority to seek authorisation to consult within the event—directly highlighting competition, risk-taking, and accountability—was passionately debated by staff and members, a debate which is still ongoing. As I move to the closing comments of this chapter, I will explain some more my thinking here.

Putting it all together: thoughts on directing as leading and leading as participating

As I began planning the 2009 conference, we had significant changes within the TIHR. The director resigned and was leaving the institute in October, and in the process of recruiting a new director, I applied and was appointed.

Recently, and in my consulting and coaching work at that time, I have become quite interested in the relationship between managing and consulting and how the two are often split in our work, and even at Leicester a typical structure for the IE or the WE is two separate arms of management and onsultant teams, distinguishing the two tasks. Although I have practiced in this way, as well as in the diabolical experience of keeping the staff as a whole throughout the IE, I am always unsure about whether or not I agree with the commonplace distinction, and whether or not it best serves our task of reflecting-in-action (as per Schon, 1991), or the studying of our behaviour in the here-and-now, as they are happening. Obholzer, in his paper "Leadership, followership, and the creative workplace" in *Working Below the Surface* (Huffington, Armstrong, Halton, Hoyle, & Pooley, 2004), talks about managers who separate their professional identities (medical doctor, lawyer, psychotherapist) from their roles as managers, and talk of doing their management tasks as not doing "real work".

In directing the Leicester conference, where the two roles of managing and consulting come together, compounded by now being the manager of the TIHR, I noticed the habit that Griffin (2002) talks about in his book *The Emergence of Leadership*, a habit that we have developed in our language and thought, of attributing direct agency to groups, leading us to think of them as objects, as things (for example "corporation" comes from the Latin "corpus" meaning "body", as does "organ" in "organisation"), but we forget that these are useful constructs which are "as if" concepts which we composed in order to help us think about managing social structures, but these are not "real" agents, they do not exist outside of human interaction.

Why are "institutions" and "organisations" so often treated with suspicion and contempt? How often have you heard consultants talk about their withdrawal from institutional life and going to work independently because they do not "trust the organisation" or are "fed up with the institutional dynamics" or "feel disappointed in the system"? What do we mean by the expression "to be institutionalised?" These are all ideas which indicate we have split ourselves from our contribution to what we have created and have reified our creation in a way that enables us to dissociate and remove our accountability from the result.

Griffin (2002) quotes Rilke in order to introduce his notion of ethical leadership as participation in the daily interaction in the "living present" (a Hegelian concept which resonates with our concept of the "here-and-now").

> Solang du Selbstgeworfenes fängst, ist alles
> Geschicklichkeit und läßlicher Gewinn -;
> erst wenn du plötzlich Fänger wirst des Balles,
> den eine ewige Mitspielerin
> dir zuwarf, deiner Mitte, in genau

gekonntem Schwung, in einem jener Bögen
aus Gottes großem Bruckenbau:
erst dann ist Fangen-können ein Vermögen, -
nicht deines, einer Welt.

(R. M. Rilke, cited by Hans Georg Gadamer in the beginning of *Warheit und Methode*, 1960)

Catch only what you've thrown yourself, all is
Mere skill and little gain;
But when you're suddenly the catcher of a ball
Thrown by an eternal partner
With accurate and measured swing
Towards you, to your core, in an arch
From the great bridge-building of God:
Why catching then becomes a power –
Not yours, a world's.

Reiner Maria Rilke (trans. Marshall & Joel, in Gadamer, 1975)

He then suggests that "ethics, that is, good conduct, is the social process of individual participants knowingly interacting with each other and having to account to each other in an ongoing, ordinary, everyday way for the detail of what they do in their local situation in the living present" (Griffin, 2002, p. 160). And since leadership is essentially a question of good conduct, he continues, the leader, in the course of his/her life, has acquired a greater spontaneity, a greater ability to deal with the "not self", the ongoing purpose or task that others are interacting for.

Drawing on the American pragmatist, G. H. Mead (1934), Griffin writes that the leader is an individual who is "capable of entering into the attitudes of the other members of the group". In that sense the leader is acting "with reference to a form of society or social order which is implied but not yet adequately expressed" (ibid., p. 217, p. 256). Leadership would be about participating in the social process of interaction in local situations in (the living present) the here-and-now without assuming a capacity to step out of, or beyond, or aside from, the interaction.

Human interaction is therefore essentially experience as it is lived in the present. Experience, as I suggested earlier, cannot be understood in terms of the individual alone but in terms of a world in which an individual "plays an active part" (Jaspers, 1931).

"All cannot be found in the individual", Jaspers writes (in Griffin, 2002), "it is in the tension between authority and freedom in which man as temporal life must remain ...". In this tension the only certain thing is the uncertainty of the possible. And this means for Jaspers, and for Griffin, and now for me, that the tension between authority and freedom is characterised by the paradox of the known and the unknown.

Earlier in this chapter I wrote that in Bion's request to work without memory or desire there is a particular understanding of leadership. I now return to this linking to Bion's writing in *Attention and Interpretation*, drawing on Keats' "negative capability":

> ... several things dove-tailed in my mind, and at once it struck me what quality went to form a Man of Achievement, especially in Literature, and which Shakespeare possessed so enormously—I mean Negative Capability, that is, when a man is capable of being in uncertainties, mysteries, doubts, without any irritable reaching after fact and reason.
>
> (Keats, *Letters to George and Thomas Keats* (1817) in Bion, 1984)

Bion quotes from Keats in order to reinforce his idea that the analyst is more able to analyse when he frees himself from the need to understand and make sense. He suggests that the more disciplined the analyst is to release himself from having any possession of memory, desire, understanding, or sense, the more possible it would become for him to work best with what the patient needs.

I think that GR conferences really grapple with these notions of acting in the here-and-now without full knowing, with uncertainty, with an ethics that relies on the commitment to relentlessly engage with the questions of task and purpose—how our choices of actions reflect what we think we need to do, what we say we do, in other words, our accountabilities to each other and to landscapes we draw together. This to me is the art of management and leadership. Directing a conference would be participating in the art of designing without assuming a capacity to know more or beyond or outside of the human interaction, and with the capacity to endure uncertainty and doubt with a touch of humility as to one's individual capability.

I am acutely interested in the questions of authority, agency and accountability. I am interested in how these are put into practice, are operationalised; how they are expressed in what we create together, the aesthetics of the design as well as the collaboration towards the emergent structure. These deliberations led me to the proposal of authorising the AP members to seek authorisation to consult within the boundaries of the WE. I was searching for a way to increase their power to participate in creating learning opportunities.

I think this work would be central to our contribution to developing ethical and sustainable future leadership for our turbulent society, using and applying GR methodology.

References

Bion, W. R. (1984). *Attention and Interpretation*. London: Karnac.

Gadamer, H. (1975). *Truth and Method* (reprinted 2006). London & New York: Continuum International Publishing Group.

Griffin, D. (2002). *The Emergence of Leadership: Linking Self-Organization and Ethics*. London & New York: Routledge.

Huffington, C., Armstrong, D., Halton, W., Hoyle, L. & Pooley, J. (2004). *Working Below the Surface: The Emotional Life of Contemporary Organisations*. London: Karnac.

Mead, G. H. (1934). *Mind, Self & Society*. Chicago: The University of Chicago Press.

Sacks, J. (2002). *The Dignity of Difference*. London & New York: Continuum Publishing Group.

Schon, D. A. (1987). *Educating the Reflective Practitioner*, San Francisco, Jossey-Bass.

Schon, D. A. (1991). *The Reflective Practitioner*, Avebury: Arena.

Notes

1. CMC = Complexity and Management Centre.
2. By the time of editing this chapter, in my fifth year of directing the conference, this picture has shifted dramatically as in the 2011 conference I had three Israeli members and two Palestinian members.
3. Later in this chapter I reflect more fully on my thinking about the experienced members sub conference and the name shift from "training to "advanced praxis" to "advancing praxis".

CHAPTER TWO

Experiential learning: the Indian experience from the proto-historic period to the present

Gouranga P. Chattopadhyay and Ajeet N. Mathur

Introduction

Experiential learning is a very old phenomenon in the Indian subcontinent. There are significant differences between the kinds of experiential learning practised in India nowadays and those we can trace back to about 8,000 BC. We trace the evolution of threads of continuities and also discontinuities over a long period of time to raise issues relevant for understanding experiential learning and traditions of succession. We conclude by discussing impediments to experiential learning with due regard to social, economic, cultural, and political factors, and raise some working hypotheses about challenges of succession that could have relevance also for persons and groups in other spaces.

Before the "beginning"

Western accounts of chronology are less than enthusiastic to proofs that collective consciousness, in which individual and group experiential learning were embedded, can predate the Christian era. The dating of the first stirrings of civilisation in the Indian subcontinent is not free from controversy. Quite a few historians, sociologists, political scientists, and so-called Indologists (such as Max Mueller) have viewed what existed previously from the perspective of what the civilising missions, of European contact brought to India and how they layered over what then existed to trigger new beginnings and awaken new potentialities. And they wondered about what they (Burnet, 1773; Hallpike, 1980; Ingold, 1994; Radcliffe-Brown, 1922) imagined as exotic (Chattopadhyay, 2001) frames in the context of indigenity and universality in knowledge traditions, as has been elaborated in a previous publication (Mathur, 2004).

It is not easy to justify a single national epithet for, or confer the status of statehood on, pre-1947 India, never, until 1947, having been invented in its present form. Yet, in the case of the Indian subcontinent, it is impossible to ignore pre-existing civilisations and settlers that, given the considerable archaeological evidence, pre-date the birth of the Christian era,. There are records of people who closely observed nature, and thinking about human nature as inseparable from Nature shaped their experience. The notion that "not even for a moment can a person stand still and do *no* work, for every person is helplessly driven to work by the forces of nature, (*Bhagavat Geeta* 3:5)[1] draws attention to this natural curiosity and the capacity to wonder at conditions born from perplexity and wonder. To wonder was to inquire into what sustains life, the significance of breathing, what is inside the mind, what is behind the senses, and whether we all share some common sensations and perceptions.

Nature, creativity and regenerativity

From trying to understand nature and the first experimentations of doing something to get in touch with the nature of authority vesting in human nature, as part of larger nature, arose the traditions of *Tantra*. The *Tantrikas* (those who followed *Tantra*) clearly made two major contributions. Both are in the realm of spirituality.

One was the idea of what made the universe tick. Their experience led them to identify a universal force manifested in two complementary divisions they called *prakriti*, the feminine aspect, and *purusha*, the masculine aspect. This idea was further developed through *yoga*. Actually T*antra* and *yoga* evolved and developed almost simultaneously.

Secondly, in their striving for better health and longer life, the potential *tantrika yogis* (*yoga* practitioners) explored their experience of animals, trees, wind, soil, water, and fire. For example, they noticed that the tall palm trees of the *Palmyra* family had the capacity to withstand gale force winds in the face of which other trees perished. So they watched how the seedlings grew to great heights and coped with cyclones, and imitated this in practices and exercises that gave rise to the *tadasana* (the Palmyra tree posture) and the *tiryaka tadasana* (the dynamic or sideways moving Palmyratree posture). They noticed how cats remain supple and how snakes raise themselves to great heights by straightening their backbones. These two experiences were applied in creating the *marjari asana* (the cat posture) and the *bhujanga asana* (the snake/cobra posture), respectively. It was possible for them to learn from trees and animals because the *tantrika* idea of an all-encompassing force meant there was no other division in the cosmos. Hence there was no question of parts and a whole. Every apparent entity was somehow a microcosm that contained the macrocosm in it.

The ideas that began to develop into a body of knowledge derived from experiential learning in *Tantra* were distilled from individual experiences of various kinds and, also, collectively valued insights from the possibilities of repeating the observations, practices, and experiments within living traditions of those times. The considerable diversity of natural habitat in the Indian subcontinent produced two processes. First, this enabled some insight-based concepts replicable across this contextual diversity that confirmed validity and reliability of certain practices. Second, and more importantly, local knowledge traditions began to value not only the transferable learning from one locality to another but also cherished the local traditions that coagulated into recipes of inter-generational value specific to the beliefs, norms, values, and attitudes reinforced within a community.

Shruti and Smriti

Many millennia later (circa 3200 BC), the convergence in the traditions, insights, and recipes was noted in verses composed with astronomical markers to signify their chronology. These were initially passed on as the early psalms and *shlokas* of the *Rig Veda* (*smriti*) through chanting (from which the significance of bodily resonance of sounds was discovered) and listening by the ear (*shruti*) to what the *rhishis* ("seers", those who had experienced enlightenment) spoke. The fixity of Panini's Sanskrit grammar, which was perfected three millennia ago, has remained unimproved to our times (something unparalleled in any other language tradition), and this enabled *shruti* to be transmitted without distortion.

The word *veda* (for works of *"vidya"* and *"vijnyan"*; *"vid"* means to realise, *"jnya"* to know) was used to signify an approach towards encompassing that which is unbounded and cannot be limited. Everything passed on was a working hypothesis to be tested for relevance through what was experienced by, thought about, and revealed for, each living generation before being passed on, *mutatis mutandis*. In this sense, *Veda* is the continuous process of inquiry into all kinds of phenomena and the reduction of any aspect of the inquiry to a fixed discrete form is no more than a text describing intermediate outcomes or routines or procedures noted or committed to memory at a discrete point in time. To fix it in form, and consider the form sacrosanct in meaning rather than in its grammar, was a travesty for the spirit of inquiry. In an inquiry into the Spencerian question, "What knowledge is of most worth?", one of us noted that this quest had been part of the *Vedic* traditions, and elaborated on the curricular design implications for education systems from this perspective (Mathur, 2000).

The compositions of the early inhabitants, especially what they learnt and passed on, got dated to the period when the oral traditions became fixed. The content of these compositions itself carries observations of astronomical markers of the fourth millennium BC that would not have been possible to imagine or fudge with the knowledge and technologies of the first millennium BC (Kak, 2000). Therefore, the dating for the early *Rig Vedic* period is 3800 BC with a lower limit at 3100 BC, around the time of the Mahabharat War. The Saraswati riverbed had completely dried up by about 1900 BC, so there could not have been any large settlements with learning traditions after 1900 BC in that area (Mishra, 1999, p. 495). The population migrated north-westwards, eastwards, and southwards.

The *Tantrikas* and the *Vedic* people had realised that it was pointless to try for mass education through written texts in an era when even the idea of a printing press was nonexistent. Also, they wanted to safeguard their knowledge from destruction by conquerors. This was not a matter of collective paranoia, because this subcontinent had been invaded time and again from the prehistoric period onwards. So all learning was based on meditation, discourse, and dialogue so that individuals carried knowledge and wisdom from one generation to the other. It was much later, in the first millennia BC, that the written tradition came, and the destructive process started then. There is very little in India's historical record from the period 500 BC to the sixteenth century AD (until the time of the poet-philosopher Kabir) that tells us anything of the living tradition except for the Sufis (Khan, 1988). Both the *Tantrika* and the *Vedic* traditions went underground to survive; these started resurfacing in a limited way in the late nineteenth century but openly only about half a century ago.

Darshan and shastra

The preceding discussion gives us some idea of experiential learning methodology of various kinds. These ideas and the methodologies are known in Sanskrit as *darshan,* a word that literally means that which has been seen or experienced. Unfortunately, as in the case of many other Sanskrit words, Western intellectuals like Max Mueller translated *darshan* as "philosophy", thereby robbing it of its basis in experiential learning. While at times in the past, the word *darshan* was also used to mean philosophy, by and large the word used for philosophy was *shastra*. Unfortunately, *shastra* was translated into English as "scripture", or more specifically "Hindu scripture". That put paid to the different notions of philosophy and experiential learning for the educated in British India. It has been further hypothesised by some (including us) that the manufacture of a Hindu religion was necessary in order to proselytise into Christianity from among many of the vast majority of the non-Moslem population of India, who were animists. Brahmins, following *shruti* and *smriti,* had by then made alliance with the *kshatriyas* to take an elitist stand and were rightly castigated as an in-group that kept knowledge to itself, by excluding others, to retain a monopoly over interpretation of codes of conduct and customary laws. This laid the foundation of the *jati* (caste system) that vitiated the occupation-based *varna* system into one in which one's *varna* and caste were determined by birth.

Neither the brahmins nor the animists had any scripture, since there was no belief system present that traced its behavioural or spiritual norms from an unapproachable supreme being, while the Oxford English Dictionary definition of the word "scripture" is "the Bible"! During the later *Vedic* period, experiential learning continued and the concepts arising out of it were recorded in the *Upanishads.* It has been estimated that there were over 130 such *Upanishads*. However, systematic destruction of these resulted in the survival of only thirty-five *Upanishads*. One kind of methodology is mentioned in the *Taittiria Upanishad* (Gambhirananda, 1989). In *gurukulas* (educational communities of habitat organised around renowned scholars known as *gurus),* students/disciples were helped to imbibe cultural values by experiencing the living methodology present there in the age group of eight to eighteen. They were taught various subjects, as much as possible through actual experience.

The idea that a hermeneutic primary task (Mathur, 2006) can be synonymous with a normative one can be traced to these experiential learning traditions where the *gurukula* was an institution emphasising experiential learning rather than instruction. This would then surface in vocational practices of apprenticeship, too. A singer (of classical or light classical songs) in India, rendering a public performance such as a musical concert, usually does not predetermine what he is going to sing before he starts singing. He feels the atmosphere of the place and the time and then begins to sing from what inspires him at that moment, in contrast to what a Western musician generally does (Khan, 1988, p. 104). The manifestation of sound on a physical plane was discovered by the influence of sound vibrations on healing. The Rafai school of Sufis experienced that the resonance of sound at a certain pitch of vibrations makes the body invulnerable to cuts and burns (Khan, 1988, p. 108). The distinction between consciousness while awake (*jagrata*) and while dreaming (*swapna*) led to recognition of the unconscious or *susupti* state. The impediments to consciousness interested those who valued reflecting and learning from experiences, and the notion of *vitarka* (assumptions or suppositions) as preparatory to clear vision about phenomenon was termed *vichara*, which has etymologically diffused to other Indo-European and Ugric language traditions, where the tradition of reflecting on the day's experiences at sunset in quiet contemplation is known as *vecher, vespers, vespera,* and *viisaus.*

Vidya and Vijnyan in the collective consciousness

The most important aspect of experiential learning was in the area of understanding the universal force—what the physicists from the West have studied for centuries, with Stephen Hawkins first stating that he would soon come up with a theory that explained everything (TOT) and later ruefully stating that such a theory may never be found. Basically it is the quantum mechanists who, through their experimental studies, have come to the hypothesis that "all things in the universe that we see" are nothing but different configurations of elementary particles, but we are not capable of actually seeing these dynamic configurations forming and dissolving because of our perceptual limitation; therefore there is no difference even between the living and the dead. Since none of the experiments allow the physicists to actually see the elementary particles, Heisenberg stated that particles like the electron, for example, had a tendency to exist. To that extent you, the readers, and we, the authors, who are actually particular kinds of configurations of elementary particles, cannot take it for granted that we exist! All we can say is that we too have a tendency to exist! (Bohm, *Cit.* Zukav, 1982; Chattopadhyay, 2000).

The notion of *anu-bhava* (the word, that comes from Sanskrit, for a unit of experience) itself captures the idea that miniscule atomistic impressions make up the mosaic of emotional, aesthetic, and psychological experiences. The taxonomy of how *anu-bhava* generates the thirty-three transitory emotional impressions recognised in the Indian system of *bhava* (sentiment), which crystallise into more durable states of aesthetic experiences (nine *rasas* of the *Rasa Siddhanta*) and undergo transformations before psychologically manifesting as basic assumption groups, has been discussed by one of the authors in another paper (Mathur, 2009).

The idea of an indivisible cosmic force—the *Advaita*—that did not have separate feminine and masculine aspects, was conceptualised in the *Vedic* period through experiential learning, and the concept called *maya* (illusion) arose. It was recognised that since everything was a configuration of something that was the basic material of all things seen, nothing really existed beyond the fantasy of the person seeing it. The corollary was that the person was also basically a configuration of the same thing that formed the illusion of existence of everything else. To that extent it was not possible to think in terms of a whole and parts in the universe. Everything was identical with the all-pervading universe that was variously termed as *atman, paramatman, brahmand*, and *brahman*. Therefore it was possible to make the statement: "There is no difference between the seer and the seen ..." (Nikhilananda, 1987).

This led to the search for that cosmic force through experience. One of the paths was through some of the branches of *yoga* known as *kriya yoga, kundalini yoga,* etc. The interesting part of these *yogas* is that those who undertake to practice these branches of *yoga* are also told that they would never get anywhere near experiencing their identity with the cosmic force unless they gave up, entirely, the desire to experience it. Instead they have to simply practice those forms of *yoga* and lead whatever life they are otherwise living. It certainly reminds us of Bion's idea of "without desire and without memory". However, since this ultimate truth could be experienced only by a few through their experience, the idea of interconnectedness was deliberately invented for the hordes of lesser beings. As a result, only a handful of people at any time would really understand the ultimate truth, and to convey this idea in a diluted form for the hoi polloi, different metaphors were used. As far as we know from various ancient and modern Indian treatises, like the Mahabharata, the eighteenth chapter of which contains the Bhagavat Geeta, through which a great yogi calle Sri Krishna had put before the public the twin ideas of Maya and its diluted version by using various contemporary metaphors (Chattopadhyay, 1997).

Metaculture of Indian experiential learning traditions

The entire focus of experiential learning in this subcontinent has been on revelation through experience. This revelation was, at one end of the spectrum, about experiencing identity with the all-pervading cosmic force. This also meant, at a metacultural level, some idea, however vague, of non-difference between not only human beings, but also between human beings and all other kinds of things in the universe. The emphasis on non-violence came from this idea of non-difference. It seems that this idea remains very deep to this day. Very recently, while analysing the reason for the Indian cricket team's "inability" to be aggressive, Paddy Upton, the mental conditioning expert attached to the team, drew the attention of the team members to the historical fact of "India never being an aggressor in wars, never having been the first to strike, never taken battle to the opposition … in comparison and historically, Indian cricket teams are not known to attack first, to dominate from the start of a cricket series …" (*Hindustan Times,* 2009).

This basic structure, if we may use such a Marxist term, is behind the Indian values on hospitality, in a guest-host relationship putting higher value on the guest, the village as a self-contained group (that resonates in some way with the idea of containers), and the spirit of the joint family system. These ideas and notions have been twisted in the later era by foreign invading powers and transformed into one of salvation. Thereafter many intelligent and highly manipulative charlatans have set themselves up as gurus in various locations in India (and abroad) and changed the mode of spiritual quest from revelation through experience to salvation through following the *guru's* leadership for their hordes of foreign followers and a sprinkling of gullible rich Indians. (See for e.g. Mehta: 1993). Apart from converting experientially learned insights, or *darshan,* into philosophy and thereby destroying the educational methodology, the idea of a Supreme Being to be worshipped as *Bhagwan* by a so-called religious group called the Hindus, was invented and taught in line with the Judeo-Christian notion of a Supreme Being. But in Sanskrit texts *Bhagwan* represents any person who has certain characteristics and qualifications. These are beauty or handsomeness, wealth, bravery, strength, and the capacity to remain non-attached to all of these. While the Bhagavat Geeta has been translated into English as the Song of God or Divine Song (Huxley, 1946), it should really be the Song of Non-attachment. Sri Krishna has been referred to as *bhagwan* in the *Bhagvat Geeta* not because he was a sort of living god, but because he was a great yoga master who possessed all the characteristics necessary to be known as a bhagwan (Chattopadhyay: 1997).

We mention the words "so-called Hindu religion" with reason. Trade relations with ancient Greece gave rise to the word "Inde" and the Arabs (sixth century AD) called the subcontinent "Hind", since both groups followed a route that brought them to the west bank of the great river Sind. Later, when Christian proselytisers came to the subcontinent, they sold the idea of Hinduism as a religion in order to convert "Hindus" to Christianity. By and by, as the British conquered most of the subcontinent, they introduced a new system of education and by using their imperial power ensured that reasonably good jobs in British India would be available to those Indians only who got educated in the new system taught through the medium of the English language. The cycle of destruction of the experience-based education, and of the opportunity through it to realise one's oneness with the all-pervading cosmic force, was completed. While in the past the struggle had been to reach out to as many people as possible to help them have the revelation that led them to avoid violence of any kind and develop a deep respect for all things in nature, the era of glittering technology and worship of Mammon was ushered in to replace a sense of oneness with envy and murderous competition. The Indian "*bhava* system" distinguishes feelings of envy and hatred that trigger projections as a separate category called *sanchar bhava*. This distinction is missing from the Aristotlian taxonomy of emotions built around the dichotomous notion of pain or pleasure.

We have already mentioned some ancient Indian values that are reflected in guest-host relationship, etc. It now seems that the value of reaching out to as many people as possible by calling out to them as the "children of immortality" (*shrinwantu vishwe amritasya putra*, translated as: Listen, O the children of immortality the world over) had been part of the *Vedic* tradition. Amrita, or immortality, here refers to the indivisible cosmic continuum discussed in the Upanishads. This scenario is today sought to be contained from spreading further. A handful of people are also trying to make experiential interventions to transform this scenario into a more manageable one, bearing in mind that what was possible many millennia ago is not at all possible in the present day, in a turbulent world with all boundaries becoming vulnerable, giving rise to anxiety in various forms in India and elsewhere.

What remains of the experiential learning tradition?

There are some institutions in India where experiential learning traditions, described in the foregoing sections, are practised or form part of education and research traditions. These include monastic communities and some ashrams like the Bihar School of Yoga. Some of them have focussed on specialised niches such as offering retreat venues, or promoting health and wellness, or developing social work or community welfare through environmental programmes and capacity building.

The sensitivity training or T-group training (developed at the National Training Laboratories, in USA), transactional analysis, and a host of branded training systems associated with profiling evaluations, also made their way to India. The T-group was introduced in India in the mid-1960s. In 1971 half a dozen or so Indian T-group trainers founded the Indian Society for Applied Behavioural Science (ISABS) as a registered society in 1972. In 1978, ISABS split, and the splinter faction gave rise to several similar organisations. In retrospect, the division came about more from inter-personal conflicts than from differences in ideology. The main problem (to which we shall return in the section on succession) was that without a notion of task, time, territory, technology with sentient boundaries, as touch-stones, experiential learning in T-groups produced painful misunderstandings that degenerated into personal value conflicts. Further, since T-groups' focus reduces all relationships to the interpersonal, the participants have little opportunity to explore their experience of intra and intergroup behaviour. Nor do they have the opportunity of exploring unconscious group dynamics. There has also been a transactional analysis society in India for several decades.

In India, team building exercises involving group work have always interested commercial organisations. Many industrial houses have included in their training and educational methodology, either through in-house application or by hiring consultants, exercises of various kinds that range from simple "games" to participation in diluted versions of outward bound programmes. These are based on the idea of experiencing reality in a different way and learning from one's insights.

Experiential learning in what is known as working conference or group relations conference (GRC) was introduced in India by the first author (who has also taken staff roles in various GRCs in Australia, Europe including U.K., Israel, and Trinidad since 1972) through the Indian Institute of Management Calcutta (IIMC) in 1973. He directed GRCs sponsored by IIMC from 1973 to 1992, a year after his retirement from there. The other author joined him as staff in the 1980s (and has taken staff roles in various GRCs in India and Europe, and also directed some of them). Several NGOs, a business school other than the IIMs, as well as registered societies, also offer working conferences. Some industrial houses; the Indian administrative service for its probationers at the L B S. national academy as well as for senior officers (in IIMC); a Delhi-based wing of the Indian police for its very senior officers; several business houses; and the British Council, jointly with the Indian Institute of Management Calcutta, have also offered working conferences in the past. The Kolkata police, too, have offered working conferences in the past, jointly with the Bengal Chamber and Concern for Calcutta. From 2005 to 2008, a media group offered four international working conferences. The Indian Institute of Management Ahmedabad (IIMA) is another institution with action research traditions where process work for managing oneself in role with respect to boundary conditions is part of the education process. The concept of primary task, so central to experiential learning in working conferences, was formulated and applied for the first time in the world in the Calico Mills of Ahmedabad by Eric Miller and A. K. Rice. Group relations conferences (directed by the second author) and organised by IIMA are now offered every academic year.

Given the size of the subcontinent, its general state of development, and the uneven nature of wealth distribution, it has not been possible, to date, to create any national institution like the Tavistock Institute, with its group relations programme, or the Grubb Institute in the UK, the A. K. Rice Institute with its many chapters in USA, IFSI in France, AISA in Australia, GRN in Holland, OFEK in Israel, etc.

Mass observation as a methodology has also been practised in India. The entire team of planners and researchers of India's planning commission think-tank, the Institute of Applied Manpower Research, conducted a mass observation exercise of Delhi on May Day in 2008. The journal diaries from this event and the working hypotheses raised by the group are in the process of being published.

There are also individuals who utilise their skill and experience from staff roles of working conferences to bring to the world of industry and commerce, NGOs, government organisations, etc., the lessons learned in working conferences as consultants and in the trainer-trainee tradition.

The earliest subcontinental philosophy that survived by going underground for many millennia and which re-emerged only in the early 1960s (i.e., about a decade and a half after the last of the colonisers had to quit India—the British from most of the subcontinent, the French and the Portuguese from small pockets in the subcontinent) is *Tantra.* There is a general belief, both in India and in many countries outside of it, that something called spirituality is to be found within various cultures of India. This sense of spirituality is generally expressed through some culture traits like hospitality, sense of neighbourliness outside the metropolises, many villages reflecting a feeling of being self-contained, and the spirit of joint family. However, during the past hundred years, the joint family as a system has gradually, but largely, eroded due to formal instructional education based on Western traditions of "skilling", opening the doors to different kinds of occupations and professions for the members of joint families, where professions and occupations were previously passed on, along with skills and traditional knowledge of crafts from one generation to the next.

Succession

It is never easy for a suppressed tradition to resurface and thrive without an abiding commitment to institutional or organisational forms from motivations supported by powerbases. In Indian metaculture, the notion of reciprocity in inter-generational relations has been strongly present. By itself, this has kept the living traditions alive to the extent that *sadhakas* (seekers) and advanced practitioners of experiential learning (self-realised persons) have reason to value both *connaissance* and *savoir*, and the capacity to establish temporary or permanent learning institutions that cherish experiential learning. However, certain processes embedded in the subcontinent over several millennia make it rather difficult for the people of the Indian subcontinent to grasp the idea of managing oneself in role (Chattopadhyay, 2004). The role models available in Indian mythology and literature may have something to do with how the exercise of authority for institution building and for social hierarchy work against each other.

The notion of human life in Indian culture visualises a life-span with four phases (Zimmer, 1951, p. 106): *brahmacharya* or the phase of conduct that promotes *jijnyasa* (curiosity) through education and socialisation into adulthood (nought to twenty-five); *vivek* (discrimination, conscience) in the *grahasta* phase of adult working and family life (twenty-five to fifty); *vairagya* (task-orientedness with non-attachment to result, which reminds one of Bion's emphasis on 'without memory and desire') all through one's working life; and dispassion in the *vanaprastha* phase of disengaging from worldly responsibilities (fifty to seventy-five). One could (and still can) enter *sannyasa* after holding one's own funeral to signify the end of all social roles, and practise *sanyam* (self-control) focus on spiritual growth. Some organised monastic orders also focus on activities that lead to the well-being of others. This does not imply that normatively predominant activities of different phases are limited only to that phase. It is merely indicative of the understanding of what is considered more important in the different stages of human life. Implicit in this model is the notion that family and society can support and sustain an individual's trajectory. Paramahamsa Satyananda Saraswati created an order called *Karma Sannyasin* (Satyasagananda & Satyananda, 1984) to replace *vanaprastha* in a way that allows adults from different walks of life to make their unique contribution to society.

Succession in experiential learning traditions involves the transfer of tacit skills through co-evolution of capabilities. The *guru-chela* (teacher and disciple) tradition in India needs to be understood both as an enabling paradigm and a constraining one. The word *guru* consists of two syllables: *gu* meaning darkness, ignorance; and *ru* annihilation of darkness by illumination. The word *guru*, although loosely used worldwide to connote 'teachers with great knowledge or glamour power', is a *sui generis* concept, where the emphasis is on learning through introspection, meditation, questioning, and dialogue rather than on teaching or being taught. The *guru* is not a mentor or an angel investor. For this reason, unless a *guru* has realised himself and resolved inner conflicts within himself to extinguish or limit desires, he is not fit to be called a *guru*, although he may make a great *adhyapak* (teacher), pundit (scholar), or *acharya* (professor) in the conventional sense. The post-independence system of education in India has drawn on this tradition, and profit-seeking in education is prohibited by law.

Neki (1973) analysed types of *guru-chela* relationships evident in Indian culture by connecting the sentient experience (*anu-bhava*) in such relationships to role models in Indian mythology. He identified seven forms in *guru-chela* relationships. Neki concluded that the *guru-chela* relationship enables succession only when unequals end up as co-equals. None of the relationships he examined could achieve co-equality except one—that between enemies—and only after one of the protagonists had been mortally wounded in battle. This could be one of the reasons why most succession struggles in India have been marked by violence and triggered by impatience, insecurity, hatred, envy, jealousy, betrayal, sabotage, and sibling rivalry, leading even to bloodshed. The cultural, social, and economic factors thus militate against the possibility of a senior acknowledging a junior as a co-equal. What makes the situation worse is when co-equality itself is denied or obstructed, both consciously and unconsciously.

Some working hypotheses

We close with some working hypotheses about why experiential learning traditions are in the doldrums in India:

Hypothesis one: The problems that make it difficult for Indians to manage themselves in their role also make it very difficult for them to reflect on and explore their day-to-day actual experience. Such reflections and explorations are very likely to *attack many of the boundaries in the mind* that have been passed on from one generation to the other over many millennia (Chattopadhyay, 2009).

Hypothesis two: The picture of relatedness held in the mind as a result of the internalised experience of an "invader in the mind" and colonialism also gets in the way of exploring one's here and now experience (Chattopadhyay, 1981, 2004, 2009).

Hypothesis three: The processes of hierarchy and of envy, embedded in the Indian psyche, make it difficult to encourage others to benefit from experiencing group relations conferences. It is not unusual to hear from senior level managers who have gained from participating in a group relations conference that lesser beings than them—meaning others in subordinate roles—are unlikely to be able to digest such strong experience.

Hypothesis four: Envy seems unresolvable in Indian metaculture (Chattopadhyay, 1999b). This destroys the possibility of engaging in elevating group relations practice to a professional system where peer group solidarity, synergy, and collaboration are important.

Hypothesis five: The problems of smooth succession and institution-building are related. People do not build personality cult-free institutions that may enable other role-holders to be recognised as co-equals.

Hypothesis six: The factors militating against sustaining container institutions include unconscious group pressure for transgression of boundaries (Mathur, 2007a) that may manifest in outbreaks of extortionary lawlessness associated with psychological and physical violence where power is used to erode authority and to corrupt notions of primary task (Chapman, 1999). This may be described as the triumph of despair over hope.

Hypothesis seven: The decline in the capability to question one's experiences makes it difficult for institutions to evolve or handle succession when they seek to change, because tensions between the old and the new are not easily resolved. This is empirically supported by the results of a recent action-research study that focussed on path-dependent outcomes through engagement with hermeneutic primary task (Mattila, 2008). While the notion of frozen boundaries of belief systems (Chattopadhyay, 2001) has been justified as an anxiety-reducing mechanism against threats of despair, what has been overlooked is that it dashes hope, removes the scope for wondering and sustaining the courage to confront and marvel (Mathur, 2007b).

We continue to think of why it is so difficult in India to cope with succession of any kind—in families, in organisations and institutions, and in public and private life of communities—and invite readers to share with us their hypotheses to add to/question/modify ours.

References

Burnet, J. (1773). *Of the Origin and Progress of Language* (*Volume I*). Edinburgh: J.Bell.

Chapman, J. (1999). Hatred and corruption of task, *Socio-Analysis, the Journal of the Australian Institute of Socio-Analysis, I*: 127–150.

Chattopadhyay, G. P. (1981). The invader in the mind in Indian metaculture. *The Economic Times, VII*: 137–138.

Chattopadhyay, G. P. (1989). Education: the authority to learn or the authority of the bowl of hemlock. *Decision, XVI*: 1.

Chattopadhyay, G. P. (1991). Hierarchy and modern organisation: A paradox leading to human wastage (with A. Malhotra). *The Indian Journal of Social Work, LII*: 561–584. (summarised in S. Long (Ed.), *Turbulence*. Melbourne: Swinburne University and Australian Institute of Socio-Analysis Joint Publication).

Chattopadhyay, G. P. (1997). *Bhagavat Geeta: A Treatise on Managing Critical Decisions*. Kolkata: Eureka Publishers.

Chattopadhyay, G. P. (1999a). A fresh look at authority and organisation: Towards a spiritual approach for managing illusion. In: R. French & R. Vince (Eds.), *Group Relations, Management and Organization* (pp. 112–126). Oxford: Oxford University Press.

Chattopadhyay, G. P. (1999b). *Managing Organisational Process: The Individual, The Enterprise, The Nation and Beyond*. Kolkata: Eureka Publishers.

Chattopadhyay, G. P. (2000). Managing illusion. *Free associations, 8*: 120–157.

Chattopadhyay, G. P. (2001). Spirituality, science and transformation versus frozen boundaries of belief systems. *Free Associations*: *8*: 653–677.

Chattopadhyay, G. P. (2004). Managing oneself in role in the Indian context (Revised version of convocation address at IMDR, Pune, 2004) *Journal of Indian Anthropological Society, 39*: 129–137.

Chattopadhyay, G. P. (2009). Colonialism in the mind. Paper presented at the National Seminar on the Contributions of K.P.Chattopadhyay and Irawati Karve to Social Anthropology, at the Asiatic Society, Kolkata, September 8–9 2009. *Journal of the Asiatic Society*.

Chattopadhyay, P. (1988). The illusion that was India. In: F. Gablenick & A. W. Carr (Eds.), *Contribution to Social and Political Science* (pp. 241–265). Washington, DC: The A. K. Rice Institute Publication.

Gambhirananda, Swami (Ed.). (1989). *Eight Upanisads, with the Commentary of Sankaracharya*. Kolkata: Advaita Ashrama.

Hallpike, C. R. (1980). *The Foundations of Primitive Thought*. Oxford: Clarendon Press.

Hindustantimes. (23 September 2009). *Vol. V*, No. 224.

Huxley, A. (1946). Introduction. In: Swami Prabhavananda & C. Isherwood (Eds.), *Bhagavad Gita, Song of God*. California: Vedanta Press.

Ingold, T. (1994). Humanity and animality. In: *Companion Encyclopaedia of Anthropology* (pp. 15–16). New York: Routledge.

Kak, S. (2000). *The Astronomical Code of the Rig Veda*. New Delhi: Munshiram Manoharlal.

Khan, Hazrat I. (1988). *The Sufi Message* (Volume II). Delhi: Motilal Banarsidas.

Mathur, A. N. (2000). *What Knowledge is of Most Worth?* Tampere: Tampere University Press. Summarised version in W. Pinar, D. Trueit, W. Doll & H. Wang (Eds.) (2003) *Internationalization of Curriculum Studies* (pp. 137–177). New York: Peter Lang.

Mathur, A. N. (2003). Who owns traditional knowledge? *Economic and Political Weekly, XXXVIII*: 4471–4481.

Mathur, A. N. (2004). Inquiring minds and inquiry frames. In: P. N. Mukherjee and C. Sengupta (Eds.), *Indigenity and Universality* (pp. 171–186). Thousand Oaks, CA: Sage.

Mathur, A. N. (2006)., Dare to think the unthought known? In: A. N. Mathur (Ed.), *Dare to Think the Unthought Known? A Festschrift in Honour of Gouranga Chattopadhyay* (pp. 1–32). Tampere: Aivoairut Oy.

Mathur, A. N. (2007a). Why does inter-group distrust turn violent? In: S. Dingli (Ed.), *Creative Thinking: Designing Future Possibilities* (pp. 240–248). Malta: University of Malta Press.

Mathur, A. N. (2007b). Whose future? Dilemma of the Gandhian Eskimo. *Futures, 39*: 895–901.

Mathur, A. N. (2009). The good, bad and ugly: distinguishing management pathologies from organisational evil. In: *Conference Proceedings* (13th APROS Conference)., Monterrey, Mexico).

Mattila, S. (2008). *Multi-Content Revelation through Dialogue Processes: A Study in Understanding the Hermeneutic Primary Task of Small Groups in the Context of Finland and India* (Publication 738). Tampere: Tampere University of Technology.

Mehta, Gita Karma Cola, Penguin Books in India, 1993.

Mishra, R. (1999). *Before the Beginning and After the End*. New Delhi: Rupa.

Neki, J. S. (1973). Guru-Chela relationship: the possibility of a therapeutic paradigm. *American Journal of Orthopsychiatry, 43*: 755–766.

Nikhilananda, Swami (1987). *Mandukya Upanisad: with Gaudapada's Karika and Shankaracharya's Commentary*. Kolkata: Advaita Ashrama.

Radcliffe-Brown, A. R. (1922). *The Andaman Islanders.* (1948 edn). Glencoe, IL: Free Press.
Satyasangananda, Swami & Satyananda, Swami (1984). *Karma Sannyasa.*, Munger, India: Bihar School of Yoga.
Zimmer, H. (1951). Citing the 'Manusmriti'. In: J. Campbell (Eed.), *Philosophies of India* (p. 106). Princeton, NJ: Bollinger Series.
Zukav, G. (1982). *Dancing Wu Li Masters.* London: Fontana/Collins.

Note

1. Nahi kashchit kshana mapi, jatu tishtaya akarma krit Karyate hyavashah karma, sarvah prakriti jair gunaih (Bhagavat Geeta 3:5).

CHAPTER THREE

Administration and creativity in the Leicester conferences: dancing on the drudge

Rachel Kelly

> *It would be difficult to find another man who lived so entirely for his duties. It is saying but little to say that he served with zeal: no, he served with love.*
>
> —Nikolai Gogol, *The Overcoat*, 1842

In this paper I will discuss the role of administrator in the annual Leicester conferences, how it is seen and not seen, and its inherent possibilities. I have administered the Leicester conference six times and also prepared the conferences beforehand and organised the post-administration between conferences. The words administration and creativity are not often juxtaposed, in fact the effect of cultural forces resulted in responses to my proposed writing of this paper that included mild bewilderment and laughter. When a similarly dull-seeming role like accounting is called creative, the connotation is that it is barely, or not, legal. My contention is that the administration function can and should be a fount of creativity. And embracing this role with any degree of passion means that the primary task of the conference is served.

Three matters I will address are: if administration is dull where is the creativity placed and what is the result of this? Administration is seen as low status (gender and class)—what or who does this hierarchy serve? Administration is on the edge, the margins, sometimes even placed outside the conference—what does this mean and where actually is it?

What do I mean by creativity? One definition is the willingness and ability to transcend traditional ideas or rules, not following established patterns or relationships and making room for meaningful new ideas, forms, methods, interpretations, etc.; using curiosity and imagination, thinking sideways. Exploring what you don't immediately understand means not doing or thinking what you habitually do or think. Or not doing what is expected of you without thinking or having reflected, opens up the field to something else, in fact to infinite possibilities.

Dullness

When you think of administration, which words come to mind? Perhaps: worker, skivvy, drone, menial, task, plodder, bureaucracy, middle management, red tape, bottom of the hierarchy, boring. In the US, it has a rather different connotation, as administration is closely associated with the political structure, but in the UK it is generally seen not just as boring but as an almost unnecessary inconvenience. It has to be paid for, albeit reluctantly, but the real work is being done elsewhere.

There is a powerful, romantic, prevailing notion of the creative genius, the lone artist in his garret or the charismatic chairman with all the ideas; the heroic celebrity CEO who single-handedly turns the company around or the "creative" in an advertising agency. If all the creativity is placed in one person or group, the others can deny their own responsibility for what is happening whilst also denying themselves the enjoyment and status that comes from engaging fully with the situation—living wholly.

If all the creativity is placed in the director and/or consultants of the Leicester conference, where might this leave the members and administration? Everyone who participates, creates the conference, and in exploring and taking up their role, more and more wholeheartedly, they make the conference more. If the administration is lacklustre, the conference will be the same; if there are administrative errors, these can serve as a distraction from the main task of the conference. Each group is a mirror of the other. But if the administrator speaks up, say in a plenary, this can allow those members who may not yet have spoken, to begin to make their mark. The administrator acts as a catalyst, the administrative charge, if you like, which fires up the dynamo of the conference (usually administrative charges are viewed with suspicion and are paid for reluctantly).

I was having many thoughts about what I might say but had let opportunities go by, never speaking for fear it was the wrong thing to say or not the right thing and so I had to galvanise myself to say anything at all. Afterwards, I felt acutely embarrassed by what I had said. Several times since, people have said to me how much they want to hear from the administration. I remember Mannie Sher, the director for my first two conferences, telling me that I could say anything. So there is no wrong or right thing to say, only perhaps what is defined by the context. Initially I also felt strongly that I didn't understand the language of the conference, whilst being amazed by the way a consultant might draw together a complex web of themes to form a beautiful hypothesis. The oblique metaphorical language was enticing but also annoying because it seemed impossible to copy: there appeared to be a certain way of speaking, a Tavistock language which I didn't know. It has occurred to me that this is how some of the members feel at times or all the time. This is how some of the staff feel sometimes. Belonging to the group means it is important to hear what everyone is thinking, whatever it is, however it is expressed, and no matter how difficult. The best moments in the conferences are when a member who has not spoken before, is able to articulate their own kind of poetry. After several conferences, the Tavistock language has become less opaque to me and I can use it to an extent, but I still want to be aware if I use it blindly in order to cover up something or to prove that I am "in the know". Not being steeped in it, I can show that this language is not a prerequisite for membership of the conference.

The role of pre-administrator includes preparing and disseminating the marketing material; encouraging members to apply, answering their questions, and managing their anxieties; organising the finances, including bursaries and discounts; preparing the timetable for the conference and staff timetables, making lists of members, compiling management statistics. Transforming the data and ideas into a concrete structure and so, in effect, drawing out the conference. Exactly how this is done each time is questionable—do I use templates from previous conferences or start afresh each time because mindlessly using templates means mistakes may creep in? Thinking about what you are creating each time means new ways of drawing out and new clearer information can be included. But what if there doesn't seem to be time to think through the process, so I forget something? Perhaps I have to learn to live with this uncertainty.

Whenever you take this risk, there is always the possibility of making a mistake, but out of what might be thought of as a mistake comes learning—you don't learn from being perfect or by following an established pattern.

To avoid uncertainty is to drain life of its excitement, to make it static. "Moving through disorder—order—disorder is an ongoing process rather than a static worldview" (Montuori, 2003). Only if we can tolerate the not knowing can we come to know through the process, rather than rushing headlong towards the goal. Often I wonder after I have had an interaction with a member exactly whether they understood what I meant, as I meant it, or what interpretation they might have made. When I pre-empt my thought process before it can reach the point of creating or conceiving, I jump ahead of myself and limit the possibilities of where we can go next. However, if I am in doubt, I may transmit my uncertainty as anxiety. Alternatively, I can deliberately take time to consider and reflect before giving an answer, which gives a legitimacy to the state of being uncertain.

There is no job description written down for the role of administrator in the Leicester conference—this means it can become more meaningful over time and each time I undertake it; I take on more responsibility (i.e., managing my responses), and I am increasingly doing things which are not in the job description I have in my mind. It is expanding. As I take up my role more and more, I become more involved and I become more myself. But rather than the well-worn phrase, "finding oneself", instead, by learning and realising, I am in a continuous process of creating myself. Brown and Starkey (2000) talk about "organizations need(ing) to be constantly rethinking their identities" which they associate with Winnicot's "playful planning", "the goal of which is to enable managers to develop alternative models of the future".

The administrative role is a dual role with an inherent tension—the administration is performing tasks that facilitate the smooth running of the conference but also has to find time to reflect and gain perspective on how and why things are being done in the way they are; what is happening in the conference as a whole; how individuals are feeling. Just like everyone else in the conference, the administration can be in a state of learning rather than knowing everything already—another tension.

Being mindful, being in the moment. In contrast to this, culturally, there is a dominating and constricting idea of what being creative is; "thinking out of the box" has become a cliché and it is mostly reserved for the "creative" or manager in his/her brainstorm meeting.

However, there is another way of being, where an attention to the myriad details, to what can be seen as the mundane and many small tasks of administration in creating the role, is the essence of creativity. To quote Mies van der Rohe, "God is in the details" (1959). And of course everyone else can do the same with their role, whatever it might be. I can bring passion to my role, which may not seem glamorous or visionary but a slow teasing out without the romance of the Eureka moment. However, feeling the moment when you lose yourself in the flow of activity, through performing a task endlessly and repetitively, is also the basis of the Eastern idea of the perfection of an art, the Zen way of living. Athletes talk about being "in the zone" when their task, say running, becomes fluid and effortless. They are not concentrating on their actions, their thinking is not separate from what they are doing.

Ask people in the street if they can sing, and an astonishingly high number will say that they cannot. The Zimbabwean adage says that if you can walk, you can dance; if you can talk, you can sing. But more recently in the West, there is a sense that, unless you are of concert hall quality, you should keep it in the bathroom. Creativity is seen as an innate gift with only a few being born with it. There is a powerful hierarchy working here. But where is the self-discipline inherent in practising, the consideration of the process rather than a focus on the end-product? The common denominator of most people who are considered excellent at their chosen vocation is a devotion to practice, and they are often hothoused from an early age. Young people are encouraged to be creative, albeit with an increasing focus on the end-product rather than the process of creating. It is in the process that creativity lies.

At Beaumont Hall, where the Leicester conferences take place at the University of Leicester, the administrator's office is the music room, a beautiful Edwardian room with a piano and views over the botanical gardens. Every time a member comes to the administration office it is a time for improvisation, even if they come for something apparently straightforward, say a computer cable; each interaction is different, the state of mind of the member is evident. "To improvise means to draw on all our knowledge and personal experience, and focus it on the very moment we are living in, in that context" (Montuori,

2003). There is an idea that improvisation is inferior to a standardised intellectual reproduction; something improvised might be thrown together, haphazardly without thought. On the contrary, improvisation can reflect a very high level of sophisticated competence which makes it much more appropriate. Improvisation means that flexibility and curiosity about what might be, are required.

Members come to the administration office during designated times, usually the breaks or just before dinner, and they come for an infinite variety of reasons—sometimes just to have a look around the room to see what we're doing, perhaps hoping to get a further insight. This is their opportunity to approach the boundary between members and staff. A few hover at the entrance not sure whether to come in, there must be others who think about visiting but never do, and still others who don't realise where the Conference Office even is. Others stride in—I had one male member from the advancing praxis subconference come with his memory stick asking to put it in our computer so he could print out a note he needed for a seminar.

Another, German, member came every morning for three days for various reasons, one of which was to ask for postcards of Beaumont Hall. On the third day she cried after asking whether she was getting on my nerves. It seemed like she needed our approval—it was a delicate moment. The postcards were being sent over from another part of the university and arrived on the fourth day and when she came to collect them she said it was her birthday so the postcards felt like a present. She'd been dancing the night before—for the first time in twenty years.

I think there's a freedom associated with administration interactions—the administration don't necessarily act like consultants might, invariably we can be welcoming and responsive (even if the response is not necessarily the one that is expected or wanted). Visiting the administration can be a testing ground—testing the boundaries, as in the male member above. Or tentative, initial explorations of what might happen on the boundary between a member and staff and reflecting how a member might be seen by the rest of the conference.

The administration is seen as representative of the rest of the staff and the director. Each time a member approaches the administration, this is an opportunity not merely to say or do the right thing (rather than the wrong thing) whatever that might be, but the administrative reaction will shape the experience of the member and will affect to a greater or lesser extent how they experience the rest of the conference. This is a responsibility but also a great opportunity.

"It is always the direction that counts" (Orwell, 1940). Directions rather than instructions are more useful for learning so I notice directions from the director or elsewhere and then interpret and apply them in different situations later on—the words pop back into my mind when they are most useful. These directions are rather like little nudges, as though the conference were a ship with the director keeping the ship on course. But they are indirect directions rather than instructing me exactly what to do and how to do it in a particular situation. This indirectness allows the possibility of new ways to emerge—I have to work it out for myself and decide to follow. This way the director also lives with the uncertainty about whether or not his/her vision is being followed, so the trust between us must be mutual.

The director can share his/her vision by official proclamations or maybe despite them: by small everyday conversations and asides (the stuff of the office) and not just by the words but more importantly by the way the words are said, the tone of voice and attitude of the speaker. S/he can't avoid being true to their vision—whatever it is. Kinesics or body language will expose what they really believe and its relative clarity and integrity. The administrator absorbs all this information almost by osmosis, and integrates/translates it into everything that goes on, including disseminating it to others, staff and members. I often hear Eliat Aram's (director of the Leicester conference, 2010) voice inside my head, or imagine her hands making pictures in the air.

Status

Administration generally has a low status. Everyone knows what administration is. Anyone can do it—over the past twenty years we have seen the democratisation of administration with the advent of email and personal computers.

And then there can be a denial of the need for administration—in the world event plenary at Leicester 2009, the world forum needed practical administrative assistance; they required music at the beginning of the plenary but they had not appointed someone to do this, either because it was not considered or not considered necessary or perhaps no one wanted to do it so it was ignored. And perhaps this reflects the low status that is attributed to it.

"Like other jobs characteristically held by women, conference administration carries less status and less overt power" (Parish, 2007). The administrative function involves serving others, caretaking and housekeeping, in effect being mother. Mothers produce and nurture babies, the ultimate creation, and yet it is ironic that they have a comparatively low status, don't get paid, and often feel isolated and undervalued in society. Historically, it has been predominantly men who have been considered creative and thus highly valued, Renaissance artists; sixteenth century British playwrights, etc.

Doing things has less status than thinking. So, for instance, manual work is seen to have a lesser role than intellectual theorising. Some people may assume that the administrative role is simply a matter of doing things. What may administration represent to staff and members in a group relations conference? Perhaps doing without thinking. Levine (2002) talks about the flight from learning "so learning by doing be(comes) a defence against learning". Further, splitting thinking from practice, whereby the thinking becomes abstract and therefore irrelevant to real life, congeals and stagnates any action that might be necessary and so can be an attack on our own potential creativity. Moreover, when thinking has a higher status than practice, there can be an increased tendency for this split of action with thinking. If administration is considered to just "do" when they actually "think", for instance by making a remark in a plenary, this can be shocking and may elicit an attack from the membership. I remember when I first made a remark in a plenary and in unison all the members' heads swivelled around to look at me. So how do we learn, by thinking or by doing? Certainly when I've been a member at a group relations conference, perhaps in an inter-group event, there can be an urge to do something, anything, in my small group rather than engage with the primary task and think about the group process instead and so learn in the here-and-now. Equally I've been in groups where all we did was "think" and didn't manage to do anything, with equally impotent results.

Since Aristotle, Western ideas about knowledge have been about a process of observation, reasoning, and logic which is then written down explicitly using language as rigorously as possible. "The history of the Western world has … been a history of rendering articulate and explicit … our knowledge and understanding of the underlying causes of phenomena in the world" (Chia, 2003). Conversely, in the East it is through direct, repetitive experimental practice that knowledge is embodied in the individual and this cannot necessarily be articulated through language but is invisible, tacit, and inferred. In the same way, the subtext in the Leicester conference becomes what the conference is all about. So the administration is the art of looking for a fine balance afresh in every moment through both thought and action.

Margins/Centre

We might imagine that in the conference or temporary organisation there is a hierarchy with the director at the top, then the consultants and the members making up the base, the classic pyramid shape, with the administration perhaps either right at the bottom or somewhere else altogether. Another way of thinking about this is as a diamond shape—director at the top, administration at the bottom, the bulge of the members in the middle surrounded by the consultants. But tip this diamond on its side and tie the end points to two trees and you have a hammock, swinging with the ebb and flow of the conference. Perhaps you could have the administrator and assistant administrator at either end, creating a cradle. Or you could think of the conference as a nest of bowls.

"Containment depends on maintaining clear boundaries and being responsive to needs". "Boundary management is part of the central, vital function of administration …" (Parish, 2007). These boundaries include those of time, that is, inviting the members over the threshold into the conference at registration; marking the beginning and end of plenaries, etc.; managing the boundaries of the conference admin office opening hours; interactions with the staff of the venue,: making numerous small adjustments to the arrangements we have with them. So the administration is at the margins, on the edge of the conference.

Furthermore, in the mind, administration can be not just on the margins but somehow doing the job completely outside the conference altogether—I've experienced a member expressing this. Conversely, the administration is placed at the centre of the conference, in the middle of everything and in the conference directorate and staff meetings. It has a unique take on the conference—having an understanding from the view of the visiting members at office opening hours; the directorate; the staff meetings; and through interactions with the staff of the venue. All the above provides the administration with knowledge and with knowledge comes power.

Administration makes the conference happen, invisibly if it is functioning well. But that very invisibility can make the administration disappear altogether—several times in conferences, the administration has been completely forgotten or almost left out when plans are being made. It is only as I have come to embrace my role more that I've realised the central connectiveness of the administration, not just holding up, but making, the invisible warp which helps to keep the weft together.

Administration looks after the details and at the same time has an overview, the context, which is more like the complex way we think. "Breaking down limiting hierarchical binary opposition such as science/art, innovation/tradition, serious/playful, order/disorder, doing/thinking." "The need for a thinking that recognizes both part and whole, contextualizes, and connects" (Montuori, 2003) We can't abolish complexity by reducing things to something simple.

If we respond to the complexities of life, or the complexities of the conference, with tension, making things difficult and complicated, trying hard, fighting and reacting, we get less than nowhere. It is a matter of practising allowing things to be simple and fluid. "Less is more" (Mies van der Rohe, 1959). Setting things in stone, trying to control through holding on rather than letting go, releasing tensions to alleviate anxiety, allows us indirect control through integrity. Part of the administrator's role is to alleviate anxiety and create optimal conditions for learning. This includes self-organisation which can then also be seen as a mirror of the organisation.

"Creative thought seeks to make sense of phenomena that appear to be chaotic, and seeks to create a higher order simplicity" (Montuori, 2003).

Sometimes the computer, printer, or the music technology breaks down or refuses to work at a particular moment in the conference. This is common at the beginning of plenaries for instance, which is an expression of the high anxiety associated with those moments. At the beginning of the 2010 conference, I was changing the coloured ink in the printer—a bit of a delicate operation which I thought I knew how to do—but it became jammed and we were unable to use the colour for the rest of the conference. Administration becomes only too noticeable when it is seen to be going wrong.

Both tradition and creativity

The Leicester conference temporary organisation is seen as the cradle of group relations tradition—2010 is its sixty-fourth recurrence; it is the original one and spans fourteen days—longer than any other. Coming to Leicester can be a long-term aspiration for people, often effecting profound and ongoing personal adaptations, developments, and transformations during and after the experience, so myths and legends have grown up about its nature. Somehow it has to remain the same as it always was when *I* attended—even though by its nature it is completely different each time it occurs. There's less room for Leicester to be about imagination, innovation, and inspiration, and there is a certain amount of resistance to the idea that these are and have always been intrinsic elements, that in fact they are what group relations is all about. There is an urge to set Leicester in stone, to finally understand it—people want to feel they *know* about it, that this is how to do it. The Tavistock group relations methodology is used in various different incarnations around the world all the time but there are variations in how adventurous these are, how willing the staff are to take risks around the methodology. There will always be a certain amount of structure set up by the pre-administration (a list of members, the timetable, etc.) but from there, how much of the group relations conference can be questioned, rethought, changed, and adapted? The world has changed a lot since 1957; the first Leicester conference, and Leicester itself, has incorporated many innovations from other group relations conferences, for example, the yoga event in 2008 and the world event in 2009 morphing into the global society event in 2010.

Similarly I can understand to a large extent the demigod status of Eric Miller, one of the originators of the Leicester conference, though it seems obvious to say that he did not know everything. In his *The Leicester Model* (1989), which still remains the main written source about the Leicester conference, he barely mentions the administrative function. The cult of the genius manifests itself.

Where the administration is creative, there may be more potential for destruction and/or the fear of such. The freedom of creativity demands a lighter touch and with that comes the fear that there is not enough containment. Then again, when something is squeezed so hard it becomes lifeless, it needs some disorder or chaos in order to revitalise it. A few years ago there was an exciting artwork in the Tate Modern art gallery in London called "Cold Dark Matter" or, more popularly, "The Exploding Shed": this was a shed containing lots of ordinary shed objects and a light at the centre which was first photographed; then the shed was taken away to be exploded and subsequently recreated in the space in an exploding condition around the light. Another artwork called "Erased" by de Kooning (Stevens & Swann, 2004) is a valued picture given to the artist Rauschenberg by de Kooning, which Rauschenberg then rubbed out and renamed. Iconoclasm has an important place—in the Leicester conference I've learnt to listen out for, and observe most intently, the one who rocks the boat, the one who appears to be going against the current. The administration has a unique position where there is more space to notice what is actually going on and to make useful observations, in the staff meetings and in the events of the conference.

In conclusion, it seems to me that, like any other role, administration can be creative, depending on what you decide to bring to it. There is a particular freedom inherent in the role which allows the possibility of continuous expansion of the role which is exciting. 2012 will be my eighth incarnation in the role at the Leicester conference and I'm already looking forward to it.

References

Brown, A. D., & Starkey, K. (2000). Organizational identity and learning: a psychodynamic perspective. *The Academy of Management Review, 25*: 102–120.

Chia, R. (2003). From knowledge-creation to the perfecting of action: Tao, basho and pure experience as the ultimate ground of knowing. *Human Relations, 56*: 953.

Gogol, N. V. (1842). *The Overcoat*. New York: Dover Thrift.

Levine, D. P. (2002). Thinking about doing: on learning from experience and the flight from thinking. *Human Relations, 55*: 1251.

Levine, D. P. (2005). The corrupt organization. *Human Relations, 58*: 723.

Miller, E. J. (1983). *Work and Creativity* (TIHR occasional paper No 6). London: Tavistock Publications.

Miller, E. J. (1989). *The Leicester Model*. (TIHR Occasional Paper No 10). London: Tavistock Publications.

Montuori, A. (2003). The complexity of improvisation and the improvisation of complexity. Social science, art, and creativity. *Human Relations, 56:* 237–25.

Morris, J. A., Brotheridge, C. M., & Urbanski, J. C. (2005). Bringing humility to leadership: Antecedents and consequences of leader humility. *Human Relations, 58*: 1323.

Orwell, G. (1940). The lion and the unicorn. In: Orwell, G., *Why I Write*. London: Penguin Books.

Parish, M. (2007). Reflections on the administrator's role. *Organisational & Social Dynamics, 7*: 61–72.

Stevens, M., & Swann, A. (2004). *de Kooning: an American Master*. New York: Knopf.

van der Rohe, Mies (1959). Speaking about restraint in design. New York Herald Tribune (28 June).

SECTION II

JOURNEYS OF CONFERENCES: GRAPPLING WITH TRADITION, SUCCESSION, AND APPLICATION

This section consists of three distinctive chapters, each dealing with a GR application in a very context-specific yet globally relevant way. The first of those describes the "Nazareth" conferences, an initiative of two psychoanalytic organisations, one in Jerusalem and one in Berlin, that came together to provide space and opportunity for the working through of the German Jewish history. It has then evolved into expanding the exploration to include the Palestinian and Israeli tension and any Other who cares. This is the subject matter of this paper. The second paper takes us through the Robben Island conferences in South Africa, which were set up against the socio-political changes in the country and have focused predominantly on race relations and diversity. This chapter explores the conference location as container for diversity from the director's lens. The third chapter takes us to Australia where the group relations network has also been active for some decades. Two veteran GR consultants invite us to examine age and generational aspects of organisational life, which include succession as well as innovation issues, exploring the inter-generational issues beyond what they term the "family psychic template".

CHAPTER FOUR

Germans, Jews, Israelis, Palestinians, and Others today: thoughts on the "Nazareth" conferences

Louisa D. Brunner, M. Fakhry Davids, and Dorothee C. von Tippelskirch-Eissing[1]

Introduction

Tradition, creativity, and succession—the themes of this conference in Belgirate—are very alive in the work we are reporting on. The Nazareth conferences now have a firmly established *tradition* of applying the group relations methodology to specific, pressing problems in the external and internal worlds, which we will describe below. They began by addressing the German-Israeli dyad, which carried within it the legacy of the Holocaust, but from the fourth conference onwards, a *creative* process of opening up began, which resulted in the Palestinians and Others being incorporated into the work. This has brought new challenges to the way of working that had been established in the series. The three of us were not involved in the original Nazareth conferences, but joined the fourth conference in 2004—Louisa Brunner and Fakhry Davids as staff, and Dorothee von Tippelskirch-Eissing as a member—so we are of the *successor* generations.

In this paper we aim to give a brief historical overview of the project. Full details of the early history are contained in the recently published book by three founder members of the Nazareth project (Erlich, Erlich-Ginor, & Beland, 2009), and we will add some material from more recent conferences to give a feel of what takes place there. We go on to discuss some ways in which this initiative differs from the general group relations approach, and raise a question relevant to the theme of tradition, creativity, and succession.

The Nazareth conferences: a brief history

There have been six Nazareth conferences. In fact the conferences began at the second attempt. The first had been scheduled for 1993, but in the event only six psychoanalysts[2] registered, so it was cancelled. The founding members of the project, who were psychoanalysts and others interested in the group relations approach, underwent considerable group relations training prior to the first conference, and formed a core group that remained quite constant over the years, setting itself the task of learning from the experience as the conference processes unfolded. Other staff members came and went, and this mix provided stability and continuity of the project, as well as leaving room for fresh input.

In 1994 and 1996 the first two conferences took place in Israel, in Nazareth—hence the name—and the third conference was held in 2000 in Bad Segeberg, Germany. These first three conferences worked under the title of "Germans and Israelis: the past in the present"[3]. As far as aims were concerned, it was recognised early on that "the power of this work lies in that it does not aim at rapprochement or exoneration" (Erlich, Erlich-Ginor, & Beland, 2009, p. 15), or, as Anton Obholzer put it in a director's report: "The focus of the conference as intended and achieved was not essentially on reconciliation and forgiveness but on learning about the dynamics of enmity".

Not long after the third conference in 2000, Rafael Moses, one of the founders of the project, and Eric Miller, director of the first three conferences, died. Mira Erlich-Ginor, in contributing to this chapter, describes their deaths as acting symbolically as "death of the fathers" and required a long period of mourning until the next move could be made. The next conference would take place four years later in 2004. A new director had to be appointed, a rethinking was in place.

Mira Erlich-Ginor goes on to describe how "a self-authorized work group for the carrying on the GIC Project", a "pre-conference think tank", addressed several questions concerning membership: the restriction to helping profession practitioners, the naming of "Israelis" but not "Jews"—which involved the question of how to open up to the perspective of Diaspora Jews, including German Jews—and the question of a third group of "others", which had been waiting in the wings for some time.

Anton Obholzer was appointed to direct the next three conferences, and he brought in two new staff members—Louisa Brunner, a Diaspora Jew, and Fakhry Davids, a Muslim "other"—concretely representing the wish to move on and open up. This reflected a degree of security about the method developed in the series. A new venue, neither Israel nor Germany, was found in Cyprus, "the interface of many social migrations and conflicts" (Conference Brochure, 2008).

The title of the next two conferences, in 2004 and 2006 respectively, was "Shaping the future by confronting the past: Germans, Jews and affected Others". Including a group of affected Others led, organically, to the Palestinians appearing as symbolically in the fifth conference, and this led directly to their inclusion in the title of the sixth one. We will describe some of this process in greater detail later in this chapter. This step, which was understood within the core group as an organic development, brought into sharp focus the question of who held authority for carrying forward and modifying the project from the original German-Israeli focus. In 2007, Partners in Confronting Collective Atrocities[4], a charity based in Germany, was formed to take responsibility for taking the Nazareth conference project forward.

This turning point in the project was again marked by a new title under which the next conference in 2008 was held. It was "Repeating, reflecting, moving on: Germans, Jews, Israelis, Palestinians & Others today". Three new members of staff were invited—Eliat Aram (a British-Israeli Jew), Adib Jarrar (a Palestinian who lives in Paris and Ramallah), and Dorothee von Tippelskirch-Eissing, one of the authors of this paper. The next conference, in June 2010, will work under the same title and will be co-directed by Fakhry Davids and Mira Erlich-Ginor.

You will have noticed that we stress explicitly aspects of our personal identity as relevant to the work. Identity is, of course, a complex phenomenon, and in our preparatory work as a staff group we try to focus on what each of us brings that is relevant to the forthcoming work. Since this is different from the way in which a regular group relations conference might begin, we would like now to give a flavour of some of the reflections that make up such personal journeys into the conference. Usually, these would be commented on by others, and it is not unusual for such contributions to elicit powerful responses, thereby opening up an engagement with emotionally charged, painful, and "hot" topics. It is this work, alongside their basic familiarity with the group relations method, that prepares the staff group for the work that is to follow in the conference itself.

Identity: personal narratives

Louisa Diana Brunner

I was born in Cambridge in 1951. My mother was born a German Jew in Mannheim; she went to Italy in the 1930s to attend university, but had to escape from Italy because of the racial laws there and she fled to England. My father was born an Italian Jew in Trieste. He had to leave Italy in 1938 to go to London. Both families suffered deeply because of the Holocaust. My parents met and married in Cambridge. In 1956 my parents decided to go back to Trieste with my sister and me.

I was the first child of the post-Holocaust and post-war generation. I always had the feeling that I had to carry hope and an opening towards the future and that pain was not allowed for me, that that was my role in the family.

In my childhood and adolescence we lived a totally assimilated and cosmopolitan life in Italy which was, and is, a Catholic country, and is quite homogenous culturally, prone to promoting conversion and to proselytism. In the 1950s and 1960s the pressure towards assimilation was very strong. I am baptised. From a sociological perspective one would define it as a majority—minority dynamic and tension where the majority strives towards homogeneity and incorporation. I always knew that I was Jewish, but I felt it difficult to make it meaningful for me; my feeling was always of being an "other", of being different, never finding a group in which to identify myself. This was extremely painful and difficult and has confronted me all my life with the issues of inclusion and exclusion in terms of class, ethnicity, race, religious identity, etc. Historically the Jews of the Diaspora have been perceived as the "other" and have undergone all type of projections all along.

In 2008, Anton Obholzer, who knew my background from our work in Italy, invited me to join the staff of the Cyprus conference for the third time. Every time I went through different emotions and anxieties on how to take up such a role. Before going to Cyprus, I went to Jerusalem. Israel is a place where I do not feel an "other", it feels safe there, although I am really an "other" there. The last evening I met a friend with whom, although our life choices are very different, I share an assimilated Jewish background, a wandering one and an international/cosmopolitan one. It is so difficult for me to find people similar to me and not to feel socially an "other". That evening I experienced once more my lifelong inner and social tension about being the "same" and an "other" at the same time. It was connecting with all this in Jerusalem that evening that helped me to prepare my emotional luggage for the conference, deeply in touch with where I come from physically and emotionally, carrying that pain and hope that is the trans-generational heritage and legacy of my family history.

Fakhry Davids

Anton Obholzer, newly appointed director for the fourth conference, knew of my work on the psychology of racism and we had also collaborated on similar events examining the inner legacy of apartheid in the new South Africa. Anton also felt that my Muslim background might add a helpful perspective to proceedings.

My early awareness of the Holocaust itself was quite limited—in apartheid South Africa we had little direct contact with Jews (who were part of the privileged white group), and the events of World War II were far less prominent than they are in Europe—unless, of course, one was actually studying European history. The most visible public references to the Holocaust occurred in the liberal press when the atrocities of the apartheid regime were likened to those of the Nazis, a case sealed by the fact that during the War the governing party[5] had openly sided with the German enemy of the then-British colonial power. This equation between apartheid and Nazism was understood in a rhetorical rather than a literal way—they invoked the Holocaust to sound the alarm as to how catastrophic a path the racist mindset had set our country on.

There was, however, a specific way in which these distant events did indeed reach into our lives. It was widely known that the state of Israel came into existence on a wave of international sympathy for the plight of Jews as victims of the Nazis. However, the birth of the Jewish state also involved the displacement of large numbers of Palestinians, sowing the seeds of an ongoing conflict that, whenever it erupted, transformed the everyday relationship between Jew and Muslim everywhere. In our part of the world, that relationship was largely characterised by mutual tolerance and respect—in Islam, Jews and Christians have a special status as previous recipients of the message of monotheism—but on these occasions that relationship became fraught with strain and tension that sometimes gave way to bitter hostility and xenophobic hatred. This I knew to be a *no-go area*, and the prospect of being able to work more deeply on the elements that went into this situation interested me. You will see, therefore, how natural it was for me to see the Palestinian issue as relevant to a conference exploring the aftermath of the Holocaust.

Dorothee von Tippelskirch-Eissing

I am German. I am Christian. My father's mother was British/Dutch, with a very international background. During the war my grandfather, who came from a Prussian noble family, hid a Jewish woman in his clinic, which was in a small German resort that had declared itself "judenrein"—cleansed of Jews. Nobody ever spoke about this, and I myself discovered it by accident in a book that I read when I was student. At the end of the war those of my relatives from my father's side who survived flight and expulsion from Prussia (now Poland), arrived and stayed in his house, most of them severely traumatised for life.

My father suffered from a hereditary disease that resulted in him being disfigured by stunted growth. However, he had nonetheless chosen to become a soldier in Hitler's army in order to be like everyone else—seeking privilege neither on account of his physical disability nor his noble ancestry (and their hygienic racial criteria were highly intolerant of anyone judged as deficient in relation to the Aryan ideal). My grandfather on my mother's side was a socially engaged protestant minister, a national conservative opposed to the national-socialist movement. Her two beloved older half-brothers, twins, both served in the army and did not survive the war.

Working on my part in this paper, I realised how difficult my German legacy made it for me to participate freely. I felt paralysed and disabled, and found it hard to imagine myself speaking to the audience in an international conference as a *German*. I realised that I did not want to be visible personally in this way. Building on his experience of the Nazareth conferences, Hermann Beland, too, has described this difficulty on the part of German psychoanalysts in taking up Freud's heritage—to speak and contribute to an exchange of thoughts and ideas in an international context[6]. He suggests that this expresses a "typical German, paranoid complex of guilt" that is a legacy of the Holocaust. It is such phenomena that we try to grapple with in these Conferences.

At other moments, I felt a tremendous amount of loneliness and anxiety, which I could only understand step by step as a repetition of being left utterly alone by my "German" parents, and later by my broader professional groups of colleagues and compatriots, all of whom remained silent in confronting these difficult and painful issues. The anxiety was related to rage and hatred on my part towards them. The fact that I was a staff member of the last conference but am not a member of PCCA,[7] may also actualise a dynamic of inclusion and exclusion simultaneously, which links with a desire to belong. However, being involved with the work of the conference—Germans, Jews, Israelis, Palestinians and Others today—also carries such destructive loadings that one might well wish to be elsewhere.

Conference structure and design

The *primary task* of the first three conferences was "to provide opportunities for participants to explore how feelings and fantasies about 'German-ness' and 'Israeli-ness/Jewish-ness' influence relations within and between the two groups in the conference"[8]. This primary task is different from that at a traditional "Leicester" conference, where the focus is on how power, authority, and leadership are played out in the event and are studied. In fact, exercising authority in a Nazareth conference is an extraordinarily complex matter—how can it not carry shades of meaning with a loaded history of fascism and Nazism, national exclusivity and intolerance of the other, racial oppression and occupation, and totalitarian leadership, all of which led to the final solution of genocide? To exercise authority in such an atmosphere is therefore fraught with difficulty.

In the first three conferences, at the suggestion of Eric Miller, there were small study groups (SSG—mixed nationalities, approximately ten members), review and application groups (RAG—same nationality, approximately ten members), and several plenaries (all staff and all members). There was no large study group (LSG) as this setting was seen as likely to stir up forces that might not readily be contained.

One problem that has been apparent since the first conference was that some members, for whom the work of the conferences was very relevant, did not fit the neatly defined categories of "German" or "Israeli". As we have already indicated, following the death of two of the founders, the membership was expanded to include "others" affected by the Holocaust. With this development and the appointment of a new director, the structure of the conferences also changed to incorporate a large study group with its own consultants. It may be that by this stage the method of working was sufficiently securely established to allow the staff to venture into this new territory. In 2008, the director went further and suggested that the management (director, two associate directors, and administrator) should work as consultants to the LSG, suggesting perhaps that containment of the LSG held a special symbolic significance in an event of this sort. Below is the programme from the 2008 Conference.

Sixth Nazareth conference programme, 2008

Repeating, reflecting, moving on: Germans, Jews, Israelis, Palestinians and Others today

	Wednesday	Thursday	Friday	Saturday	Sunday	Monday
7:00–9:00	Breakfast					
9:00–10.30		LSG	LSG	LSG	LSG	RG
10:30–11:00	Coffee					
11:00–12:30		SSG	SSG	SSG	SSG	CP
13:00–14:00	Lunch					
14:30–16:00	OP	SE	—	SE	SE	
16:00–16:30	Coffee					
16:30–18:00	SSG	SE	SE	SE	P	
19.00–20:00	Dinner					
20:30–22:00	LSG	RG	SE	—	RG	
OP—Opening Plenary; SSG—Small Study Group; LSG—Large Study Group; SE—System Event; RG—Review Group; P—Plenary; CP—Closing Plenary.						

Selected Cyprus excerpts

In the opening plenary of the first Cyprus conference—the fourth in the Nazareth series—an Israeli member asked why, given that the conference was to address others[9] affected by the Holocaust, there was no Palestinian on the staff? It was suggested that the Palestinians were indeed present at this conference—not as participants in the flesh, but within the mind. As it does in plenaries, the discussion moved on, but any hope that this comment might open the way for an engagement with the subject of the Palestinians proved unfounded.

However, there was a flashpoint *within* the staff system relevant to the Palestinian issue. On one occasion during the system event, when all the staff were together, the point was made that Hitler's explicit ideological aim was to exterminate the Jews *as a people*, which set the Holocaust apart from other instances where, usually, genocide is secondary to some other aim (e.g., the conquest of land). It was suggested that a case could be made that Golda Meir's much-publicised assertion that Israel was a land *without* a people for a people without a land[10] contained an explicitly genocidal *idea* in that it necessarily obliterated the existing Palestinian population of the land. At that very moment there was a knock on the door requesting the staff member responsible for this comment, together with a colleague, to consult to an inter-group meeting, which meant that the conversation among staff was abruptly interrupted.

After their departure this remark sparked a heated furore in which the staff member concerned was accused by an Israeli colleague of minimising the Holocaust by equating it with events involved in the creation of the state of Israel. We did not return to these matters, and this flashpoint involving conflict between a Muslim/Palestinian perspective and a Jewish/Israeli one was not contained in the structure of our proceedings, and thus underwent repression.

Return of the repressed

In the closing plenary of the fourth conference an Israeli staff member noted, in the dying moments, that there had been no comment on the fact that one of his colleagues has a Muslim name. Did this silence have a meaning? The gaze of the membership settled on, the colleague in question, who felt completely paralysed by this intervention. After a few moments a voice inquired what it had been like for him to be at the conference. A pregnant pause followed, before he shrugged, "What can I say?".

Our colleague's comment had had a violent impact on our Muslim colleague, leaving him enraged, which he spoke about in the hour-long debriefing meeting afterwards. He returned home still feeling violated, and was determined not to have anything further to do with "so-called colleagues for whom he was nothing but a token 'Muslim' in their midst". He felt they now stood revealed as wanting a token, rather than a real, Palestinian—the question raised in the opening plenary.

Moving on: staff work

We learnt from that conference that work on "hot" issues like this was relevant to our task, yet was left uncontained. We therefore added a full working day for staff before the members' conference and one after to address this omission.

This was a fortuitous decision, for the next conference took place just after Israel's invasion of Lebanon. In addition to discussing the left-over Muslim issue, we now found ourselves plunged into a heated debate over whether an international Muslim conspiracy, with the Hamas-Hizbullah-Iran axis at its core, directed against the West and the state of Israel, existed. In this scenario Israel faced the prospect of a Holocaust all over again—had not Ahmedinejad, the Iranian president, explicitly denied the Holocaust, all the while openly voicing the wish to wipe Israel from the map? Given this threat it was surely understandable that Israel should defend herself—and Western civilisation—by whatever means possible, with considerations of proportionality an academic luxury.

Fakhry Davids argued that a current of Islamophobia coloured Western views of motives in the Middle East, the aim of which was to reduce complex social and political reality into a simplified us-them polarity. Once deployed, we are all drawn powerfully into stereotyped mindsets that make objective observation and critical thinking very difficult: each side tended to justify their position as right, and to demonise the other. Perhaps you will have guessed that this view generated a heated debate, with others arguing that it either ignores or minimises real threats from extremists. The exchange between us would, in diplomatic language, be characterised as "full and frank" and generating intense feeling and passion.

From our point of view, the important thing was not who was right and who was wrong, but that a setting had been created where these issues could be voiced. The viewpoints were true and held with conviction, and afterwards many members of staff suggested that it was this engagement, at the outset, that equipped us, as a staff group, for the task ahead. We had begun to put right the failure in the previous conference highlighted by the Golda Meir remark, namely that a powerful conflict between two different views of Israeli-Palestinian situation had been left uncontained. A split previously unattended to was now in the open, hence its ability to sow the seeds for further conflict and enmity was now known openly and its dimensions had been gone into. In that conference it became possible for us to recognise, with emotional conviction, that an unwanted and displaced group in the system event was, indeed, the Palestinians. We had grown organically and in the next conference we incorporated the Palestinians formally—they belonged to the work.

A large study group

We would like to describe two incidents from a large study group, where Fakhry Davids and von Tippelskirch-Eissing were two of the four consultants present. Early on, a conflagration flared up between an Israeli and a Palestinian member. Previously, a number of relevant issues had been raised and were still alive. For example, the fact that the conference flyer had been translated into Arabic (and not German or Hebrew) had been raised, bringing a protest that Arabic, and hence the Palestinian situation, was being given preferential treatment at this conference. Was this sending an unconscious signal about which issues, and hence groups, were to be given priority here? Speaking to the theme of equality and even-handedness, a Palestinian member contrasted the journey of a typical Israeli to a conference like this—book the tickets, take one's passport, and pass freely through security and custom controls—to that of a typical Palestinian journey—apply for official permission to attend well in advance, be subjected to interrogation of one's motives etc. and kept waiting endlessly, be held up at checkpoints, be singled out for humiliation at the airport, supposedly on security grounds but really on account of being Arab, and thus risk missing flights.

An articulate Palestinian woman—the only person at the conference with a *hijab* (headscarf) which she wore tightly around her head, concealing all her hair—had thus far contributed substantially.

A German woman commented on how she reminded her of Hamas, a provocative comment that succeeded in bringing her to her feet once more. An Israeli woman now interrupted, saying that we had already heard a lot from her—could she not shut up and take in what others said for a change? The Palestinian would not oblige, and instead accused the Israeli of "killing us" back home. Here, however, that would not be tolerated and she would just have to listen to Palestinians. Before we knew what was happening the two of them were involved in a vicious shouting match—the Palestinian woman on her feet and the Israeli sitting some distance away. A German member now got to her feet and, raising her voice over the two of them, said that they looked like someone in a watchtower shooting at another on the ground who, in turn, was returning the fire. This mindless, heedless violence distressed her, especially as a German. It reminded her of being inside the Holocaust memorial in Berlin from where, paradoxically, one cannot hear anything going on outside, just as Germans did not "hear" the murder going on in their own country during the Holocaust. This description, and her pain at witnessing such unstoppable violence afresh, struck a deep chord with the group.

Compared with the earlier conferences, we see here that a German found the position of a "third" opened up, allowing comment from an observer position that offered a possibility of containment through thought. For Germans, it came as a surprise to be located outside the perpetrator-victim dyad. Could they become a container for the anxiety, hatred, and despair between Jews and Palestinians, paradoxically introducing an element of hope? In previous conferences this possibility had been unthinkable; it also highlighted the need to differentiate between this "third" position, which involves tolerating the anxiety of getting caught up within the lines of confrontation, and the position of a bystander, where one tries to lift oneself manically above the fray.

When the consultants discussed this incident afterwards, we felt that it indicated that the large study group setting must have felt sufficiently secure for an issue as powerful as this to surface so directly, an impression that was reinforced by the way in which the process moved on in the course of the conference.

The second incident was a moment of great relief, when some younger members, including Palestinians, Israelis, Germans and Others, started to talk about a "party" they had had the night before. It began at the pool, then a young woman, Palestinian, retreated to a bedroom with several young men, where it continued. How could she manage all these young men? Had anything happened? The atmosphere in the large study group was now highly charged and expectant. With delicate innuendo, she explained that their sexuality was not a threat—at least some of the men were homosexual.

As the sexual tension gradually dissipated, some older members spoke of how much noise the younger ones had generated. In self-mocking tones an older member noted that what used to be quite an "old" conference, in terms of the age of members, who mostly belonged to the "second generation"—children of war and post-war times—was now a much "younger"-looking Conference, with a number of younger Germans, Israelis, and some from other countries, and nearly all the Palestinians being in their twenties or thirties. Would the "second generation" allow the next one to move on or would this be judged as too noisy and risky, and would the "old" issues be forced into them, making for an endless repetition?

System event: a site of difficulty

In recent conferences the system event has emerged as a site where difficulties have been located. At the last conference (the sixth, in 2008) we left it to the membership to decide which groups they would form, without any suggestion or reminder as to the groupings that were in fact present (i.e., Germans, Israelis, and Palestinians etc.) In the event, groups were formed mostly resembling a small study group in composition—that is, with mixed composition—each setting out to reflect on and study issues relevant to the conference theme (e.g., "Mourning and moving on", "Hopelessness and desperation", "Aggression—cold hate", "Tower", "How Germans fit in", "Sex and what if we can't fight and feel burnt out?", "Separation—cooperation—identity", "Feel the pain of the others"). It is significant, we think, that the membership resisted forming "nationality" groups. This can be seen as anti-task in that it prevented the sort of flashpoint that we reported from the large study group being studied in greater depth, which is the very task of the system event.

There was awareness in the system of this difficulty, and later on an attempt was made to put things right. There was an invitation (on the system event notice board) in which a sort of mini system event within the system event was proposed, where the nationality groups would be allowed fifteen minutes to consider issues relevant to themselves, but *in the presence* of everyone else. This suggests that the system event itself was felt to be insufficiently secure to contain dynamics that might arise once people broke into their national groupings. In a similar vein, there was a late attempt to set up a "Palestinian" group—made up of an Israeli, an East European living in Israel and one Other, but this drew a hostile response. A note appeared on the notice board warning that groups can be driven to violence if they feel their identities have been taken over.

If we bear in mind that the aim of the system event is to allow the dynamics between groupings present at the conference to come to life and hence be experienced, observed, and reflected on, and thus give depth to the proceedings, we have here a serious obstacle to deepening our work. We will not dwell any further on the meaning of this issue except to say that management did eventually point out that this was defensive, and there was widespread recognition that people were just too afraid to go there. We raise it here as an instance of the sort of difficulties that come up and which the staff group try to bear in mind for future work.

Discussion: Nazareth conferences and group relations

In dividing the work for this paper, we decided that Louisa Brunner should be responsible for bringing forward discussion points situating the Nazareth conference developments within the broader group relations and psychoanalytic traditions. A management and organisational consultant by profession, Brunner felt initially immobilised by this task, especially by its psychoanalytic dimension. Her reflections on this problem and on why her colleagues, who are practising psychoanalysts, unconsciously gave her this task, illustrate one aspect of the work of these conferences:

> It may be that the process of writing the paper mirrored or enacted something about shifting roles. In the Holocaust genocide the Jews were the victims and the Nazi Germans the perpetrators. But as time passes, in the present Israeli-Palestinian conflict (a war), things are different as one has to deal with foes. Namely the role of the aggressor is not to be found only in one subgroup as during the Holocaust; it can shift and change, and this can be very painful. Furthermore, as previously described, in the conference a German

could take up a "third party" role between Israelis and Palestinians. In this process, however, the Diaspora Jews and the Others—in theory, the expected "Third"—were sidelined and silenced. This, I think, also enacted a stereotype of the passive Diaspora Jew versus the active Israeli Jew. I saw that I was re-enacting something of all this in writing the paper, and this helped me to move forward. I started to think about the theme in terms of group relations, which comprises both psychoanalytic ideas and the systemic dimension, which is indeed "my cup of tea".

A more psychoanalytic conference?

On the flight back from Cyprus in 2008 two of us (Brunner and von Tippelskirch-Eissing), who have considerable experience in the group relations tradition, discussed with Hermann Beland, one of the founders of the series, our observation that the psychoanalytic dimension is more prominent in these conferences than any other in the group relations movement. There are different aspects to this. First, although Nazareth conferences were conceived on the basis of group relations theory and methodology, they arose out of the need to access and address the inner legacy of the Holocaust, which Israeli and German analysts (and others) recognised as being alive within them. This is important, for analysts have all had an extensive psychoanalysis, and it was recognised that these aspects of their inner world had not been fully accessed in that process. This gave these conferences an explicitly analytic task from the outset.

Second, and following on from this point, a large proportion of the membership of the Nazareth Conferences have been psychoanalysts and psychotherapists and, alongside sponsors from the world of group relations (OFEK, Tavistock), the conferences are uniquely sponsored by psychoanalytic organisations (International Psychoanalytic Association, German Psychoanalytic Societies, DPV and DPG, and Israeli Psychoanalytic Societies).

Third, a shared culture has evolved over the years. Within the group relations movement we think of the conference as a temporary learning organisation. However, in the case of the Nazareth conferences this concept must be extended to recognise a "continuing learning community of practice". In addition to the conferences themselves, there are "in-between activities among members and staff, the staff is quite stable and the same, etc." (Erlich-Ginor, unpublished note on the history of the project), which impacts on the culture of the conferences. Shein (1996) defines the culture of an organisation as "the basic tacit assumptions about how the world is and ought to be that a group of people are sharing and that determines their perceptions, thoughts, feelings and their overt behaviour". In the Nazareth conferences this culture, which functions unconsciously, is expressed in a common psychoanalytic "language" (e.g., the desirability of reflection rather action, and the use of technical terms like projective identification etc.), which is noticeable to those of us (Brunner) who come from outside that tradition. This language reflects a strong bond among participants, expressing hidden aspects of the identity of the project. It is shared by most of staff and members—there is little need for detailed explanation—which makes for a known and safe environment in which to address topics that are uncanny, scary, poignant, painful. But the existence of this shared culture could also exclude and alienate those who do not "speak" that language, and whose potentially valuable contributions to the project might therefore be lost.

Presence of the Other

As stated earlier, these conferences do not aim at reconciliation, but recognise that past atrocities continue to impact on relationships in the present, underpinning them with "hidden prejudices, stereotypes, fantasies and fears" which the conference simply aims to bring to the surface (Brochure, 2010).

The discovery in the Nazareth series is that to work properly on the conflicted dynamics stemming from past atrocity the physical presence of the Other is essential; it is not sufficient to have them "in the mind". Erlich-Ginor notes that "work in the presence of the Other is ... probably the unique contribution of the conference ... in order to get out from the imprisonment of the past"; Beland stresses that the Other "is the counterpart of one's burden of guilt and shame ... suffering and pain" (Erlich, Erlich-Ginor, & Beland, 2009; pp. 175–176).

Why is the presence of the Other so necessary? Breckner and Rupp (2002) see a "told story" as a changing biographical text that is a human strategy to make sense of lived experience. However, such stories can serve defensive functions, and the presence of the Other brings an element in the story dramatically alive. You are in front of a real person with her or his own emotions and pain, not your imagined ones, a real life, not a "told story". This reveals our projections or stereotypes, thus creating a permeable boundary between internal and external, and lays bare the role of fantasy in the way the Other is perceived.

Group relations conferences are temporary learning organisations that create, reflect, mirror, and reproduce collective fantasies about the "organisation in the mind". The apex for learning about this "organisation in the mind" is the institutional/organisational event (the system event in the Nazareth series conferences), and it is for this reason that we have referred to the difficulties in the system event of our conferences as the site where problems are located and hence new learning can be sought. This work is, at one and the same time, most interesting and most difficult, since defining the field (which, in order to understand group dynamics, Lewin's field theory (1997) requires us to do) is a slippery business that involves continuous interweaving between past and present, and ethnic and national identity boundaries, which are inevitably fluid and mobile.

Personal involvement of staff

Beyond the professional investment that all group relations conferences look for in their staff, the Nazareth conferences also require a personal investment in the work on the part of the staff member. The national, ethnic, and religious identity of the staff group mirrors, as far as possible, that of the membership. This is necessary because the conference addresses not the traditional issues of authority, but a particular theme that involves those very identifications. It is only through a deep connection with one's own personal and social history, and a willingness to work at it honestly and authentically, that we can become supportive and empathic whilst at the same time facilitating an engagement with painful issues that is, by definition, difficult. However, this sets up a powerful unconscious identification between staff and membership.

We have already described how this personal involvement with the issues leads to important work in the staff group that prepares it for the task ahead. However, strong identification also invites projection—by members into staff and vice versa—which can interfere with the capacity for abstinence and thinking/reflection. Do we unwittingly "assimilate ourselves" with members' issues, pain, and suffering, and support or protect, where asserting our "otherness" as staff would be more on task? Do we then miss the opportunity to work directly with "hotter" material?

Concluding thoughts

Commenting on the responses to questionnaires sent to 2008 Conference participants, our colleague Shmuel Erlich says "... the 2008 Cyprus conference seems to have shaken up many persons and issues ... I believe this is actually what it is meant to do".

From a systemic point of view one can view the conference as a "fractal" that represents whole society dynamics—the broader picture in a nutshell, so to speak. It is, therefore, encouraging that the deep exploration aimed for in these events seems to produce "learning" that extends to the wider world—an incidental benefit. If these conferences can shake things up with respect to fixed, polarised positions that ordinarily produce hatred and feed cycles of enmity, should we do more to make it available beyond the narrow group of professional practitioners who usually attend?

Finally, we would like to return to the link between the work we have presented and the theme of tradition, creativity, and succession. As we indicated at the outset, the conferences have moved on in two ways—first, negotiating the transition in directorship forced by the death of the "first generation", and secondly, by expanding the focus of the conferences. The first, succession in directorship, was made possible by the work of mourning on the part of the organisers, and resulted in a transition that preserved the essential tradition of the series. However, the new director also brought in a new perspective that placed greater emphasis on broadening out. For example, can what has been learnt be applied to present-day conflicts? This change in emphasis, which can be seen as a creative development, was embodied in the fact that he brought two "others" onto the staff (Brunner and Davids), and coincided with the emergence of "Palestinians" and "Others" as a focus of work. In one way, these developments involved considerable conflict, which was contained within, in the staff group. That would suggest that we have managed to move on in a creative way whilst preserving the essential traditions of the Nazareth project. However, we may also ask whether there is a level of difficulty of conflict involved in this transition that has hitherto been avoided as a focus of work and dealt with through enactment. For example, all three of us are, as we have pointed out, part of the successor generation. Does the absence of the earlier generation in this outreach venture indicate a successful handing over to the next generation, or does it signify a level of opposition to that change which has yet to surface in its own right? Only time will tell.

References

Breckner, R., & Rupp, S. (2002). Discovering biographies in changing social worlds: the biographical-interpretive method. In: P. Chamberlayne, M. Rustin & T. Wengraf (Eds.), *Biography and Social Exclusion in Europe*. Bristol: Policy Press.

Brunner, L. D. (2002). Groups and work in the past and at present: A conversation with Eric Miller. *Organisational and Social Dynamics*, 2: 156–171.

Erlich, H. S., Erlich-Ginor, M., & Beland, H. (2009). *Fed with Tears—Poisoned with Milk. The "Nazareth" Group-Relations Conferences. Germans and Israelis—The Past in the Present* (With a Foreword by Archbishop Desmond M. Tutu). Giessen: Psychosozial-Verlag.

Lewin, K. (1997). *Resolving Social Conflicts and Field Theory in Social Science*. Washington: American Psychological Association.

Schein, E. H. (1996). *Organisational Culture and Leadership*. San Francisco: Jossey-Bass Psychology Series.

Schein, E. H. (2006). Culture: the missing concept in organization studies. *Administrative Science Quarterly*, 41: 229–240.

Notes

1. We are especially grateful to Veronika Grueneisen for her contributions and comments in the preparation of this presentation.
2. Mira Erlich-Ginor in her paper "The story/history of the project" notes that this restricted membership enacted "at the start a dynamic of exclusion. Of course turning to psychoanalysts was a way to handle our anxiety, it felt that addressing a wider audience would be too risky and that psychoanalysts will be able to deal with the explosive material."
3. See *Fed with Tears—Poisoned with Milk: The "Nazareth" Group-Relations-Conferences: Germans and Israelis—The Past in the Present*. With a foreword by Archbishop Desmond M. Tutu, edited. by H. Shmuel Erlich, Mira Erlich-Ginor, Hermann Beland., Giessen, 2009. See: The story and history of the project, pp. 17–33, by H. Shmuel Erlich and Hermann Beland; The process of conference design, pp. 35–43, by Eric Miller; Supplementary comments on design and structure, pp. 43–47, by H. Shmuel Erlich.

4. PCCA, Chairperson: Veronika Grüneisen; www.p-cca.org.
5. The National Party, architects of apartheid.
6. The idea that Christians are illegitimate inheritors of the Scriptures, the Hebrew Bible, is one I am familiar with in my work as a Christian theologian.
7. Since writing this chapter I have become a member of the Board of PCCA
8. E. Miller, *The Process of Conference Design*, p. 38.
9. "Shaping the future by confronting the past: Germans, Jews and affected others".
10. Fakhry Davids writes: "I have since learnt that there is no record of Golda Meir using this emotive phrase, which has a long and controversial history. It may have become associated with her on account of an assertion (in 1969) that when she arrived in Palestine in the 1920s the 'Palestinian people', as a national entity, did not exist (Erlich-Ginor, personal communication)".

CHAPTER FIVE

Robben Island as a container for diversity dynamics: the directors' experience

Michelle S. May and Frans Cilliers

The South African diversity challenge

Globalisation and democratisation are the most important forces changing the face of the workforce in South Africa (De Jager, Cilliers, & Veldsman, 2004; Myburg, 2006). The complexity of globalisation is enhanced by Africanisation (Coetzee, 2007). Whereas the apartheid South African corporate world was almost exclusively Western in its focus, and disconnected from the rest of Africa, the 1994 government started building strong political and economic connections with neighboring and mid-African states. This political democratisation of the workplace from a mainly homogenous (white male) to an increasingly multicultural and diverse workforce, as well as the fast growing black middle class, changed customer demographics, expectations, and the ways in which organisations do business.

South Africans experience many diverse and unresolved emotions from the apartheid era, associated with racial segregation, minority domination, and inhumane acts (Human, 2005). The Truth and Reconciliation Commission (TRC) and new legislation on employment equity and affirmative action authorised the black voice and forced whites to investigate their denial (Asmal, Asmal, & Roberts, 1997). Yet, the diversity discourse stayed filled with high levels of competition, conflict, fear, anger, hate, resentment, hurt, hopelessness, and helplessness, which imprisoned citizens privately, as well as in the workplace (Cilliers & May, 2002; Pretorius, 2003). This makes the workplace ideal to study "diversities" of social and cultural backgrounds, religious practices, rites of passage according to ethnic or religious roots, perceptions about politeness, social correctness, generosity and time, languages, dietary laws, dress codes, and cultural taboos in the organisation (Cilliers, 2004).

Since 1994, many South African organisations have implemented diversity management programmes to address the above (Coetzee, 2007). Such programmes, designed eclectically from many paradigms and using mechanistic "exercises" based on the assumption that diversity can be trained and the outcomes controlled, show very little scientific effectiveness (Cavaleros, Van Vuuren, & Visser, 2002). Diversity programmes presented from a systems psychodynamic consulting stance, view the workshop as a microcosm of the organisational diversity dynamics where the macro organisational diversity issues play out in the micro workshop here-and-now events (Czander, 1993). Such programmes indicate movement towards increased systemic awareness and the owning of projections onto and into "the other", authorising the subsystem to take up a leadership role, and to move from the paranoid-schizoid to the depressive position (Cilliers & May, 2002; Cilliers, Rothmann & Struwig, 2004; Coetzee, 2007; Myburg, 2006).

Exploring the directors' experience of working with diversity dynamics

Over the last ten years we have been involved in the Robben Island diversity experience (RIDE) presented annually in November in South Africa on Robben Island in Cape Town's Table Bay. This six day event is attended by (up to eighty) representatives from organisations tasked with transformation, diversity management, and implementing employment equity. The island serves as a symbol of both past denigration and current liberation and hope with regards to South African diversity dynamics (Cilliers & May, 2002). It is our belief that in order to harness our diversity, we need to deal with our differences and similarities as construed by the previous dispensation and then work towards celebrating our diversity. This can best be done by studying the underlying human dynamics referring to relatedness between people, the identity of those involved, the role of power in these relationships, as well as the effect of reference systems in understanding diversity dynamics.

RIDE is designed and presented from the systems psychodynamic perspective. The primary task is to provide opportunities for participants to study South African diversity dynamics as they unfold in the here-and-now of the event and to transfer their learning to specific organisations. The programme consists of large group, small group, inter-group, and institutional events, as well as reflective events. RIDE is staffed by (up to ten) competent organisational consultants working in the systems psychodynamic consultancy stance, chosen in a representative manner with regard to diversity characteristics, including gender and race.

Systems psychodynamic research on diversity has been presented and published internationally (Foster, 2004; Foster, Dickinson, Bishop, & Klein 2006; Levine, 2002; McRae, 2004; Nichols, 2004; Skolnick & Green, 2004) but with little reference to the experiences of participants. In South Africa, Cilliers and May (2002), De Jager, Cilliers and Veldsman (2004) and Pretorius (2003) referred to participant's experiences in group relations conferences, but the role of the director has not been investigated. We will explore our experiences of our role as director of RIDE by describing and analysing through discourse analysis (see Brewerton & Milward, 2004; Camic, Rhodes & Yardley, 2003; Denzin & Lincoln, 1994) various vignettes about RIDE. This analysis and interpretation involved exploring the self as instrument in what an older (fifty) white male and a younger black woman in a South African organisation in the twenty-first century, represents, holds, and contains in terms of various defenses such as introjections, projections, and projective identification (Czander, 1993). Through the findings we will report on our experiences as director of RIDE in terms of containing diversity dynamics, and specifically the dimensions of race, gender, and age.

Diversity characteristics of the directors as containers

Frans' experiences as white male director

My first recollection of seeing the island was on holiday at Bloubergstrand ("Blue Mountain Beach") with my parents when the children were told that the island was used to lock up people who do not fit into society "to protect us from the black danger". In planning and directing the first RIDE, I had positive expectations about the work, which I only later realised was naïve in not realising that my object representation will get me into very difficult situations.

Right from the start, I was challenged by the manager (of the hosting organisation) and his colleague, as well as by two co-consultants (four white males). It was as if the white males had to fight for the first position on the island that now belonged to white *and* black South Africans. My working as a directorate pair with Michelle (a black female associate director) was under attack by participants. In old South African apartheid terms, this is an illegitimate and shameful relationship. It was as if participants unconsciously struggled with the conflict between the old and the new authority configuration.

Historically, I am from French Huguenot and Dutch decent. As such I represent the National Party government and its apartheid policy. In the Robben Island context I represent the prison wardens who suppressed the imprisoned freedom fighters (like Nelson Mandela). Although I consciously experienced being authorised by participants in how they took up their membership roles, my unconscious experience was of a simmering ganging-up amongst black participants to act out violently against my authority. I remember that I had two dreams about my father warning me about the dangers of the 'darkness'. It was as if black men's script was: "One of you had your chance—now get out of the way"—as if white leadership had become irrelevant. This experience was strong when some participants revealed that they had been actually imprisoned on the island some years ago or when others revealed that their family members had been imprisoned and died on the island. It was as if the shame of the past had to be carried by me as the white director.

When Michelle became the director of RIDE in 2002, I took up the role as associate director. This *support role* felt more comfortable—as if the South African system prefers the white man in a second role in terms of diversity.

Michelle's experience

It is very difficult for me to write about my experiences, not because the experiences were that unspeakable, but because I am challenged to explain my race. In apartheid South Africa I was classified by the government and society as coloured, but amongst those who were involved in the struggle I was classified as black. In post-apartheid South Africa I am classified as black and further classified as coloured. Within my own community I will be classified mainly as coloured, but by those with a particular kind of political consciousness, I am classified as black. I am also not seen as African—the term non-African black has been used to describe me. My race identity oscillates, for others, between being black or coloured, with most South Africans classifying me as coloured. I grew up in a rural town, Genadendal (Valley of Mercy), one and a half hour's drive from Cape Town, as well as in Cape Town. I was part of the political struggle during my high school years and to some extent during my tertiary education. I felt that I belonged to Robben Island and that Robben Island belonged to me—that those who were imprisoned on the island were the reason why I could walk onto Robben Island to do diversity work. Thus, I have never wondered whether I belonged on Robben Island, but I have wondered, and at times been certain, that I am not qualified to direct RIDE. However, I have taken up the role to the best of my abilities, working towards providing a containing RIDE, for staff and participants.

In June 2006, Lerato Motswoaledi, a black, Tswana woman, took up the role of Director of ride.

Working on the boundary between ride and macro role players

The management and staff of Robben Island

The hosting organisation planned RIDE from Pretoria (1,000 km north of Cape Town), and the island management is split between Cape Town harbour and the officials on the island. This logistical split led to what seemed to be the island system's rebellion against the presence of RIDE. We saw the task of the island management as being to contain the revered space and entertain the curiosity of daily tourists, who leave the island at sunset. RIDE possibly represented an anti-task in its focus on organisational learning and development. It seemed that the RIDE staff and participants were seen as people from affluent organisations coming to *plak*[1] on the island for their own benefit. To include RIDE as a diversity laboratory where participants study unconscious aspects of employees' diversity struggles, must have created high anxiety.

This anxiety on the boundary influenced the service rendered by the island's management, especially concerning the accommodation that was provided in the early years. It was not the best of accommodation and it was not always ready, regardless of days of negotiation between island staff and the hosting organisation. We believe that RIDE participants could have felt that we did not provide accommodation for them in a contained manner—probably impacting on the overall experience of RIDE as a container.

The hosting organisation

RIDE was conceptualised by the directors, Marius Pretorius and Derek Hendrikz, of the hosting organisation (TDCI). In 2000 they approached us to plan and design RIDE in collaboration with them. They seemed to have very clear expectations about the design of RIDE. They understood the demands of the group relations approach, but they also wanted to generate future business from those organisations attending RIDE. We had no difficulty with this endeavor, although this task impacted on the boundaries of RIDE. Our experience was that we had to adjust the boundaries of RIDE to accommodate participants where required. This, of course, resulted in conflict between the organisers and us. In retrospect this was very difficult to deal with because the organisers wanted to preserve RIDE as a business endeavor, while we wanted to preserve RIDE as a container. Of course, we believed that by preserving RIDE we would not damage their business.

Perhaps contained in the split between the directors of TDCI and the directorship were the demands made by the RIDE staff members from the directors across diversity characteristics. Instead of working more actively with these demands, it may have been projected and contained in the relationships between TDCI and us, in an attempt to preserve the relationship with staff while working in this volatile, chaotic container. What remains unknown is how working differently with the conflict between staff and directors could have enhanced the veracity of RIDE as a container.

Thus, we became part of a macro intergroup event with unclear boundaries between directing RIDE, the hosting organisation with their expectations, the island's management, the expectations of participants to be "on holy ground" or to revisit the island where some of them were imprisoned, as well as the anxiety around the different representations in the minds of all those present and not present.

Attacks on the RIDE programme as container

The boundaries of task, time, space, and consultancy in RIDE were attacked in all kinds of ways. We considered this an attack on the programme as container and ultimately an attack on our ability to provide containment for membership and staff participants during RIDE.

Crossing the sea boundary by boat from Cape Town to Robben Island

This created difficulties and anxiety for the directors. On one occasion, a staff member (a black female from the Eastern Cape) did not arrive on time at the Cape Town waterfront for the boat taking all the consultants to the island. She did not phone or answer our calls. She arrived the next day on the same boat as the participants, without any apparent realisation of the boundary issues involved. Also, arriving on the island, starting the first staff meeting, and exploring the meaning of possibly working with minus one consultant, another (white female) consultant loudly declared that she did not feel contained, and went to her room to lie down and read a book. These serve as examples of how the role of male director was challenged by female consultants in different ways. It laid the table for some difficult gender issues to be explored in the coming week.

On another occasion, when the consultants arrived in Cape Town ready to depart for the island, the so called *cape doctor* (the fierce southwest wind with rain) was blowing, and all boat trips to the island were cancelled. We slept over in the city and took the first boat on the following morning. At midday, when the participants embarked for the island, the wind blew again to the extent that most got sea sick, arriving "in different (facial) colours" on the island. Participants were angry during the opening plenary—they came late, dragged themselves into the room, complained loudly about not having been able to eat lunch, still feeling sick, the consultants not caring about their terrible experience, their physical discomfort, and worse, not even listening to their anger. Later during the week, some participants referred to how bleak their crossing of the boundary experiences seemed, and compared them to the experiences of the prisoners on the island during the apartheid era. Thus, studying diversity on Robben Island became a comparison between the experiences of the "haves" and "didn't/don't haves".

The prison tour

Late afternoon of the fourth RIDE day, a participant tour of the Robben Island Prison was scheduled. Normally, an ex-prisoner would act as their guide. Participants returned quite filled up by the intensity of the experience—enhanced by the work they had done up to that point and the intense looking—back on apartheid. The impact of the prison tour was such that it was very difficult to work with participants on diversity dynamics immediately after the tour—their immediate emotional experiences transcended the RIDE programme. This was further impacted by participants' different reasons for attendance—for example, a pilgrimage to Robben Island. Consequently, the evening session was removed from future programmes to facilitate reflection of the day's experiences. This change may also be indicative of our inability to contain the enormity of the participants' emotional experience. It also felt as if an interpretation at that point was like venturing on to immensely painful ground.

Mandela's visit to Robben Island

During one RIDE, we received news that President Mandela would visit the island as part of the FIFA world soccer cup inspection of South Africa's infrastructure. This acted as a threat to and attack on the RIDE boundaries—the realisation was that although boundaries were held by directors and consultants, organisers and membership may be tempted to shift boundaries. Membership and some staff members wanted to "see Mandela". Several discussions in the staff room entertained our fantasies about how island staff could be approached to ensure that Mandela address RIDE during a large group. Should such a request be agreed too, we were aware of the implication for the boundaries of the programme. The conflict was between the excitement around Mandela and preserving the boundaries of RIDE. On the morning of the visit, a black female consultant realistically reminded us that RIDE is more important than seeing Mr. Mandela. This comment allowed space for contemplating the breaking of the boundaries and shifted our response towards wanting to preserve the boundaries of RIDE to work with the task. Several participants left a small group session to have a glimpse of Mandela—but this was brief and, in our fantasy, not very satisfying.

The boundaries of RIDE feel immensely fluid, leaving in me (Michelle) knowledge of what the decision should be, but waiting for a decision to emerge from amongst the staff. This could point to my capacity for negative capability (French & Simpson, 2009). On the other hand it raises the question about how much authority does a coloured, black woman have as the director of RIDE. I have appropriate authority from the hosting organisation, the directorate and the staff members. I think that it is my self-authorisation that is problematic—I am not free from the diversity dynamics that come with my race, gender, and age. The role in my mind of who I am in the South African diversity hierarchy, impacts on the extent to which I can work with the authorisation that I receive. The director (of RIDE) will be attacked, but the way in which I work with my diversity dynamics impacts my ability to deal with the attack. A constant struggle in RIDE appears to be that the containment provided by the director through constant reflection on diversity dynamics should not become so "passive" and turn into paralysis when difficult decisions must be made (see Nutkevitch, 2001) due to the diversity hierarchy in the mind.

The training group

We have both fulfilled the role of associate director and training group (TG) director for RIDE, which proved difficult. (Subsequently a white woman, Hanna Kotze, has taken up the role of TG director). The practical reason for our investment in having a TG is to have consultants-in-training to ease the load of staff members, especially for the reflection events. Although the TG usually consisted of four to five participants, it remained difficult over the years to have enough TG participants, which resulted in

- a scramble to find participants for the training group
- a power struggle between the director and the organisers with regards to the viability of the TG
- a situation where we had to cancel the TG at the last minute, asking the potential participants to become part of the working conference, that is, demoting TG participants

- not holding the TG in mind. One year, after the usual difficulty to have a training group, I (Michelle) forgot to introduce the TG director and participants (which I eventually remembered to do towards the end of the plenary)
- creativity on the part of the organisers, the TG director, and director to create an attractive-enough TG design to entice participants. Their training included attending certain staff meetings and giving feedback to the staff regarding participants' reflections about diversity dynamics in there-and-then events.

The TG made the pre-conference work for RIDE fragile and the TG became the container for the organisers, the director, and the TG director having to deal head on with the possibility that RIDE would not take place at all. It appeared that the organisers and the director could work with the fragility of RIDE as a container in the pre-conference work only through frantic efforts of preserving the training group, as if the working conference would magically fill itself. These frantic efforts to fill the TG are also linked to the marketing of the event that starts after July. This could indicate ambivalence within the organisers and the director about hosting RIDE. We tried to address this ambivalence by starting the preconference work earlier, but these attempts never really came to fruition. In retrospect, the ambivalence could be about dreading the work needed to contain volatile and chaotic diversity dynamics

- within oneself
- within the organisers ("will their business survive?")
- between the organisers, the director, and the staff ("will we survive and get or provide the necessary resources/boundary conditions to contain the event?")
- between us and the island ("will we be able to forge a working relationship with those on Robben Island to ensure a solid container?")
- between the organisers, the staff, and new membership ("will staff be able to create a good-enough container for working with diversity dynamics?").

Membership and the challenges they bring

Participants, through several incidents, mirrored many of the difficult South African diversity dynamics, with the potential to elicit even more volatile (diversity) dynamics. We felt challenged about how we could contain these dynamics *and* make them available to be worked with by membership and staff.

Stale diversity relationships "in the kitchen and the garden"

The madams and the maids

One inter-group event took place in an old prison wardens' house. The event had a "woman's group", which consisted of black and white women and a black female consultant, working in the old kitchen of this house. After deliberations the group eventually sent out two black women to "inform the director of what happened in their group". As they left, the consultant remarked that the group was sending the maids to do the work on their behalf. This caused quite a stir in terms of the diversity relations in the group. Later, two white females left the group to also speak to the white male director (consulting in an open space) about how the group did not want to work as a team and how frustrated they were by the consultant's way of "joining the enemy". The director knew the two women from a previous consultancy in a financial organisation. This complicated the consultancy, which seemed to be about the white women reporting (gossiping about) the black consultant's negative behaviour to the white director (as her boss). This was interpreted as how a group of South African women acted out the colonial white madam/black maid race and status diversity and how they had to report non-performance to the male authority, representing the "boss"/husband in the household. The nature and intensity of this interaction spread itself through the whole event and was revisited in the large and small groups. Even some time after RIDE, the consultants still processed the interaction which had such a profound effect.

The madam and the garden boy

Another example was a white female (who declared herself as affluent, living and working in a very rich part of Johannesburg), who in the large group spoke about her difficulty in interacting with her newly appointed black male manager. Her only memory of working with a black male was the typical colonial scenario of giving orders to her "garden boy", who stayed in a small room in her back yard.

Her experienced relationship with a black man was so set in her own authority hierarchy in the mind that any role difference created unbearable anxiety and detachment. She simply did not have any frame of reference of how to behave—similarly or differently.

"Fufulala"

On several occasions participants communicated their dissatisfaction with the demands of the programme and challenged our authority—on one occasion this was done in an amusing and creative manner. During the institutional event, a group introduced themselves as "fufulala". I (Michelle—director) could not hear the name and asked the administrator to spell the name for me. He did so twice ("F. U. F. U. lala …") but I could not understand, while Frans (as associate director) was very amused by the name. While on the task level, the attack on the management of the institutional event was addressed, this was also an example of an attack on the directors which raised the question of whether we can contain what is being projected onto us while being attacked (see Nutkevitch, 2001). It was very difficult to work with the attack as it was directed at us, and it was reflected on again during the closing plenary.

The white male from a mining company

Often a block booking was made by a particular company. In one RIDE (consisting of eighty participants) there were at least twelve participants from a big mining company, of which one white man was very vocal about the lack of "facilitation" by staff. His behaviour was often discussed in staff meetings, and we hypothesised that his complaints about our containment were done on behalf of the membership. He represented a white man with a voice in a context where it appeared that white men were not easily heard. Perhaps this was due to his experience of being backed by the power of his male colleagues from the biggest and richest gold mining company in the world.

Alternatively, I (Michelle) could be openly challenged by a white man and not by women or men from other race groups. It was as if membership was watching my reaction to the behaviour of this white man and my response could help them see how they could respond to him—how will I exercise my authority in relation to him? The staff did not work with this aspect—seemingly it was not available for us to work with. We worked with what the participant represented while also attending to other participants and what they represented in RIDE. This enabled us not to spend *all* our time on this participant. The apparent preoccupation by membership and staff with the white man could denote attempts at trying out a "new" relationship with the same role players with "new" authority, that is, black female director, white male conference participant. Perhaps through RIDE as a good-enough container, membership and staff could explore a relationship across race marked by a "new" authority relationship.

The pilgrims

Some participants came to the RIDE on a pilgrimage. They had either themselves been imprisoned on the island during the apartheid era (one was known as "the general" and some were referred to as "the black mafia") or had family members having been imprisoned there. They came to see and honor the place where so many of their own and veterans have struggled and died.

This sent a message to the director and staff to be very careful with regard to what they raise within sessions and thus how the roles are taken up and the primary task is consulted to. It was as if there was a fight around who belongs and who has entitlement to be and work on the island. When this was raised in sessions, it was met with a revered silence, as if we were on holy ground, and that those who had intimate experiences belonged more. This "subliminal" message became a fear and a control mechanism between director and staff versus participants. It was as if consultants were seduced into the pain of the participants. The participants then became the director of the task—what can be ventured into and what not, and how tentatively the work will be done. It was as if the anxiety underlying diverse relationships has the potential to seduce authority relationships into becoming spectators of the struggle drama. These discussions went on in the staff room and sometimes also threatened to derail the reflective consultancy work.

Foreigners

RIDE was attended by foreigners from Africa (Swaziland, Zimbabwe, and Nigeria), Europe (Netherlands, Sweden), USA, and Australia.

These participants expressed their expectations to learn about diversity in and from a country that struggles with reconciling differences. As the events progressed, they became less verbal, as if they were silenced by the intensity of the South African experiences and by the diversity examples used in the events. Some of them later spoke about their experiences of being sidelined, which resulted in some of them taking up an academic role. It was as if the foreigners were excluded from the heat of the experience, taking up a role where they could hold on to the rationality and intellectual parts of diversity, while the South Africans could fight out the diversity issues of the past.

The participants from African countries appeared to be treated with more disdain than those from Western countries. A woman from Swaziland was referred to as a Swazi princess. She was treated as "royalty" and experienced as arrogant. Participants from Zimbabwe and Nigeria were mostly ignored. This could relate to issues of xenophobia (which flared up in South Africa in 2008). However, the issue of the foreigner from Africa was not really explored, possibly due to the South African preoccupation (almost obsession) with our diversity dynamics. It seems that our narcissism inhibits the conversation with other Africans who may have similar experiences. Alternatively, deep seated despair and rage, experienced by South Africans about unresolved issues pertaining to injuries inflicted in the past, impacts this conversation. We are unclear about what diversity dynamics were projected into these foreigners to contain on behalf RIDE as a whole.

Thus far, only South Africans have consulted in RIDE. On the rational level, this could relate to the financial implications of having international consultants. On the irrational level, our uncertainties about taking up the role of director may also relate to projections, introjections, and possibly shame about our diversity issues—not wanting to wash our dirty laundry in public.

Conclusion

Below the surface the South African diversity scenario is packed with history, complex and diverse perceptions and experiences, extreme levels of fear, anger, hate, aggression, competition, rivalry, competition, and envy between the different diversity groups. Surprisingly, this chapter has presented for us—and, we hope, for you the reader—a reflective space to think about how our individual diversity dynamics are used (in RIDE and other daily contexts) in the service of unconscious relations across differences. We have been aware of some of the ways in which our diversity is used in RIDE. We have created spaces through staff meetings and in personal reflective space to explore how our diversity impacts our role as director. Although these opportunities improved our effectiveness as directors, we have also realised we cannot be aware of all the ways in which our diversity, which is integrally linked to our authority (Skolnick & Green, 2004), are used, especially the way in which our race and gender are used to negotiate and experiment with new relationships across difference in the unconscious. This has left a real impression about the importance of membership's need to negotiate and experiment with new race and gender relations, and how they use us in our authority roles to unconsciously role model these new race and gender relationships. It seems that the preoccupation with these new relationships across race and gender occurs at the expense of working with other diversity characteristics and issues. It also highlights the need for those in authority positions, whether in organisations or as directors in group relations events, to be aware of how their diversity dynamics may be used by their followers to negotiate and experiment with new (race and gender) relations on their behalf.

Although on a national and international scale, the effect of RIDE is small. It is our experience that RIDE offered to the participants an event filled with intense confrontation with diversity dynamics, opportunities to listen to the other, and a shift in the quality of the relationships between differences. The most obvious recommendation is that South African diversity work must never stop, informally as well as formally, in organisations, seeing that organisations are where most people spend most of their lifetime. Also, organisations are places where the complexity of irrational behaviour can be studied (Huffington, Armstrong, Halton, Hoyle, & Pooley, 2004). This makes organisational diversity work, informed by systems psychodynamics, accessible and meaningful.

References

Asmal, K., Asmal, L., & Roberts, R. S. (1997). *Reconciliation through Truth: A Reckoning of Apartheid's Criminal Governance.* Cape Town: David Philip Publishers.

Brewerton, P. & Millward, L. (2004). *Organizational Research Methods. A Guide for Students and Researchers*. London: Sage.

Camic, P. M., Rhodes, J. E. & Yardley, L. (2003). *Qualitative Research in Psychology*. Washington, DC: APA.

Cavaleros, C., Van Vuuren, L. J. & Visser, D. (2002). The effectiveness of a diversity awareness training programme. *South African Journal of Industrial Psychology, 28*: 50–61.

Cilliers, F. (2004). A person-centered view on diversity in South Africa. *The Person-Centered Journal, 11*: 33–47.

Cilliers, F. & May, M. (2002). South African diversity dynamics. Reporting on the 2000 Robben Island diversity experience. A group relations event. *South African Journal of Labour Relations, 26*: 42–68.

Cilliers, F., Rothmann, S. & Struwig, W. H. (2004). Transference and counter-transference in systems psycho-dynamic group process consultation: The consultant's experience. *South African Journal of Industrial Psychology, 30*: 72–81.

Coetzee, O. (2007). Exploring interpersonal and inter-group diversity dynamics in South African organizations by means of a theoretical model. Unpublished DCOM thesis. University of South Africa, Pretoria.

Czander, W. M. (1993). *The Psychodynamics of Work and Organizations*. New York: Guilford.

De Jager, W., Cilliers, F. & Veldsman, T. (2004). Leadership development from a systems psycho-dynamic consultancy stance. *South African Journal of Human Resource Management, 1*: 85–92.

Denzin, N. K. & Lincoln, Y. S. (1994). *Handbook of Qualitative Research*. Thousand Oaks, CA: Sage.

Foster, A. (2004). Living and working with difference and diversity. Paper presented at OPUS, London.

Foster, A., Dickinson, A., Bishop, B. & Klein, J. (2006). *Difference: An Avoided Topic in Practice*. London: Karnac.

French, R. & Simpson, P. (2009). "Negative Capability": A contribution to the understanding of creative leadership. In: B. Sievers (Ed.), *Psychoanalytic Studies of Organizations. Contributions from the International Society for the Psychoanalytic Study of Organizations (ISPSO)*. London: Karnac.

Huffington, C., Armstrong, A., Halton, W., Hoyle, L. & Pooley, J. (2004). *Working Below the Surface. The Emotional Life of Contemporary Organizations*. London: Karnac.

Human, L. (2005). *Diversity Management for Business Success*. Pretoria: Van Schaik.

Levine, D. P. (2002). The ethical organisation and the ideal of diversity. *International Society of the Psychoanalytic Study of Organizations.*, 2002 Symposium, University of Denver Graduate School of International Studies.

McRae, M. B. (2004). Class, race and gender: Person-in-role implications in taking up the directorship. In: S. Cytrynbaum & D. A. Noumair, *Group Dynamics, Organizational Irrationality, and Social Complexity: Group Relations Reader 3*. Jupiter, FL: A. K. Rice Institute.

Myburg, H. S. (2006). The experience of organizational development consultants working in the systems psychodynamic stance. Unpublished M.A. dissertation. University of South Africa, Pretoria.

Nichols, L. (2004). When faith eclipses hope; forgiveness within reparation. Paper presented at OPUS, London.

Nutkevitch, A. (2001). Is containment relevant? *Organisational & Social Dynamics, 2*; 270–271.

Pretorius, M. (2003). An exploration of South African diversity dynamics. Unpublished M. A. dissertation. University of South Africa, Pretoria.

Skolnick, M. & Green, Z. (2004). The denigrated other: Diversity and group relations. In: S. Cytrynbaum & D. A. Noumair, *Group Dynamics, Organizational Irrationality, and Social Complexity: Group Relations Reader 3*. Jupiter, FL: A. K. Rice Institute.

Stapley, L. F. (1996). *The Personality of the Organisation. A Psycho-dynamic Explanation of Culture and Change*. London: Free Association.

Thomas, R. R. (1996). *Redefining Diversity*. New York: American Management Association.

Note

1. Plak—informally and illegally creating a settlement on Robben Island. Often in South Africa this is how an informal settlement (squatter camp) develops illegally near to more affluent suburbs and impacts on the value of the properties in the suburb.

CHAPTER SIX

Beyond the family psychic template

Brigid Nossal & Susan Long

Introduction

In this paper we put forward the working hypothesis that the family as a psychic template applied to organisations has a) moved from an explanatory hypothesis to an almost exclusive principle in group relations thinking and b) as a consequence, excluded other possible explanatory hypotheses and the use of other psychic templates. Beyond this, we explore the idea that the group relations community of practice may identify with the application of the family psychic template to the extent of at times acting it out rather than using it as a tool for thinking. We stress that this is a working hypothesis and that it has emerged from a collaboration that goes broader than ours. Former members of the Australian Institute of Socio-Analysis (AISA) executive and conference members and staff have also contributed to the findings and ideas presented here.

We attempt to build our argument from experiences in group relations conferences in 2002 and 2008 and from within our community of practice in group relations and systems psychodynamics (socio-analysis) in Australia and consider the implications for group relations conference design. We hope this may also further our thinking about authority relations, leadership and traditional organisational structures.

Generational Identifications

In defining generations there are two major influences. The first is the family, the second is group history. Most basically, the generations are defined in terms of lineage from parent to child. The incest taboo and the development of the human family generally keep this clear so that generations are not confused. Of course, generational identification goes beyond the family to cohorts of people in history, although the overlap in terms of ages within a cohort can be broad. Definitive historical moments generally define a generation—a war or the introduction of culture-changing technologies: the atom bomb or the micro-chip, for example. People grow up in the shadow of such influential events (Hopper, 2003).

Much of what is said about inter-generational issues must also be considered in terms of age and life stage. Our focus will primarily be on the way that family dynamics and their analysis influence how people consciously and unconsciously identify with generational positions in their workplace relations. The psychic phenomena and anxieties aroused in inter-generational dynamics in the workplace might be seen to have their origins in early family experiences. Sophocles' tragedy, *Oedipus the King*, which Freud used as a poignant analogy for the psychic journey of the child, is essentially an inter-generational drama. It has an almost unquestioned currency within our community of practice vernacular.

Our enquiry begins with our learning from a group relations conference in 2008, exploring intergenerational dynamics in the workplace. This seemed to offer a framework for thinking anew about the events that gave rise to its theme. These events include the closure of the Australian Institute of Socio-Analysis (AISA) in 2004. AISA was the home of group relations in Australia from 1983–2004. While the material causes for the closure were multiple, there is a strong case to be made that inter-generational dynamics (if only as a frame of identification) had a lot to do with it.

We acknowledge that family as a "psychic template" or framework for understanding intra-organisational dynamics has been explored elsewhere (Long, 2006; Morgan, 1997; Sievers, 1995). In this paper, we hypothesise about the impact of the predominance of "family-as-psychic-template" applied to organisational settings. Further, we speculate about the power of the leadership/followership relation to (possibly inadvertently) invoke this identification with family, which, once invoked, acquires its own, seemingly intractable, momentum. In this particular instance, we explore AISA's director/member relation. We argue that there is a somewhat taken-for-granted transposition of family and related inter-generational dynamics into organisational contexts that can give rise to the very dynamics that they seek to explain. That is, there is a circular causal relationship between the group identification that is invited and invoked (often by leaders and consultants and offered as an interpretation of events) and the ensuing group dynamics and emotional experiences. It is hard, if not impossible, to know the *original cause* in this often escalating spiral: primitive dynamic or its invocation? We argue that perhaps the idea of cause and its interpretation is problematic.

We maintain that similar to, but qualitatively different from, Bion's basic assumption group processes (Bion, 1961), primitive anxieties, anchored in early experiences in the family, can resurface in organisational life in ways that can effect a swing in individuals and groups to paranoid-schizoid or other primitive emotional functioning. Like BaG processes, they seem unavoidable and can function in ways that also support work group and task-oriented functioning. In recent years there seems to have been a preoccupation with inter-generational dynamics, in both our field and the organisations that we consult to, that may serve to preclude other frames of reference and group identifications that may better serve to engender creative and collaborative task-oriented group and organisational functioning.

Group and intergroup identifications (a theoretical framework)

Alderfer's (1987) theoretical framework of intergroup dynamics, inclusive of his reference to Devereux's articulation of "group level transference" (p. 201) reminds us of the power of group identifications to "prime" our perceptual and emotional experiences:

> To the extent that group memberships and relations among groups shape how others react to us and how we perceive those reactions, we are indeed captured by the groups to which we belong.

> We are, of course, most fully prisoner of those groups of whose membership we remain unaware. (Alderfer, 1987, p. 202)

This framework is useful for considering inter-generational dynamics because there is evidence to suggest that many of these dynamics are concerned with group identifications. As Alderfer claims, we all belong to multiple groups and an awareness of group membership becomes most obvious when interacting with other groups:

> … which group will become focal at the moment will depend on who else representing which other groups is present and what identity group and organizational-group issues are critical in the current intergroup exchanges … How group members relate to each other within their group, and to the expectations placed on them by others, is highly dependent on the nature of both the intra-group and intergroup forces active at the time. (Ibid., p. 205)

Alderfer concludes:

> Intergroup theory proposes that both organization groups … and identity groups … affect one's intergroup relations and thereby shape one's cognitive formations. (Ibid., p. 219)

We can add to this last quote the words "both consciously and unconsciously".

Members of generational cohorts might be seen in terms of "identity groups". They provide points of identification, found for example in terms such as "middle-aged", "teenagers", "young adults", "the aged", or more recently "generation x", "generation y", or "baby boomers". Such cohort/age identity groups may provide identity through reference to age/life related issues such as parenting, education, music, or public and political events one grew up with.

Long (1984) argues that when joining a new group, members will identify with the group on the basis of its somehow "belonging" to a pre-existing authority. "The group-that-was-joined" is conceived by a founding authority, and members only gradually come to see it as a "group-that-is-created" through their own exercise of authority. Age or generational-based identity groups may unconsciously be seen to belong to their members only after having won them from a previous generation.

Identity groups may exist for extended periods of time. For example, men and women; young and old; conservatives and liberals; blacks and whites. But new identity groups may form as part of social history, for instance, professional groups, "the class of '89", "those in the 2009 bush fires in Victoria", or "group relations communities of practice". Each identity group has its authorities and often has distinguishable founders: the founders of group relations work, for example. From this perspective, those who form for work purposes on the basis of identity groups and who interact with those from other identity groups will have both internal and external dynamics to contend with.

Internally they must find ways to work within the parameters first devised by the founding authorities, perhaps changing, augmenting, and developing them, in order for the identity to become internalised and open to development and transformation; this is lest the identity remain outside and still only belong to the founders or older generation. In tandem, the founding authorities must find ways to leave the parameters open to development and transformation that might be initiated by those who join or by the founders themselves. A failure of this openness on either side creates the circumstances in which the newcomer is at risk of either remaining a disenfranchised "child" in the system or having to wrest the purpose and leadership of the group from the existing authorities. The existing authorities risk their own stagnation or redundancy. None of these are particularly attractive alternatives. Externally the group members must also find ways to take on the chosen or given identity in such a way that it does not prevent working creatively with other groups.[1]

Learning from the 2008 group relations conference

The theme for the 2008 conference emerged from two places. First, within the community of practice here in Australia and internationally we seem to be dealing with inter-generational phenomena and, in particular, the issue of succession. We use the words "seem to be" because, on closer examination, it seems this may be just one interpretation of the dynamics involved.

Looking more broadly, we can see these issues alive in various forms in the media and the organisations to which we consult. To hold a group relations conference on the theme of inter-generational dynamics was an opportunity to examine both the creative and destructive potential of these dynamics.

From the conference, we discovered a number of interesting things. For example, in the inter-group event we discovered that the so-called "generation X", who were the middle group in this conference (and mostly middle-aged women) when thinking and working within an inter-generational frame of reference, became silent, sapped of energy and somewhat paralysed. It was as if they were conforming to the stereotype of the "silent generation".

The so-called "baby boomer" generation (those fifty-five plus) might have all been in their eighties (although most were in their fifties) for the preoccupation that younger members had, while in their company, with anxieties associated with ageing and mortality. However, in this inter-group event, where people were grouped according to their generation, the older generation were predominantly energetic and playful in a way that was possibly enhanced by an awareness of "deadlines"—the expression they used was being "closer to the end of the twig".

By contrast, the "young", or "generation Y", showed an initiative for systematic hard work. They were anxious to demonstrate their intelligence, perhaps as a cover-up for their internal rivalries. They also celebrated their youth and beauty. Interestingly, the young group were keen to interact with the oldest group and more or less ignored the two groups who were their immediate seniors. The older group spoke of feeling protective and "sort of like grandparents" to the young ones.

When mixed age groups worked in the small study group system, what emerged included a stifling "political correctness" that may have doubled as a mask for more primitive defences and anxiety about death or anxiety about the appropriateness of really engaging creatively across the generational divide, as if it might have been incest. It's hard to describe how tense and polite people were, while at the same time there was an undermining and dismissiveness occurring at a subtle level. As an example, a dialogue began with an older woman talking about how uncomfortable and guilty she felt about how her generation had "stuffed up" the planet and how anxious this made her for her grandchildren's future. As the discussion unfolded, it didn't seem possible to consider that the young people might be resourceful enough to find new solutions. Unlike the stereotype of generation Y being brash, demanding, loud, and only out for themselves, the young people were deferential, meek, and tried hard to put things in ways that would neither offend the older people nor draw attention to the possibility that a fifty- year- old might feel envious of their youth. At the same time, one young man (thirty) said on a number of occasions, "I don't know why the older generation are so hung up about succession and why they can't just bow out gracefully." What this communicated to older members of the group was that they were already redundant and he had nothing to learn from them. Interestingly, in his case, the older person in the organisation referenced was only fifty-five. He was finding it difficult to assert his authority and demonstrate his expertise out of deference and for fear of offending her. It was put to him that if he focused on those work-related issues in which he had considerable and superior expertise rather than the interpersonal sensitivities, these supposed inter-generational dynamics would probably cease to be relevant.

In the frame of studying inter-generational dynamics, conference members seemed to identify with, and "act out", the stereotypes of the generation that they had been assigned to: "grandparent approaching death and being delighted in and protective of the grandchildren", "boring, silent middle-aged person", and "young person who knows nothing, has no competency and acts to prematurely push the oldies off the twig". Significantly, it was as if these relations belonged to a family constellation.

As a staff group, we wondered about the terror that was palpable. Terror appeared in the small study system, the large study system, and in dreams in the staff group leading up to the conference. At first, unconscious anxiety about death seemed a plausible hypothesis, but we speculated that this might only serve to mask the more terrifying anxieties associated with the incest taboo. As Freud (1917) maintained, the Oedipal story invokes terror as we recognise the truth of it as our own unconscious story (in Strachey and Richards, 1981, p. 374). The lines between family relations and inter-generational relations became blurred. At an emotional level, we can hypothesise that the feelings present found their antecedents in early childhood relations in the family and as remnants of the Oedipus complex and its associated feelings of guilt.

As the week progressed, people reflected on the impact of these dominating stereotypes. They questioned how accurate and/or useful they were and witnessed how imprisoning they were. It was as if members then collectively broke free of the shackles of these stereotypes and what resulted was an explosion of creative exuberance across and linking the generations. A cross-generational singing group was formed, for example. As one member described it, "once the prison walls we create for ourselves are challenged by real relationships and interaction, they become more fluid." In the institutional event some groups moved outside the spaces designated by management. For a time, it was as if the staff as management group became completely redundant while groups explored something other than the seeming hierarchical structure provided. As a management group we asked ourselves if this was an act of rebellious flight from the work and an attack on our authority or a genuine attempt to explore a different way of being an organisation. Something seemed to be pushing against the boundaries of normal and familiar models of organisation, albeit, still mostly within them.

This raised the question of what it is about the way we structure our organisations that may serve to reinforce the inter-generational stereotypes that keep individuals stuck and that work against inter-generational linking, bridging, and collaboration. It showed how the group-that-was-joined, provided by the conference management to study inter-generational dynamics, was augmented by the group-that-was-created through the members taking up their authority for membership in new ways. This augmentation was not so much a rebellion as an extension of what the founding authorities had provided. Inter-generational relations were able to move away from the debilitating anxieties raised around the incest and murder of the Oedipal story, so evident in the large study group experience, to a trust in being able to work creatively together. It was not that Oedipal anxieties were totally dispelled. It was more that they had been explored and contained enough so that other dynamics could come into play. We could look at this as developmental movement beyond the Oedipal complex. Something that helped with this was the development of new cross-generational identity groups (groups-that-were-created) that could include mutual histories and shared experiences within the conference, much as broad generational cohorts share histories and experiences (Hopper, 2003).

Evidence from the AISA story

Our learning from the conference offers a perspective for the exploration of events leading to the closure of AISA and, more broadly, speaks to the potential destructiveness of working *from* an inter-generational and/or family group identification rather than *working through* such dynamics. The events have often been spoken of in our community of practice in terms of inter-generational dynamics. As already mentioned, they had some influence on the choice of theme for the 2008 conference. We can trace the origins of the ideas involved back to the international conference in 2002, held in Lorne, "Exploring Being in Global Systems", where an idea emerged in our community of practice that may have gone to work in creating some of the cultural conditions for the closure of AISA.

This 2002 conference contained members from group relations organisations globally. During exploration of the dynamics a hypothesis was advanced that the "younger generation" were enacting the Oedipal drama and were seeking to "kill off" the older generation. We link to this hypothesis an association of "transference vampires", which strongly caught part of the mood during the social dreaming and pointed to the transferences occurring between the generations. The idea hovered around that the generations were enacting the Oedipal scenario from both sides: the younger generation with murderous and ambitious intent and the older with murderous and infantalising intent (one must remember in Oedipus that Laius' intent was to kill his son in the first instance); unconscious, of course. This was all complicated by gender, interpersonal, and country-of-origin dynamics.

Since then, the Oedipal hypothesis has seemed pervasive in exchanges with many colleagues in the work. In conversations at subsequent annual meetings of the International Society for the Psychoanalytic Study of Organizations (ISPSO), for example, dialogue for Brigid with peers was often dominated by thoughts about the role of the "younger generation" in the field and the need to think about succession and leadership. In relations with the "older generation", quite often there would be remarks about the risk to the quality of the work by younger members or the risk of prematurely being "pushed out". One might argue that thoughts such as these are always and inevitably so, but we have cause to challenge the particulars in this case and question what purpose it serves and how it comes to pass.

Evidence from the AISA executive would suggest that its members' struggles with the challenges of addressing questions of leadership succession and organisational development were permeated with anxieties that might have been linked with the Oedipal hypothesis.

> Most of us are locked into a dependency-transferential position as a product of working with [the Director], who appears to foster a contradictory relationship with members: one of growth and

> learning through taking personal authority and simultaneously, one of dependency in looking to the father figure for direction. (Nixon, Edwards, & O'Malley, 2001)

Many of the AISA executive members were either current or past students of the director; at the same time they were charged with the task of being his employer and responsible for the governance of the organisation. This director had held the role for twenty years and since the organisation's foundation (thus, truly a "founding authority" in Long's 2005 terms). As one executive member commented, it seemed difficult to find a boundary between the director's role and the person and, indeed, between the organisation of AISA and the director. Some executive members reported feeling that any critical comments and questions about the organisation were received by the director as if they were a personal attack. The director may have experienced them this way and reportedly said so. While executive members believed they were executing their roles as managers of the organisation in critically examining AISA's structure and position, the blurred boundaries between the person of the director and the organisation meant that their experience of questioning policies or practices was difficult since it was always infused with the risk that this might be experienced as an attack and/or may indeed have been the enactment of an unconscious attack.

Members of a socio-analytically minded group, if challenged by such a hypothesis, are duty bound to examine it for its veracity. However, as one member commented, this turning of the focus in on themselves (set in train by an interpretation) "takes the focus away from healthy positive enquiry from the external situation which might suggest that in reality issues are ... more about probity, transparency, fairness, and integrity." The dynamics in the executive seemed at times to be driven from a paranoid/schizoid state of mind, and its members found it difficult to think.

At the time AISA was going through a period of growth, or at least there was a desire for growth. Through the fellowship programme, for the first time, there was a critical mass of people training to be professional socio-analysts who had a vested interest in AISA's development. While AISA was known internationally within the field, members spoke often of how little known it was amongst prospective client organisations and in Australian society more broadly. They saw the potential for the organisation to play a more meaningful and influential role in society through the expansion of its activities. While over the years, many members had dedicated a lot of time (much of it voluntary) to the success of AISA programmes and GR conferences, the director was the one constant who worked in and on AISA full-time. In Australia, we owe a debt of gratitude for the dedication and persistence of this director in ensuring the high quality of the programmes and training offered by AISA. However, after twenty years, there was a strong push for change, and in particular, a change in leadership structures and tenure.

To this point, the director, from a variety of authorised roles, oversaw and made decisions about many things—from the selection of staff for conferences and training programmes to the choice of consultants for any consulting work that came in. If the organisation was to grow and develop, it was no longer feasible, nor desirable, for it to continue to be managed by one individual. The director and the executive recognised the need to think about succession, but this proved dangerous territory:

> The issue of succession, or of moving past [the Director's] leadership, seems exceedingly painful and is treated with dread, as if dealing with the issue would have catastrophic consequences. The often unconscious phantasies around this issue are very dominant in the membership and get in the way of creativity and generativity. (Nixon, Edwards, & O'Malley, 2001)

In response to the push for change and a concern that the organisation had become overly dependent upon the role of director, in 2003, the director proposed a new design for the governance structure based on principles of distributed leadership. The role of director of AISA was to be replaced with a number of activity "directors". Members of the executive would take up these roles or portfolios. This design effectively did away with the role of director of AISA as a single point of accountability for the organisation. The new model was welcomed and embraced by members of the executive, and a rigorous process of appointing individuals to roles was commenced. However, it was reported that about six months into this restructure process, the director had a change of heart and announced that he no longer supported the idea of AISA not having a director role as a single point of accountability, suggesting that it was untenable; the organisation would not survive, and he threatened to, and then subsequently did, resign from his role. At the same time, according to an outline of events that was distributed to the membership by an executive member, the director asserted that the executive were acting to "topple the director".

At least one executive member subsequently reflected that perhaps the organisation needed a primary director, but it seemed impossible to think about anyone in this role but its current incumbent. Thus it was not clear whether or not the executive (acting on behalf of the membership) were unconsciously holding onto this new design so as to avoid the issue of succession in the role of director—easier to do away with it. This member recalled that executive meetings seemed to be characterised by paranoid anxieties:

> The stress in the room was enormous, I felt mad at times—the dynamics in the exec were so toxic.

As it was related, the toxic dynamics were between other members of the executive and the director. Others in the group described feeling paralysed by the director's presence and his hostility. The director believed that his previously proposed model would not work, and he strongly opposed it. It seemed impossible to have a reasonable dialogue since the dynamics were felt to be pervaded by paranoid-schizoid processes. Consequently, the very thing that brought the group together (a shared passion for and commitment to socio-analysis) was not able to be put to use in the service of the group.

In early 2004, the organisation was discovered to be at risk of trading while insolvent. A number of planned programmes had been cancelled due to lack of applicants. The executive took the decision to cease trading and, in effect, to close the organisation. We recall two predominant reactions to this. On the one hand, it was as if there was a huge collective sigh of relief, and on the other, people were left feeling scarred and bereft by the experience. As one director reflected five years on, "the damage and trauma to me personally was incalculable." Others also spoke of how shocking and damaging the experience had been.

During this time, the hypothesis about an Oedipal enactment (linking back to its introduction some years previously) was in members' minds and on their lips. Gouranga Chattopadhyay, a fellow of AISA, sent the executive a message putting forward the hypothesis again that an Oedipal dynamic was being enacted and the "children" were "killing off the father". Chattopadhyay subsequently wrote about it this way in *Dare to Think the Unthought Known:*

> AISA professionals recognised the heavy dependence on [the Director], but did little about it. However, the baD was covertly setting a process of counter-dependency until early in this century a new Executive Council figuratively (also literally almost financially) "killed" the father figure ... and thoroughly fucked the Mother AISA. This acting out of the unconscious Oedipal drama exhausted the children after [the Director] left ... I have given the Oedipal hypothesis and circulated it to all members. (Chattopadhyay, 2006, p. 248)

At the same time, an executive member, Allan Shafer, offered an alternative hypothesis about a reverse Oedipal enactment in which the "father", unwilling to allow the "children" to grow up, "kills the children off". One might think of this as a Kronos myth, Kronos being the Athenian god who ate his own children to prevent being overthrown. As indicated earlier, attempted murder of the child is also prominent in the Oedipal myth. These two sides of the primitive phantasy led to a "group that could not be created". Neither could the founding authority, nor the potential successors, achieve a new identity.

With hindsight, it seems possible that the director, the executive, and AISA's members were in the thrall of a set of identifications that had little to do with the task of the organisation. As described, the emotional experience was filled with terror and paranoid-schizoid functioning. The result was the resignation of the director and the closure of AISA. It seems reasonable now to hypothesise that the introduction of the family psychic template of Oedipal relations into the system in relation to organisational succession during the 2002 conference, and its acceptance by many leaders in the field, may have invited and/or reinforced a collective identification with the Oedipal drama, giving it predominance and power—at both a conscious and an unconscious level—to function as a major operating assumption in the community of practice.

It may seem a blatant heresy to question a fundamental assumption of psychoanalysis and one that is strongly invoked in group relations work—that is, that Oedipal relations and dilemmas are integral to all relations. However, we argue that the family/Oedipal psychic template, while being one important source of dynamics, may not be the only one. It may be possible to activate other forms of organisation. Indeed, Lawrence invites us to think of organisations from the perspective of the Sphinx rather than Oedipus (Lawrence, 1997).

The inter-generational group relations conference taught us that if you invite people to explore inter-generational dynamics in the here-and-now and to identify with a generational group, they are likely to initially conform to the stereotypes therein. This is done both in terms of how they behave and, most importantly, in terms of how they feel about themselves and, consequently, how they feel about relations with others. In the inter-generational conference, when this became explicit other identifications became possible, and indeed choices about these could be made. So when a group chose to identify itself as the singing group, for example, or the outdoors group, this identification became the basis for assumptions and group functioning. The dynamic was that people at first took up an *assigned* identification and later developed their own *chosen* identifications (see Long, 1984). They first joined a group and later made one.

As Freud observed, the drama of *Oedipus the King* has a power to move us at a deeply unconscious level. It could be said we all have a valency to identify with it and respond with strong emotions. If this identification is invited by a tradition and its leaders, what power might it have to make manifest the emotions and ensuing dynamics that it was intended to describe? Brigid has experience of being in its thrall in her relations with older members in the field—in little ways plagued by the thought that she might be engaged in "killing them off". It was not until she began to think about this paper and the power of group identifications to elicit a particular emotional response (or in Alderfer's terms, our cognitive formations) that she also began to question the validity of its place of prominence either in our community of practice or in organisations more generally.

It is a big question to pose. If the Oedipal family psychic template is not *the* fundamental descriptor for all groups and organisations, what might be the alternatives?[2] Is the child always "father to the man" in organisations, as in the vision of developmental psychology, or might sometimes the culture of the adult become fundamental to organisational life? Or at least might there be a place for Bion's view of the work group where maturity and a scientific valency are the fundamental principles?

Implications for future GR conferences and their design

We are arguing that group relations must include the capacity to identify a number of psychic templates within organisational life and that the family Oedipal one is too often unconsciously adopted as *the* template when dealing with dynamics within its own community of practice. If a working hypothesis of Oedipal enactment emerges, this in turn influences how people take up their roles, perhaps sometimes enacting the hypothesis as the fulfilment of a prophesy. Such working hypotheses, if presented as definitive interpretations from authorities, may counteract the emergence of other psychic templates, such as the work group or the democratic assembly.

In this, we must draw the obvious distinction between running an institute or association that sponsors group relations work and running a group relations conference. Although learning from the latter may be applied to the former, they have different tasks and warrant different structures. We are not arguing the Oedipal family psychic template is never relevant, just that its privileged position in thinking about our own communities of practice blinds us to other possibilities, invites collusion in the dynamic, and curtails further creative development.

Form and function, structure and dynamics, co-evolve and are intertwined. In another conference held at RMIT University in 2009, the institutional event was re-designed using the world event (Green & McRae, 2009). Member groups were asked to elect leaders who then became members of a leadership forum with responsibility for running the event in collaboration with management. This provided a structure for distributed leadership and democratic decision making. The members learned a lot from this redesign, not least how to think about the move from imposed hierarchy to elected representation. The relatedness to the management group was one that was less obsessed with "what management was thinking" and more about negotiation in the development and fulfilment of task. The transferential issues of parent/child became less important than the process of collaborative effort and the analysis of resistances against this. In this another aspect of the family template could be explored—that of sibling rivalry and its possible transformation (or not) into mutual work.

All this implies that the conference design of the future requires a form that might encourage more distributed leadership or other less hierarchical structures. It implies that rather than primarily straining after a hypothesis that describes the unconscious nature of the total institution, a structure emerges to look at the implications of different hypotheses arising in different parts of the institution. This may involve a design for more fully studying change as it occurs in the conference. It may involve a task of more than studying, but also one of developing working communities (Long, 2009). We are sure that all this is done to some extent within the group relations methodology, but we wish to make this more explicit.

Conclusion

An observation we make is that family is such a dominant model for relations between people in organisations—what we think of as a "psychic template"—that it leads to unconscious impotence. What psychoanalysis discovered as an explanatory concept has, at times, become an unconscious directive in our community of practice and in group relations fundamentalism. We repeatedly learn from clients that organisations are too often regarded as places where the children never grow up and the parents/teachers hold all the power, control, authority, and decision-making. This cripples the capacity to be creative, to take up authority for work, to have robust debates, and to be thoughtful agents in adapting to complex and changing external and internal circumstances.

Age-related stereotypes are another such "psychic template" or, in Morgan's (1997) terms, "psychic prison", that serves to keep people stuck—perhaps because they invite a preoccupation with mortality and an ensuing political correctness that is both stifling and false. False because it is anchored in untested and unchallenged stereotypes. Members of the 2008 conference discovered that if they could abandon these stereotypes and instead build their group identity and relations by reference to a shared task, the energy levels rose and a joyousness and appreciation for each other and each other's differences emerged (regardless of whether this was to do with age, gender, race, culture, or work experience).

We reflect that trying to imagine moving beyond the fact (or metaphor) of the Oedipal drama and the "family-as-psychic template" may be a futile enterprise. What might there be to take its place? Yet, the work of group relations, and systems psychodynamics more broadly, is fundamentally about creating a learning environment in which the transformation in the individual's and the group's capacities to take up authority, to think, to reflect, to be an active agent in the making and taking up of roles within organisations is possible. We appeal to and engage with adults in this enterprise and we respect adulthood. The Oedipus complex describes and belongs to a developmental process in childhood, adolescence, and regressive states. If it is not possible to move beyond family, in organisations, we wonder if it is not more useful to think of the relations between adult members of families

References

Alderfer, C. P. (1987). An intergroup perspective on group dynamics. In: J. W. Lorsch (Ed.), *Handbook of Organizational Behaviour.* Englewood Cliffs: Prentice-Hall.

Bion, W. R. (1961). *Experiences In Groups*. London: Routledge.

Bion, W. R. (1970). *Attention and Interpretation: A Scientific Approach to Insight in Psycho-Analysis and Groups.* London: Tavistock Publications. Chattopadhyay, G. (2006). A conversation with Gouranga: Candid reflections. In A. N. Mathur (Ed.), *Dare to Think the Unthought Known.* Tampere: Aivoairut Oy.

Green, Z. G., McRae, M. (2009). A world of difference. In: E. Aram, R. Baxter, & A. Nutkavitch, *Adaptation and Innovation: Theory, Design and Role Taking in Group Relations Conferences and Their Applications.* London: Karnac.

Hopper, E. (2003). *The Social Unconscious.* London: International Library of Group Analysis.

Lawrence, W. G. (1997). Centring the Sphinx for the Psychoanalytic Study of Organisations. Philadelphia: ISPSO Symposium.

Long, S. D. (1984). Early integration in groups: A group to join and a group to create. *Human Relations, 37*: 311–332.

Long, S. (2006). This used to be my playground: Family/work dynamics. In: A. Mathur, *Dare to Think the Unthought Known.* Tampere: Aivoairut Oy.

Long, S. (2009). The community system. In: E. Aram, R. Baxter & A. Nutkavitch (Eds.), *Adaptation and Innovation: Theory, Design and Role Taking in Group Relations Conferences and Their Applications.* London: Karnac.

Morgan, G. (1997). *Images of Organization.* Thousand Oaks, CA: Sage Publications.

Nixon, S., Edwards, M., & O'Malley, M. (2001). Working note to membership. Melbourne, Australian Institute of Socio-Analysis.

Sievers, B. (1995). Characters in search of a theatre: Organization as theatre for the drama of childhood and the drama of work. In: S. Long, (Ed.), *International Perspectives on Organizations in Times of Turbulence.* Hawthorn: Swinburne University of Management.

Smith, K. (1983). Social comparison processes and dynamic conservatism in intergroup relations. In L. L. C. a. B. M. Straw (Ed.), *Research in Organisational Behaviour, 5*: pp. 199–233.

Strachey, J., & Richards, A. (1981). *Introductory Lectures on Psychoanalysis, Sigmund Freud*. New York: Penguin Books.

Notes

1. This seems to fit with Smith (1983) and his concept of dynamic conservatism. It also puts us in mind of Bion's container/contained and the container not being too much of an 'obstructive rigidity' (Bion, 1970). The point about working with other groups is very germaine to the GR context.
2. A colleague, Himadri Potter, has pointed out to us that Norman O. Brown in the mid twentieth century also examined the possibilities that the Oedipal hierarchical form of organisation might be a deviation from other forms. Also, although the "modern" form of family post the incest taboo has been a central basis for our civilisations, the primal horde discussed by Freud may also provide a psychic template for some aspects of organisation—a pre-family form.

SECTION III

LEARNING THROUGH EXPERIENCE: WRESTLING WITH CREATIVITY AND INNOVATION IN SUCCESSION AND APPLICATION

This versatile section offers four chapters, all of which explore at least one of the conference title's themes, reflecting on the negative as well as the positive aspects at work. The first is an examination of learning from and through a GR conference method in an academic setting in Israel, where learning already carries a particular meaning which, with GR, opens up new possibilities. The second is Beverly Malone's exploration of the adaptive potential of the GR method to the one-to-one context of mentoring and coaching. The third is a painful account of the struggle for a creative succession in the GR Netherlands context, and the fourth is the vivacious account of the innovations and application of GR work to the Latin American setting, and to Peru in particular. Reading the chapters in this section poignantly brings us in touch with how to think about and make sense of the group relations global network. Where do innovations take place? How is succession carried through? What usefully can we draw from the GR methodology to work in other, more specific, work areas?

CHAPTER SEVEN

Learning from experience and the experience of learning in an academic setting

Oren Kaplan, Judith Levy, Avi Nutkevitch, and Miri Tsadok

The title of our paper comprises two subjects. The first, "learning from experience and the experience of learning", relates directly to one of the central issues in group relations conferences—that of learning. What is the relationship between learning from experience and the experience of learning? Are they one and same? This question, to which the theoretical literature on group relations has not provided a conclusive answer, is also a central one in our course—"Psychological Aspects of Management"—and is the subject of this paper. It is not only an open-ended question with which we are preoccupied, but the way we try to understand that relationship underlies much of the course's structure and design. In addition, the problems posed by this question, and the ways we try to act on it in our course, are compounded by the subject expressed in the title of our paper: the academic setting of our course. How can learning, as we may want to relate to it and understand it from group relations conferences, and the way we grapple with it, be implemented in an academic setting in general, and in an MBA in business administration in particular?

We have coined our course in its setting as a "meeting of cultures": it is regarded or experienced by us as the "grandchild" (as will be explained) of Tavistock or OFEK conferences set in an MBA programme in business psychology, part of the College of Management, Israel. Whereas in group relations conferences the question of learning, although central, is firmly and ideologically rooted in "experience", in an MBA programme, other kinds of learning prevail. What kind of learning do we want to invoke in a course on the psychological aspects of management? How does that learning fit in with the general aims of the MBA programme? These are the questions that underlie many of our attempts at innovation and development, and these are the questions, as well as some of our answers, that we will try and discuss in this paper. Whether such integration is fully possible may very well remain an open question.

Our presentation, then, follows three prongs. We will begin with the background of the course and the complex setting, both academically and historically, within which it functions; we will continue with our ideas about learning and the ways in which we have tried to implement them, illustrating this through two activities/events that are part of the course; and we will conclude with the nature of the organisational holding environment that we have created, or need to create, to promote the kind of learning we hope to achieve.

The course

The course "Psychological Aspects of Management" has been administered for six years in the MBA management and business psychology programme (henceforth MBPP) at the college of management. The four authors of the present paper serve as the faculty of the course, which is spread over a full academic year and includes about eighty academic hours.

The primary task of the course was defined as "the development of understandings and insights regarding role, management, and group and organisational processes from a psychoanalytic-systemic perspective", and it includes workshop-type activities as well as theoretical classes. Thus, in addition to the theoretical classes, there are modules such as "mental maps"—sessions that explore the role of the manager and the role of the student in his/her organisation; an inter-group "visiting exercise"; "organisational topography", which investigates individual and group identity issues; "history of the future," which explores strategic processes in an organisation; "role analysis," which analyses the current role of the individual in the context of his past and familial roles; an "organisational event" (which will be discussed later on); "critical event" case studies brought by the students, which are used to apply the psychoanalytic-systemic understanding gained during the course; and "observations in organisations", including a diagnostic process on an organisation. Many of these activities were inspired by the programme in organisational consultation and development: a psychoanalytic-systemic approach (henceforth POCD), currently sponsored by Ofek, the Israel Association for the Study of Group and Organizational Processes, and the Tavistock Institute, and by other group relations activities in the world. They were further elaborated upon and developed by the writers of this paper. Symbolically it can be claimed that the POCD is an offspring of the GR framework and that our course is an offspring of the POCD, thus, to us, a "grandchild" of group relations conferences.

Our course functions, as noted, within a very complex setting, which is a meeting of cultures in more than one sense. It is the most psychological/experiential element in the MBPP and thus serves as a focus of both alienation and envy within the programme and the college in general. As a descendent of group relations, it carries that identification into the business world, which is the main identity of the college. This identification/identity not only arouses suspicion on the business side, but harbours its own ambivalence towards the business world, as we all recognise from GRC organisations the world over. Finally, the students themselves, in their choice of degree, are creating a hybrid identity, a process which does not always go smoothly. It is this complex network of ambivalences that we must contain and work with in our course.

"A meeting of cultures"

The school of business administration at the college of management is the largest in Israel; it includes of 4500 student out of which 1500 are MBA students. It was founded about thirty years ago and was the first academic institution in Israel that broke out of the university system and was authorised by the Israel council for higher education to give academic degrees.

Each class of the MBPP, a two-year programme, includes about thirty-five students, most of them women. They are bachelors in psychology, social work, or other social science fields, who wish to qualify in business and management. The objective of the MBPP is to provide its students with wide theoretical and practical knowledge in traditional

MBA areas while delving deeper into the psychological aspects of these fields. A significant emphasis is put on the personal development of the student/manager, and the present course is part of this objective.

In the past, applicants with a psychological background did not consider the MBA programme as a relevant master's degree for them. Although the faculty of the course always saw the value of a business-psychologically oriented programme, the school saw it mainly from an economical perspective. As the college is not supported by the government, the school can only afford to run programmes that can pay their way. It was expected, therefore, that the BMPP would attract psychology and social work students with high grades, who otherwise would not consider studying in the MBA programme, and thus extend the school's potential attraction for applicants. The MBPP programme has met these expectations. However, from an inner organisational culture point of view, it has remained alien: psychology in general is not perceived as a business hard-core subject and within that, the idea of small workshops seems not academic and not economical. Luckily, the dean of the graduate school at the time of the inception of the programme knew Rina Bar Lev (an OFEK member who was a co-founder of the POCD), so there was a certain fondness towards the new born exotic "baby" in the school of business.

As mentioned before, the students of the MBPP come mainly from a background of BA degrees in psychology, behavioural science, or social work. The MBA is often a significant change in their career track, and in spite of their enthusiasm for the new direction, they still carry ambivalence towards the business world they encounter.

When introduced to our course, they are often confused and suspicious. On the one hand, it takes them back to the experiential world, which they think they have left behind when entering the MBA programme; on the other, our version of the experiential, based as it is on group relations, with its orientation towards the organisational, is alien and even threatening. Doubts are expressed whether this kind of approach can have any practical bearing on their roles as managers and their route along the business world.

However, if we look at this more closely, we see that their confusion and ambivalence is, in fact, a mirror of the difficult meeting between the world of group relations and the world of business in general. In our case this is reflected, for example, in the ambivalence that still exists between OFEK—the main disseminator of group relations in Israel—and the college. All four faculty of the course are OFEK members, and OFEK's annual international conference is sponsored by the college, which gives OFEK a financial security net and sends eight students to the conference on a full bursary. Nevertheless, the affiliation with the college is still regarded with some suspicion within OFEK, as if a business college must in some way threaten the purity of a group relations organisation.

But are not all GR conferences and their organisational environments trapped in this same conflict? There is a wish to be practical and to contribute significantly to the management and business world, but, nevertheless, this wish often gets permeated with ambivalence. The business world, the GR world, the students—they all carry suspiciousness about this attempt to combine the psychoanalytic world with the business world.

It is against this background that we have developed our ideas about the kind of learning we wish to invoke and the ways of achieving it. We will now go on to describe some theoretical underpinnings to our approach and then give two actual examples of events from our course as a way of illuminating both our thinking and the practical issues that arise.

On the relationship between learning and experience

T is a student in the MBA programme. He holds a senior position in the municipal educational system in the West Bank. He is a settler, and he is religious. Last July he participated in OFEK's "Israeli" group relations conference, thus named because its working language is Hebrew and all staff are Israeli. T is one of eight MBA students who came to the conference with a full scholarship given by the MBA programme.

It was the closing plenary of the conference. Participants were reflecting on their conference experience. At some point T started talking, increasingly emotionally:

> All year we have been learning at the college about valency, but it was only here that I really understood the meaning of the term, as I have felt it deeply in myself. I am the only religious member of the conference (at least as can be seen from the outside), and I live in a settlement. All during the conference I felt how difficult it has been for me to deal with the projections that those labels have drawn.

> I am still religious, and I live in a settlement, and I do not intend to change, but I have now experienced, most profoundly, the gap between how I see myself and how others see me. I still do not know how to separate myself, as I know myself, from that.

He then proceeded to read, most movingly, a passage from the Bible, concerning Elijah the Prophet, which he compared, verse by verse, to his experience at the conference. These were very poignant moments but also relevant to our discussion. What did it mean in terms of the learning in the MBA programme that only at that moment did he understand what valency was? How important was it for an MBA student training for a managerial role not only to experience "valency", but also to be able to know—and learn—that the experience he was describing could be so termed? We believe it is important. It was therefore a moment of satisfaction and a sense of achievement for those conference staff members who are also part of the faculty team at the MBA programme. The opportunities for learning provided by the staff at the conference had led to an experience of learning.

Yet at times this is not the case. We often come across a closing plenary in a GRC, or for that matter a review session in the MBA programme, where participants report not having learnt. In a closing plenary of one of OFEK's international GRC several years ago, S described with much anger her experiences in the organisational event. She exuded frustration and criticism. It was "obvious" to staff members that S was describing experiences which contained issues of taking/being given authority which reflected her own personal dynamics, the dynamic of that particular group she referred to, as well as a possible reflection of the system as a whole. Something in this spirit was said by a staff member. However, S stuck to her guns. Her frustrating experience did not turn into an experience of learning. Some staff members were frustrated, too. Here they had provided rich opportunities for very meaningful and deep learning, and here they had a conference member—S—who did have experiences; however, her experience had not turned into an experience of learning. What had happened? Was it S's problem? Was it S's defensiveness or her suspicious attitude? Or was it, perhaps, a certain aspect of the conference or staff dynamics that was not recognised/owned/worked through; if it had been identified and worked with, might that have created the conditions where even this "stubborn" member could have had an experience of learning? When S spoke other members remained silent. Did they have a similar experience? As staff members in GRC we often wonder not only about what members have learnt—an elusive subject in its own right—but whether they had an experience of learning, and was having such an experience enough?

Learning from experience is—as we have stated—a major axis of our course. But equally important to us is the experience of learning. What do these two entail? What kind of events leading to learning from experience do we provide during the year-long course? And not less important, what could be the faculty's contribution, or perhaps even responsibility, in assisting the students in their process of transforming an emotional experience into an experience of learning?

To relate to these questions we would like to turn to Bion. Bion is the "father" or "mother"—depending on whether we ascribe fatherhood to the psychoanalytic leg and motherhood to the open systems leg or the other way round—of the ideas and theories underlying group relations conferences. One of the main notions presented by Bion regarding learning from experience is the notion of alpha function.

Alpha function is a mental activity or a set of mental operations that transforms beta elements into alpha elements (Bion, 1991). Beta elements are the most rudimentary impressions that experience makes on the mind and are prone to evacuation, especially via projective identification or some form of acting out. They are mental parts that are "things in themselves", unknown to us, and they are experienced as undigested facts. They might be split off, denied, or disowned psychic elements. Alpha elements, on the other hand, are mental parts that are at times conscious but might also be unconscious, yet are "lying there", serving as the raw elements for thinking, dreaming, reasoning, and also conceptual thinking. Antonio Ferro (2005) conceptualises an alpha metafunction as a higher level of a thinking apparatus, where thoughtful reflections can take place and a higher level of learning can occur. This thinking can move and develop from a more basic level, such as "I feel blamed", or "I feel related to as an extremist and I am not recognised for what I am", to a higher level of thinking, such as, "Now I understand what valency is and feels like". That is, perhaps, what happened to T in the closing plenary.

Bion states: "To learn from experience, alpha function must operate on the awareness of emotional experience" (Bion, 1991, p. 8). In group relations conferences, as well as in our course, we create opportunities for learning from experience where we encounter in ourselves emotional experiences, which can be seen to be rudimentary beta elements that are often unconsciously painful, shameful, or filled with anxiety, and where our alpha function might enable us to transform these beta elements into alpha elements which will be used by us to understand and thus to learn about unconscious processes. These might be related, for example, to our perception of what managing is, or what internal authority is, or how childhood experiences are connected to our current dilemmas at work, or our tendency to wait to be given authority by a group and not to dare and take it. Thus we hope that the experiences students have in the various events we design will produce an experience of learning, both emotional and conceptual, with regard both to themselves in role and to group and organisational processes.

We now turn to two activities within our course which, we hope, will illustrate our thinking on learning and its implementation, as well as our attempt at integrating all the elements of our course into a learning whole.

Yoman massa: on the ability to introspect and reflect as a tool of management

> Thoughts, emotions, sensations, try to put in order
> Am I again in a "dance therapy" school
> I though I am done with that
> Done, haven't done, never done really.
> But wait a minute, where am I again?
> Master degree, MBA
> Specialization in business and management psychology.
> Uhh!!! sound so big!!
>
> (From a student's first travel diary)

Last year we asked our students to write a diary after each lesson. We gave them two or three open questions regarding the experience of the learning that had taken place, which they were requested to answer in a few paragraphs and to send to us via an internet portal. The diaries were distributed randomly among us by Keren Lipinsky, the course assistant, who read all the entries and sent us her overall impressions. Towards the end of the year, as part of their final assignment, the students were asked to review their diary entries and to choose three that represented three meaningful points in their learning process.

Writing these diary entries (called *yoman massa* in Hebrew, meaning "journey diary") was a task we assigned only two years ago. The idea was to add another way of communicating between the students and faculty and to provide a means for the students to digest their experience. In retrospect it was much more than that. We want to suggest that the diary is part of a structure that enables the containment of the anxiety that accompanies the learning process. We feel that we created a kind of transitional space in which the diaries serve as a means for individual internal expression, which, nevertheless, gets read by the faculty. On the other hand, it is not a direct dialogue, since we do not respond directly to the personal material. We use it in the service of their learning and for us to understand something about the state of the group and the learning process.

In his final entry, summarising his learning during the year, M wrote: "Dear reader, on this occasion, I want to thank you for your listening, for being faceless but full of meaning; thanks."

Writing the diary was a way to reflect and introspect. The writing of it as a regular task after every lesson turned reflection and introspection into skills one could practice and be trained in, and this links to one of the basic notions that leads us in this course: the idea that people can learn and be trained to use introspection and reflection as a tool of management. It is not something you either have or do not have. Reflective thinking and introspection imply the ability to self-observe and to think retrospectively on one's activity, experience and thoughts. We often use these words when we describe the favorable outcomes of participation in group relations conferences, but it is useful to reflect more precisely on these terms.

Introspection could be defined as self-observation and the reporting of inner thoughts, desires, and sensations. It is a conscious and usually purposeful mental process relying on thinking, reasoning, and examining one's own thoughts and feelings.

Reflection, the ability of a system to contain a representation of itself, is closely related to introspection, and like introspection, it links awareness to the act of observation, to the act of visualising. To watch, to see, is to know. The emphasis in this term, however, is not on the "intro" but on the "re"—the return of the image: the "second degree" quality of the act. The root of the verb comes from Latin: *re* plus *flectere*: to bend back. We would like to suggest that both introspection and reflection are terms that are linked to circular movement as opposed to a linear one. It implies directing oneself towards a goal with the ability to "bend back", where bending back could mean to suspend one's reaction and avoid an instinctive-automatic one. It means to look backward in order to progress in the future. It also means to look inside in order to better understand the outside. For us the ability to reflect and introspect is closely related to the notion of reverie and thus, also, to alpha function: it is the ability to contain and own the experiences and thus learn from them. When alpha function operates, reflection and introspection are possible, but we might also say it the other way around: creating space for reflection enhances the operation of alpha function.

This is a state of mind that enables creativity, a condition in which there is enough calmness and relaxed space to think "out of the box"—inward, outward, backward, and all around. As we know, to acquire this state of mind is not simple, especially when it comes to the business-management world. Directors are often carried away by "strong winds" that push them to react quickly and impulsively. Suspension of reaction seems like a hesitation, a kind of weakness. Sometimes it is. There are urgent situations that leave no time and no space to reflect and introspect. But most of the time, even in stressful situations, there is some time and some space that can be used less or more effectively. One could argue: why bother to stop, to reflect, instead of moving spontaneously? When we ride on bicycles or swim, over-consciousness could hinder and might even cause a fall or delay.

At the beginning of the year we often encounter remarks such as "well all of this is nice and convincing but outside in the real word, in our office, who can afford to search and reflect on what goes on below the surface? One should act, the faster the better". Or: "As a manager I can't elaborate and go into all these emotions. I must cut through them and get the job done".

All of this is true in a way: in stressful and emergency situations, it is better if one can rely on virtually automatic reactions, like a reflex reaction, with no need for contemplation. (By the way, the common origin of the terms "reflex" and "reflection" makes one think about the wisdom of the language that teaches us that sometimes words having the opposite meaning have the same origin.) Our working hypothesis is that a regular creation of a space for reflection and introspection enables their transformation into an integrated, and thus natural, skill. As in the case of walking, swimming, riding, and driving, there are different stages. The first demands a slowing down, an awareness of every part of the act in order to enable the later smooth motion. Ongoing practice transforms the reflective thinking from an alien and unnatural act into a dynamic flow that assimilates the reflection as an integral part of role taking and management capabilities.

The organisational event: an integrated experience

In the middle of the course we run an extended organisational event. It is inspired by the OE event in GR conferences, but it has a more structured design. Rather than the usual two-hour a week sessions, we build it around an introductory session, a marathon of six hours the following week, and then a concluding session the week after. This way, we can capture something of the intensity of experience that the OE generates in a group relations conference. Furthermore, the task to be accomplished is taken from the world of reality and business.

The heart of the OE event comprises the simulation of an organisational merger—"Coca Cola Israel has purchased three companies (three dairy firms) and merged them". In reality, Coca Cola Israel did purchase a medium size dairy firm a few years ago in order to expand its business into new arenas. In Israel there are two large dairy firms that dominate the market, and a few additional small and medium size dairies (including the one that was bought by Coca Cola) that are not very dominant. In our simulation, Coca Cola Israel decided to purchase two additional medium size dairies, in addition to the one it had already bought, and merge the three of them into one big company that could compete head to head with the two other dominant firms currently leading the market.

When we built the event we did not pay much attention to the latent meanings of the business structure that we created. In retrospect we can see that we chose a commercial firm which is one of the top brands of the world. In addition, in the background of the merger (as in any merger) there is much emphasis on leadership and competition—Coca Cola Israel wanted to be a market leader in the new arena it conquered and, therefore, applied an active competitive attitude in order to gain this position. We were captivated by the idea that we were bringing a hardcore business element—a renowned brand name at that—into our psychological course, and we paid less attention to the competitive elements that were thus brought into the event. It is not surprising, therefore, that leadership and competition were at the heart of the processes in this event, even more than we see in traditional organisational events. One piece of evidence for this is the management structure we designed for it. In traditional GR events, the management is usually the management of the conference, while some of the staff members function as consultants. In our event, our role as staff is only to consult, while the managerial roles are allocated to the students. During the event, the students function as a directorate representing Coca Cola, which manages the event, and as management members of each of the three merged firms. The aim of the event is to create a new senior management of the combined companies that represents the resources and needs of each company.

In the two events we have run in the last two years, we discussed the role we wanted to give to the top management from Coca Cola. Should this management negotiate the future merger (where the results of the negotiation would be unclear), or should it represent Coca Cola after having purchased the three companies, thereby increasing the dependency of the employees of these firms on the top management. We decided on the latter option, perhaps thinking that this is also the realistic structure of an organisation with a real management at its head. In retrospect there were probably additional unconscious elements in this decision. We worried that the extreme competition between groups that were having to give up their freedom and be swallowed by a big company would "blow" the whole merger, and perhaps the whole event. But behind that realistic "pedagogical" thought there might have been another layer. Not once during the event did we discuss the notion that the top management of Coca Cola was actually a shadow management of the course that replaced us as the faculty. The question of how much we compete with them and how much they compete with us was raised. But if we combine the above two thoughts, it could be suggested that we had a fear that if the merger failed, and with it the top management of the students who represented us, the failure would be actually ours as management of the whole system. The structure we designed was therefore also a defence against such failure, and we are still considering how to design it in the coming year.

One of the most dramatic occurrences takes place at the beginning of the last third of the event. At this time the students are required to liquidate one of the territories "in an effort to cut costs". In the earlier phases of the event, the groups discuss and negotiate the decision about which factory (territory) will be liquidated and where its employees (group members) should move, that is, to one of the other territories. This issue attracts much attention during the event and represents the core of the competition between the groups. The organisational myth is that the group that will be evacuated from its room will be the loser. Therefore the three groups struggle, mainly in the negotiation with the top management, not to be the losing team. However, the outcomes of this liquidation have not always been the expected ones. In one year, the two groups that were joined (the one that was evacuated and the one which they joined) were occupied in constructing their new realm, whereas the third group, the one that remained untouched, and therefore was the "winner", became "boring", without much interest. In fact, after their victory and survival, there did not seem to be much meaning to their existence.

The given structure of the session is such that at the end of each subunit, the teams must take time for a review session—a group reflection—to look at the way they have worked, how they have dealt with their objectives. The aim is, on the one hand, for the students to experience competition and decision-making, but, on the other hand, to integrate the tools that we have given them for reflection and review into that experience.

It is interesting to note that when we first ran the event two years ago, the students, despite interpretations from us as consultants, often skipped the "review section because of the stress of time and the important tasks they had to do". To a great extent this can be seen to parallel the everyday happenings in organisations. There is no time for reflection, and the burning necessities push the privilege of stopping and observing out of the system, despite the cognitive understanding that such a pause may contribute a great deal to the general proceedings of the organisation. The third time we ran the event, we decided to change the setting and declared in advance that the review sessions (ten minutes here and there along the event) would be facilitated by us, the course faculty. We compared this function to the role of organisational consultant in an organisation. The review process then assumed important meaning, both to the way the virtual organisation functioned but also as a modeling for the students. We believe that such review processes, though not easy to implement, are important to the health and success of an organisation. This is where, we feel, the "meeting of cultures" mentioned earlier comes into play on all levels. It is not only the meeting of the psychological with the business world. It is also the place where the learning from experience becomes, we hope, an experience of learning.

The end of the organisational event is actually a broad review session. In its first part, the top management of the event invites the whole organisation to a closing plenary in which the final organisational structure is presented and a discussion on the process ensues. In its second part, all of the participants leave their roles, and the faculty returns to its original role in a review session of the event as a whole.

It is beyond the scope of this paper to describe the complexity of this event in more detail. However, what is notable is the amount of energy and involvement it invokes on the part of the students (even after the event, they report that when shopping in the supermarket, they feel loyal to the real life dairy they represented), together with questions and criticism of the way it evolves: does the "real world" really behave in this way? Would a real business firm give so much space for processes such as review and reflection? As the most business-oriented event in the whole course, the ambivalence around the psychological materials that the group relations world brings in is very marked and very pertinent, and we, as faculty, do not always have a full or convincing answer.

The "holding environment"

We turn now to our third "prong"—the conditions necessary for this course to work and for learning to be achieved. This contains our challenge as a faculty team to create such conditions, when, as has been noted already, the setting differs from that in a group relations conference and we aim not only at the emotional understanding of experience but at developing a vocabulary and a body of knowledge based on the psychoanalytic-systemic perspective.

We identify three factors which we deem crucial in providing the "organisational container" that will enhance this kind of learning.

The first is the management of group and organisational conditions and boundaries in both the internal and external environment. In an earlier part of the chapter we described the "meeting of cultures" and the organisational context in which the course operates. There are three boundaries which we have to manage: the boundary between the course and the MBPP; the boundary between the MBPP and the MBA track; and the boundary between the course, the MBPP, and OFEK.

These boundaries are suffused with envy, competition, ambivalence, and differences in the culture of learning and operating. All this may affect the course directly and indirectly, emotionally and practically (e.g., how and when to grade the students—an issue which is a problem in a mode of learning from experience). These boundaries have therefore to be managed politically, emotionally, and practically. We cannot go into the details of such boundary problems here, but the fact that one of us—Oren—is the director of the MBPP and part of the faculty team of the course provides the optimal management of these boundaries and contributes significantly to the flourishing of the course. Without his holding this multiplicity of roles, we believe that the success and perhaps even the survival of the course would have been compromised.

The second factor is what we see as creating space for "play". It could be said that the learning and the training in our course take place by providing a playground—in the sense of a space that provides the opportunities to practice in the here-and-now real situations that require management skills and self-management in teams. We call these situations play, not because they are unreal or unlike the outside reality, but because the primary task here is to learn and to practice. The cost of feeling a failure is real, but it is not an existential threat.

At the beginning of the year we use the metaphor of a training swimming pool for the space of the learning. The swimming pool is quite safe but not totally protected; we, the staff, are there to help the learning and to lessen the danger. Of course there is the risk of getting hurt, feeling ashamed, and the possibility of failure. The wish to succeed and to be recognised is there, but we suggest that all of this helps the play to be real and vivid. Hopefully, when no serious pathology interferes, there is no need to fight for survival, and there is an opportunity to keep the play as a learning space. One might derive very successful learning from an experience of failure. Let us quote from the diary of one of our more criticising and challenging students, K, who wrote, following the organisational event: "The most striking thing was the fact that D lied to the girls from Gad company, which means taking the game much more seriously than I would have expected. I myself adopted this behavior later with the representatives of Yotvata (another company) ... kind of getting involved deeply in the game. I believe something in the way we acted faithfully represented real reactions in this kind of event: panic, chaos, the shaking up of the entire system and the controls, everyone running with no clear destination, running for the sake of running."

In this respect, the fact that the course takes place once a week during a whole academic year and lacks the well-known intensive quality of the group relations conference experience, is not only a disadvantage. It also allows for the practicing of this interweave between the reality of the workshop and the outside world. There is time to reflect on the different modes of coping, to try new and unfamiliar ones, to reflect on the group processes throughout the year and to have time to digest—to be swept in and then to observe from some distance; in other words, it is analogous to what we in psychoanalysis call "working through".

In his book *Playing and Reality,* D. W. Winnicott beautifully expresses this idea of the play as a place of real and creative existence: "Playing is an experience, always a creative experience, and it is an experience in the space-time continuum, a basic form of living" (Winnicott, 1971, p. 54).

Later he reminds us of the importance of play as an area that holds together and allows the interweaving movement between inner reality and the outside:

> "... and on the basis of playing is built the whole of man's experiential existence. No longer are we either introvert or extrovert. We experience life in the area of transitional phenomena, in the exciting interweave of subjectivity and objective observation, and in an area that is intermediate between the inner reality of the individual and the shared reality of the world that is external to individuals." (ibid., p. 75)

We hope that in some ways we have succeeded in playing and have provided both our students and ourselves a transitional space that enables all of us to learn from experience, to harness the subjective and inner experience to the comprehension of the outer world.

The third factor relating to the conditions necessary to achieve the kind of learning we aim at is what we term the "organisational alpha function" (which is somewhat similar to working on the countertransference, or containing).

As already noted, we are preoccupied with the conditions that can enhance the possibility for the student to "play" and to learn from experience, that is, for his alpha function to transform emotional experiences which are carried internally as beta elements into alpha elements Bion described the crucial role that the mother has in the development of alpha function. If the mother has the ability for reverie and for containing anxiety—either her own or that projected into her—the baby has a better chance of developing his alpha function. We see a conceptual correspondence between this process and the dynamics existing in the faculty-student matrix of our course. What we call the organisational alpha function is the mental activity which takes place in the organisational sphere where beta elements get transformed into alpha elements. And it is the faculty's responsibility to take a leading role in this process. Thus, the more the faculty is able to contain what is projected into it (those unthought, undigested beta elements roaming in the faculty-student space) as well as recognise its own anxieties and unconscious split-off parts, "digest" them, and own them explicitly when appropriate, the better are the conditions created for the alpha function of the students to operate, and thus for productive engagement with the process of learning, especially learning from experience.

We would like now to describe a particular faculty-student dynamic that takes place in the area between surrender and submission. For that let us turn to the first session of the course, in which we tell them about the course, about its primary task and conceptual framework. But how can we explain what and how we are going to learn? We have already had the experience of five such courses. The year before last was difficult. A relatively large number of the students were not satisfied, were like K in the vignette. How can we "explain" better? How can we make it easier for them to grasp what they will get out of the course, and how can we make it easier for them to join us with a curious and trusting heart on this journey? To help them in this initial phase, we came up with three metaphors which we hoped would be illuminating:

a. "Eyeglasses": we said that we assumed/hoped that the course and the learning would be experienced as wearing eyeglasses that enabled a sharper, deeper, and wider view both inwardly and outwardly.
b. "Night vision binoculars": we suggested that in some respects the experience of learning would be like using night vision binoculars so that we can see in a clearer way what transpires in the darkness under the surface. This metaphor was useful for the introduction of the notion of the unconscious and of unconscious processes.
c. "A training swimming pool": here we moved from the individual learner to the context of learning. We said that this learning swimming pool was a kind of container/pool in our psychoanalytic-systemic

> language. This raised both the association of daring to jump into the water and the responsibility and challenge of the faculty to build a swimming pool that is felt to be safe enough to jump into.

It was a bit disappointing, but not really surprising for us, to find out that quite a large number of students wrote in their first travel diary that "the aims are foggy" and that they are "confused". Our explanation, including the metaphors, did not clear the fog. In a way we, the faculty, could identify with them. We ourselves could not know what exactly would evolve and what would then be learnt. Nevertheless, we trusted the process. We also knew that the kind of learning we offer requires the students' willingness to go along with us. We tried to use our metaphors to make it easier for them to follow our lead and to trust in us to take them to safe enough, though challenging, places. What do the students experience internally vis-à-vis this predicament?

These questions take us to Imanuel Ghent, the New York psychoanalyst who wrote a seminal paper regarding the relation of submission to surrender (1999). For Ghent the term "surrender" has nothing to do with hoisting a white flag. In fact, rather than carrying a connotation of defeat, the term conveys the letting down of a defensive barrier. Surrender means giving room to forces working towards growth; it actually represents the longing one has to open oneself up and to let down defenses.

Contrary to that is the fear of letting down defenses, the fear of letting the "true self" be exposed to the danger of hurt and disappointments. In such a case, "joining the journey" is experienced unconsciously as submission. When this is the dominant feeling we might expect suspiciousness and resistance.

We believe that the primary task, the structure, and the modes of teaching and learning in this course, put the students in the emotional—mostly unconscious—state between "surrender" and "submission". Our explanations of the primary task and the associated "friendly" metaphors do not prevent this internal predicament (this is obviously true in GRCs and in almost any experiential, and not only experiential, teaching situation). The range of emotions between these two polarities exists in the class and is distributed among the students. Some—even most—are positive in their attitude, and, although a little anxious, seem to be willing "go with us". This reflects surrender. Others are suspicious, closed, and exude an oppositional stance. They are often seen and defined by us faculty as problematic students, oppositional and resistant. Naturally, we like them less. At times we get angry with them, and at times we regret having accepted them into the course. We claim that our attitude, as well as that of other students who consciously at least resent these oppositional students, could be understood as a failure of the organisational alpha function. We understand group processes. We know that the opposition belongs to the group as a whole. We know that these "resistant" students are carrying the resistance to experiencing submission for the whole group, which is the way they experience our call to follow us and lower their defenses.

By naming students as problematic, as oppositional, as stubborn, and as resistant—as we referred to S in that closing plenary—by being angry with them, or in a way "hating them", we are in a sense projecting into them our own resistance to acknowledging the complicated predicament between surrender and submission that we put them in. In our course, we do not acknowledge our own ambivalence and uncertainty regarding the various events we designed and regarding the fogginess of these events and our thinking about them. We should find ways to acknowledge and perhaps communicate the complex predicament they are in. Such work by the faculty, such acknowledgement, is the work of the organisational alpha function. The more the faculty is engaged in such work, the better will be the holding environment we provide for the students, who invest in the programme not only a great deal of money but especially their hopes and longing for professional and personal growth and development.

References

Bion, W. R. (1991/62). *Learning from Experience*. London: Karnac.

Ferro, A. (2005). *Seeds of Illness, Seeds of Recovery. The Genesis of Suffering and the Role of Psychoanalysis*. London: Brunner-Routledge.

Ghent, E. (1999). Masochism, submission, surrender: Masochism as a perversion of surrender. In: S. Mitchell & L. Aron (Eds.), *Relational Psychoanalysis: The Emergence of a Tradition*. New Jersey & London: The Analytic Press.

Winnicott, D. W. (1971). *Playing and Reality*. London: Penguin Books.

CHAPTER EIGHT

Leadership: a song of mentoring and power

Beverly Malone

This chapter explores the power of mentoring as a tradition nestled in the hills of Kentucky by a woman whose mother was a slave. It is amazing the creativity necessary to visualise a future of leadership for her offspring when her own academic background only included an elementary level of preparation. And yet, this daughter of a slave was clearly committed to succession planning for a role that she had never experienced; a role that she had only dreamed and envisioned, a role of leadership. In the rural, harsh hills of Kentucky there was a woman dreaming, setting forth a way of knowing and caring through mentoring that could be a template for succession in global organisational work.

A song of beginning

Mentoring is a type of nurturance. Women are genetically structured and psychosocially developed in the art of nurturance. Our babies arrive with the view, according to Melanie Klein (1932), that they are one with their mothers, unable to distinguish between the "me and not me", reveling in the security of connectedness and wholeness. But even before their arrival into the world our heartbeat carries the rhythm of life, a song of constancy and expectation to our unborn babes. As mothers (most of us), we sing songs of love, encouragement, and growth to our children. These songs before and after birth are songs of power. With songs that declare, "I love you a bushel and a peck … a bushel and a peck and a hug around the neck", we instill in our children an inner reserve of hope, confidence, and power for meeting and shaping their futures.

The nursing profession of which I am a member is established on the solid rock of nurturance. We call it caring. It can be defined as promoting health, healing, and hope in response to the human condition (NLN, 2007). Nursing excels at providing nurturance to patients—the other identified in the role of patient. But the gap that must be filled is how to nurture one another, nurse to nurse, as well as consultant to consultant. Colleagues, we must sing songs of power to our potential leaders, songs of advocacy for our most fragile others, including the most fragile part of ourselves; songs of opportunity when faced with adversity and songs of knowing that assure our future leaders that they may be delayed in their journey but not defeated.

Mentoring is a song of power that becomes embedded in the very fabric of one's existence. In your darkest night, it is the song that comes to your memory in dreams, phrases, smells, and sensations, speaking of strategies, tactics, and visions of transformation. It is the song of reassurance that provides reason for one's existence and for choosing to continue to lead in this time in this place.

Learning to sing the song—a personal song

I first learned to sing the song of mentoring from my Granny, the child of a black slave and a white master. She was sixty-five when I was born. She taught me songs of healing, the song of laughter, and the song of power. She was an extraordinary healer. As a child I naturally assumed that she had magic in her hands. "Bev Lay", with a strong, maple syrup slow Kentucky accent, she would sing, "Go pick that leaf, and over there that root." And from the leaves and roots, she would mix a salve that grew hair on a baby's bald head.

She stood almost six feet tall, with lovely long silver hair and the long nose and dramatic facial features of an American Indian. Her skin was copper and she told me that her hair had been red when she was young. She taught me to read from the Bible by the time I was three. Friends and visitors were expected to bring me books to read or they were not truly welcome in Granny's house. Granny's house was a container of drama, joy, danger, and power, a mini organisational behavioural conference. Every so often, my Granny would step outside and shoot her gun, a little .25 automatic, in the air. She carried it rolled up in her stocking on a daily basis. As a child, I would ask her why she was shooting and at whom. Her standard answer was that she was just reminding folks that she had it.

With limited resources, she effectively positioned my world for me to succeed. As I watched this elderly agile woman wield power and authority, I treasured her songs of endurance and creativity. She was a matriarch, a widow who clearly expressed her desire to make her own decisions as well as yours. During my time with her, she raised, housed, fed, and healed more than thirty different people in our home. There was always food enough, room enough, and love enough to include others.

Yet I never doubted that I was the centre of her life. I received her song of commitment, clearly understanding that more would be required of me. As a business woman, she was a bootlegger, she was too astute to invest so much without demanding maximum return. The cloak of leadership and responsibility would be passed to me. I was anointed her successor. By the time I was eight years old, Ms. Addie, my Granny was very ill and over the next several years, our roles were reversed. The cloak of leadership and responsibility came early but the song of mentoring is with me forever.

Mentoring: a song of change and perhaps transformation

Mentoring can be defined as an endeavor for organisations to use and share human capital, knowledge, and job-related support (Hezlett, 2005; Young & Perrewe, 2004) or, on an individual basis, as simply a transaction to reveal and provide a faster journey for the protégé to move through and up the system's career ladder. The characteristics of mentoring can include: role modeling; counseling; acceptance of the protégé; coaching; sponsorship; and validation (Offstein, Morwick, & Shah, 2007). Other researchers have added competency, compassion, courage, commitment, and integrity (Blass & Ferris, 2007).

Mentoring changes the protégé and the mentor. Both have unmet needs and desires. The protégé is in need of knowledge but, even more importantly, also in need of the hidden pathways in systems known only to mentors with special passwords. These are the maps to the treasure chests of success. The mentor is in need of affirmation and adoration that is reflected in the eager attentive face of the protégé as he/she assists, supports, worships, and works with and for the mentor.

The mentor has the power to distinguish between a wall and a door. One of my mentors has said to me: "If you keep travelling in the direction you are going, you will invariably hit that wall. Feel the knots on your head. Those identify the number of times and the intensity with which you have hit the wall. Step over to your right, turn the knob and walk through the door." A mentor can guide the protégé through the maze without crashing into walls.

How does a protégé search for a mentor? There are four steps that may be useful:

1. The searcher must identify him or herself as seeking a mentor. Wallflowers, who pass through the crowd with little notice are not as likely to be chosen by a mentor. Let prospective mentors know that you are looking for a mentor.
2. The searcher must bring something of worth (e.g., creativity, competence, skills, talents, and abilities) to negotiate the transaction with the mentor. It is this same something of worth that can move the protégé into a highly competitive relationship with the mentor.
3. The searcher must exhibit a level of respect underpinned with a degree of passion for the mentor and the mentor's work. Choose and approach your potential mentor.
4. Give in return.

From a different viewpoint, the mentor may be searching for a protégé. Whoever initiates the search, this one-on-one joining in a power-differentiated relationship is the traditional form of mentoring.

Less traditional, but possibly as effective, is peer mentoring. This does not require the same level of intensity or commitment by the peers or each of the participants as classical mentoring, described above. There is an agreed-upon illusion or contract that the peers are all equal yet different, bringing distinct gifts to the relationship but none of them rising to the elevated platform of mentor. To escape the reality of the differential power between classical mentor and protégé, peer mentoring can be seen as a milder form of mentoring.

There are several other types of mentoring, including:

- Paid contractual, such as a coach; mentees have been known to relish this type of mentoring as they describe their feelings of not owing anyone or bowing to anyone in their career journey.

- Assigned mentoring has been frequently used in corporations. In this situation novices enter the corporate world and are assigned a mentor to assist in navigating through and, at times, up the system.

These non-traditional types of mentoring may lack the passion and the commitment, or in some situations the relationship may develop into a more intense experience for both the mentor and mentee.

The mythology of mentoring is interesting. Mentor appears in Greek mythology, as Odysseus's trusted friend who cares for his son when Odysseus leaves for the Trojan War. Merlin, part-sage and part-magician, mentors the young man about the subtleties of leadership that prepare him to become the legendary King Arthur.

There are also current day myths about mentoring. Following are two examples:

1. You only need one mentor for your career/life. Since mentoring is about the development and enhancement of the person, the multifaceted nature of the person attests to the insufficiency of having only one mentor. If you are an African-American female who is a nurse as well as a clinical psychologist involved in organisational behavioural work, you may need a mentor for each of the descriptors, as well as combinations of the descriptors, if the goal is to truly enhance and transform the person. The descriptors above reflect my own person and I have mentors who are white, Jewish, clinical psychologists, African-American psychiatric nurses, and women and men involved in organisational behavioural work.
2. The mentor is all giving, receiving very little. Mentoring is a reciprocal process. Both the mentor and protégé gain. One of my mentors once explained to me about the establishment of power bases. She pointed out that she had more than a hundred protégés, all feeling in great debt to her and humbled by her willingness to mentor them. These protégés had done well in the world and were powerful and now well-established in various parts of the country and the world, always ready to be available for a request that she might make.

Leadership: a song of power

Mentoring and power are inextricably linked by the concept of leadership. While mentoring is part of the preparatory process of leading, power is the fuel and the execution. Women may shy away from both the concept of power and mentoring, publicly avoiding the shadow of assertive, goal-oriented behaviours that potentially mold and shape others. For example, with a quick scan, one may conclude that the delicacy and propriety of the predominantly female nursing profession precluded such deliberately, competitive, male-type behaviours such as mentoring and power, designed to influence and control individuals, groups, and organisations.

Another perspective is that power has been deliberately packaged to be aversive or inaccessible to women. This argument is easily supported by the term "MEN tor." The traditional mentor in the US has been white, male, and a powerful senior member of the organisation. Mentors tend to be attracted to protégés with whom they can identify. The mentor's selection of the protégé tends to be narcissistic. It is the unrepentant seeking of immortality camouflaged by the appearance of generativity as described by Ericson (1950). Historically, women have often found mentors to be scarce. Nurses in particular have found a void of accessible, available mentors in health care organisations. In other words, mentoring has been wrapped in a package that is foreign, mysterious to nurses, and difficult to access.

This perspective is not to deny that there are powerful female leaders in nursing, but many of these leaders may suffer from the queen bee syndrome. This female syndrome is based on a model of the oppressed. There is only one position at the top and only one privileged female can occupy the position at a time; therefore, all other females are viewed as competitors who must be actively or passively eliminated. The withholding of mentoring to potential protégés is an attempt at passive annihilation of contenders for leadership. However, I must stress that the queen bee syndrome, while labeled with a female title, is not restricted to women. We can travel back in time to Freud and Jung, as their mentor/protégé relationship exploded due to succession issues of the protégé growing into his self-authorised being. Or, only look within our present organisational behaviour work in 2009 to see the negative competition and rivalry that seems to plague the collaboration and alliance of many of our organisations.

Power is not the deadly enemy of those with integrity. Power is simply moving an object from point A to point B. Moving one's self from the bed (point A) to work (point B) can be considered the most powerful act of one's day. Moving someone's mind from point A to B is known as education. Moving one's own mind from point A to B is frequently labeled a miracle since there is little belief that there is a need for us to change our own minds.

The nursing profession has experienced considerable difficulty with the concept of power. As giving, caring, mostly women, in our career decision-making, we have often chosen nursing as the discipline with the greatest distance from the concept and implementation of power. The picture in the mind of power, resonates more strongly with those who choose to work in the financial markets and business operations. Those individuals could be described as the Genghis Khans of business or the manipulators of the economy from a base of monetary greed. Yet the experience of being a patient in any health care setting, whether community or hospital, demands a nurse who can use power. Power is an essential ingredient to the provision of safe, quality care.

For example: in the early hours of the morning, a nurse walks in to the hospital to greet her patient: "Good morning, my name is Sarah Kirk. I'm your powerless nurse for the day." This greeting and its implications provide little hope for a positive journey through the health care system, but rather leaves the patient and family experiencing the overwhelming anxiety of being in a vulnerable role in a chaotic organisation without a navigator or an advocate to manage and extract the healing resources needed from the system.

The rhythm of leadership: an overall model

1. **Dreamer**: Leaders are dreamers, whether from the times of Mary Seacole and Harriet Tubman or Ms. Addie, they are always looking down the road past their own personal obstacles sometimes determined by the present exclusive culture of their world. For some, especially those balancing a number of responsibilities including children, school, and work, for example, dreaming is a luxury or an underdeveloped talent. It takes permission and time to dream. Very useful is a designated space and, when possible, a designated time, with some degree of protective boundaries that provides the dreamer with enough safety and time to dream.
2. **Vision** (picture in the mind of who one wants to become. At first it may resemble one's mentor or one of the mentors): Dreaming is usually a precedent to a vision. A vision is a relative of a dream, not constrained by logic, time, or place. And, as many others over time

have come to the conclusion, without vision there is no leadership. One leader described a vision like a tree without any leaves and that, as others share and invest in your dream, the leaves appear and the picture of the tree changes into a more vibrant but different image.

It is the shareable vision that is meaningful and achievable, particularly in relation to the nation's health care. As a psychiatric nurse, I have often considered the difference between a vision and a hallucination. After several years of thought, I've come to the conclusion that a hallucination is simply vision without action. It's the personal ownership of the would-be leader who yearns to keep the vision/hallucination perfect, as conceived without any input from others, and yet simultaneously yearns to lead those others.

With our hyper-speed lives and minimum response time communication, the opportunity to dream may be infrequent. Dreaming may be experienced as a luxury rather than a necessity for leadership.

3. **Mastery** (one's gift, contribution, work, skills, talents): Mastery holds the concept of overcoming or of coming into one's own abilities, talents, and skills. The acknowledgment of this accomplishment may be a position, an award, or an academic credential that tends to be as universally transferable as the US currency once was. Leaders need to acknowledge their need for mastery. This ability to humble one's self into the learner role is important. The pursuit of mastery indicates that there is a gap and work yet to be done.
4. **Boundary management** (where one starts and stops even with one's mentor): Boundary management is of particular importance to the mentor and protégé. Leadership roles frequently reflect cutting edge behaviour. An edge is a boundary that separates entities and immediately alerts a leader to the need to design transactions across the boundary. In any system there are living and dying edges. For example, being placed on a minority task force or committee, even as chair, may mean being pushed to a dying edge where others really want to deny and forget the existence of the task force, its mission of diversity, and its members. Leaders need to be at the living edge of the system where transformation and excellence are the essential operational values, and creative action is the modus operandus.

   The leader must be able to define the current reality, which includes the identification of boundaries. Once the boundaries are located and noted they can be extended through risk taking and collaboration. Leaders must be adept at temporarily overlapping boundaries with other entities while maintaining the integrity of their own boundaries.

5. **Extended Power**: Mentoring is an intense relationship/informal contract of learning between two individuals (one identified as the coach and guide) with differentiated levels of power and authority, with the fuel of power, and the grounding of integrity. Mentoring may be one of the most exquisite forms of power. It is generous and generative, for it salvages and enhances the best of us to continue on into the next generations. However it is also narcissistic—just slightly—since the mentor usually chooses someone, the protégé, who reminds him or her of self; but what a gracious and giving way to be narcissistic. Mentoring can be defined as intense career building, a mutually beneficial relationship between two individuals of unequal power. It is for the protégé to clearly acknowledge this inequity with a respect and a desire to shorten, if not close, the gap. The mentor has the ability to provide career-saving direction to the protégé. A mentor can distinguish between a wall and a door. In the middle of the minority nurse leader's career, that distinction and its communication to the protégé can be immensely powerful.

   The protégé brings vitality, commitment, and youth in age, career, and spirit to the relationship. The protégé also brings information, especially if the mentor and protégé are employed in the same organisation. The information, at times known as gossip, that was once accessible to the mentor is now cloaked behind employees who will not speak about certain issues in the presence of an executive. The protégé still has access to a different level of communication. This sharing of various levels of communication can be mutually beneficial. For most leaders, a mentor is essential to survive the challenges and macro/micro inequities that are frequently presented or discovered along one's career path.

Closing notes

Throughout my career journey I have found the song of life to be immeasurably challenging and yet easily sung. When one realises that one does not have to sing alone, through collaboration, partnerships, and mentoring transactions, the opportunities outweigh the difficulties. And as a result, leadership with creative, daring ingenuity is a natural step. The protégé can be moved (powered) to the fast track of the organisation and can learn to lead with and without the safety net of his/her mentor. With the mentor's support, the novice learns to risk. Without risk-taking there is no creativity and no leadership. The song of beginning can come full circle until the protégé becomes a mentor, ending a phase and simultaneously beginning a new song, searching for immortality as the new protégé extends the life of leadership.

In organisational systems, the need for succession planning is required and yet neglected. Mentoring is a critical tool in extending the life of the system. The lifeline and knowing of our work must be transmitted for the 'now' and future leaders. We must dream and envision a new reality where tradition and creativity collide making wonderful music. Our global relations network of organisational learning is in desperate need of the songs of power, leadership, rhythm, and mentoring. We cannot wait to mentor until we have aged beyond action; we need to mentor as we are mentored: develop others as we are developing, and share the creativity and power of our traditions, the uniqueness of our differences, and the harmony of our similarities. The song, the music, is there to be made and heard and to provide inspiration to move forward.

References

Blass, F. R., & Ferris, G. (2007). Leader reputation: The role of mentoring, political skill, contextual learning and adaptation. *Human Resource Management, 46:* 5–19.

Erikson, E. H. (1950). *Childhood and Society*. New York: Norton.

Hezlett, S. A. (2005). Protégés' learning in mentoring relationships: A review of the literature and an exploratory case study. *Advances in Developing Human Resources, 7*: 505–526.

Klein, M. (1932). *The Psycho-Analysis of Children*. London: Hogarth.

Malone, B. (1998). Mentoring: a song of power. In: C. Vance & R. Olson (Eds.), *The Mentor Connection in Nursing*. New York: Springer Publishing Company. National League for Nursing. (2007). Strategic Plan.

Offsteing, E., Morwick, J., & Shah, A. (2007). Mentoring programs and jobs. A contingency approach. *Review of Business, 27*: 32–37.

Shoaf, M., & Britt , M. (2009). Leadership and mentoring: How different are they? *Proceedings of ASBBS, 16*.

Young, A. M. & Perrewe, P. L. (2004). The role of expectations in the mentoring exchange: An analysis of mentor and protégé expectations in relation to perceived support. *Journal of Managerial Issues, 16*: 103–126.

CHAPTER NINE

Beyond succession: learning from experience of being the board of Group Relations Nederland[1]

Pim Stafleu, Doris Gottlieb, Janine van Oosten, and Gerard van Reekum

This chapter consists of five parts, dealing respectively with the context and genesis of Group Relations Nederland, the significance of writing it for its transformation, the subject of succession and how that has changed in the experience of the authors, and a description of recent transitions that illustrate the application of the authors' learning and the emergence of a new paradigm for the institution. We appreciated the invitation to present its content as a paper at the Belgirate 2009 conference, as it offered us an opportunity to jointly explore what David Armstrong named *in-actment*, by drawing the picture of a turbulent and transformational episode in the history of the institution with ourselves in it (Armstrong, 2005). In turn, our commitment to jointly produce this text has been instrumental to *enact* its transformation, as will be explained in the following parts.

Context and genesis of the institution

Group Relations Nederland was incorporated on 19 October 1992 in a notary office in Haarlem. The charter of foundation lists the members of its first board in the following order: Erika Stern (university lecturer),

Servaas van Beekum (consultant/trainer), Katherina van Lohuizen (psychologist), and Elisha Davar (clinical psychologist).

The bylaws already indicated the aspiration to create a space in the Netherlands for inquiring into current developments and themes alive in society at large. Besides promoting its objectives in speech and writing, the organisation of group relations conferences and study days were the only activities mentioned in this document. The rest of the bylaws were concerned with regulating the position and authority of the board, which would remain the sole organisational unit in its formal structure until July 2009.

Although having been colleagues in another setting before, the four members of the first board embodied, and in that sense represented, two separate educational institutions. At the time, Elisha Davar and Erika Stern had become a work pair that would be lastingly engaged with training counsellors at Utrecht University; Servaas van Beekum and Karien van Lohuizen, who as a couple had become a work pair, ran a two-year programme for professional trainers from their private company "IAS International".

In both curricula, students were required to take part as members in a residential group relations conference. The initial idea was to jointly offer one event for the two institutions and have Group Relations Nederland provide the necessary legal and psychological container.

It was thought beneficial for the students' learning climate if they were to meet with others apart from peers in their own course group. In the same spirit, participation in Group Relations Nederland's conferences has always remained open to people from outside the two institutions and their programmes. As this saved the temporary institution of the conference from the risk of degenerating into a closed system (in terms of members, funding, and staffing), it also provided the natural basis for making a distinction between the conference sponsor and the two educational institutes involved. Fuelled by experiences from when the founders had been direct colleagues in a different setting, there was an informed expectation that should the university or a competing institution contain the conference, its dynamics might easily become contaminated with the political interests of management. This fear of interference in the "business" of the conference was first and foremost projected towards the university. The larger and more bureaucratic of the two institutions was expected to be least inclined to respect the boundaries around a seemingly insignificant and vulnerable temporary institution. Although such a process of infection would in itself be educating, the founders reasoned that this particular type of dynamics might divert the members' attention too much away from the realities in which they were to apply their learning.

We must acknowledge that this defence proved effective, although it came at the cost of considerable effort and sometimes of painful personal sacrifices by the founders and those who have succeeded them on the board.

From its origin, the institution was encompassed by a fear of interference. Only with hindsight is it possible now to see more concretely how this may have unintentionally encouraged the import, or even creation of, some elements that one had wished to avoid. In the course of this paper we address a few of these elements, as far as we've been able to learn from the experience of being the board.

As stated above, the institution started off as a legal vehicle for a joint venture by two work pairs. Their venture was conceptualised as a temporary institution, recurring but never permanent. If Group Relations Nederland itself existed as an organisational entity in the world at all, it was in the shape of its conference.

> The relations to other institutions and individuals, which developed over time, were linked to one or more of the founders personally or with the institutions they represented. Their recruitment efforts were understandably geared towards promoting enrolment in their own courses, recruitment to the conference being secondary, and involvement in Group Relations Nederland not being an issue or concern.

Although an identifiable aggregation of people formed around the Dutch conferences over the years, in terms of organisational structure Group Relations Nederland remained solely a legal solution, with no opening for significant involvement by those who might feel they belong to this entity. As a consequence, most, if not all, of the work came down to the members of the board.

Another illustration of the institution's low profile can be drawn from an exchange, not too long ago, with an authorised delegate of a group relations institution from another country. It appeared that neither he, nor anyone in his institution, ever thought of their extensive connections with the Netherlands as a link with the institution Group

Relations Nederland, but instead with Utrecht University. To the board, this sobering discovery was in contrast with our institution being frequently represented in their conferences and actually in their institution's governance structure, and to how we had always felt it was on behalf of our institution that people from theirs were invited into the staff of the Dutch conferences. Exploring this it became apparent that Group Relations Nederland developed as an appendix to the projects of its founders.

The organisational culture resembled family life rather than professional work. In such a culture, the personal involvement in each other's private lives dominates over people's commitment, as a board member, to the objectives and interests of their institution. Thus, Group Relations Nederland, and especially its activities, could become seemingly synonymous with the whole of one's lifework, instead of more realistically being an element in it (regardless of how significant that element might be). This point can be illustrated by the phenomenon that repeatedly in the past board members have thought of the idea of using the institution as a vehicle for generating personal income, for instance through the marketing of branded consulting services. We have since learned that the Netherlands is not unique in this respect. In the history of a number of group relations institutions this has contributed to rather unmanageable tensions.

The type and style of leadership during approximately the first fifteen years of Group Relations Nederland's history must be described as centralist and charged with a certain amount of impulsiveness. As already indicated by the otherwise puzzling order in which the founders were listed in the charter of foundation, Erika Stern has been in the lead positions from the start and for a very long time. She chaired the board from October 1992 until March 2003 and was the first director of a Group Relations Nederland conference able to address the membership in Dutch, holding the role of conference director six times from 2001 through 2006 (succeeding Siv Boalt Boëthius and David Armstrong, who were early supporters from abroad).

By the end of 2004, Erika Stern was the last of the four founders to leave the board. Those of us who were board members at the time experienced that moment as the demarcation of a new phase. From this point on Group Relations Nederland was to prove its ability to survive and really start existing and functioning as an institution, independent from the minds that conceived it.

In view of this it was interesting to see how the three founders who still resided in the Netherlands responded to a suggestion of the new board in 2005. The suggestion was to think with the board about a possible task for a so called "foundation group" and if they would wish to take part in it. This group then appeared to have come together, even before responding, and prepared a meeting with the board. Already during the period in which Martha Mens was the chair of Group Relations Nederland, and especially from 2005–the period after Erika Stern stepped down—the board found itself confronted with various overt and covert directives from "the elders" (so to speak) on how to properly manage their heritage. The underlying fear seemed to be that the institution would fall apart, its international network dissolved, the yearly conferences no longer mounted. Were the "parents" afraid of the successors being not "good enough" to make the transition and/or carry on the legacy? Or were the "adolescents" reacting against them? No doubt, there was a good deal of extractive introjection to this experience of being the board.

Not having a way of knowing if things would have developed differently under easier circumstances, the board experienced a prolonged period in which it appeared very hard to keep thinking clearly, especially about succession-related issues. In June 2006 Erika Stern announced she was suffering from an incurable illness. She passed away in March 2007. A year later Karien van Lohuizen suddenly died. This sequence of events confronted the entire aggregation with disorienting trauma and a profound sense of caesura. Again with hindsight, we can now see how this tear exposed the unconscious understanding of succession that had existed until then around Group Relations Nederland.

This paper as a catalyst

The invitation to Pim Stafleu, then chair of the board, to write a paper for the Belgirate 2009 conference came in July of 2008, in the midst of the board searching for a way to open up the institution. How we responded to this invitation has contributed to both the way the text took shape and to the way we have begun to understand tradition, creativity, and succession within our group relations institution.

The first question that we began to ponder was how to interpret the invitation. As an invitation for the individual "heir" to the legacy that was left by the former founders and the previous chair, or as an invitation to the institution made up of people who are taking up a linked and complex set of roles to reflect upon how it has engaged with the themes of tradition, creativity, and succession?

Related was the question of how to write it. The invitation to the individual who had taken on leadership of the institution could be seen as evidence of the Belgirate III conference management following a concept of succession based in a person. Discussing this, our own thinking about succession and how it has evolved from the traditional view became evident.

Correspondence with the conference management left us with the possibility of interpreting the invitation as we saw fit. We decided to use the invitation as an opportunity to explore elements of succession anew. Key to this approach was that we realised that each of the members of the board has a unique perspective to contribute, based upon their position within the whole. One of the guiding principles of systems theory—that one's position in the system will also condition the view of one's reality and that each view holds only a piece of the larger picture, which (overall) is most likely unknowable—informed how we were to produce the text. Instead of one person telling *the* story, or writing it out for commentary, we came together over a series of meetings to explore our memories of the past years and their relation to the chosen topic. Two things came to the fore while doing this: the compression of time and sequence of events, and the multiplicity of interpretation.

One of the phenomena that appeared was the confusing experience of time compressed. It appeared very difficult to recall the sequence of events. Instead of being held in the mind as a chronological sequence, it seemed more that events were grouped illogically. By working together we slowly were able to untangle the series of events and come up with a verifiable timeline together. Within this reconstruction we counted more than twenty-five major events to which this board had responded over the last years. These ranged from small but important events, such as inter-institutional discussions, to big and, for some of us, calamitous events, notably the death of colleagues and the cancellation of the annual working conference in 2007. This experience sharpened our understanding of how we had lived in the different moments and the different situations: it brought out some of the inherent tensions of hierarchies and power that can exist. Whose story get's told, who's memory takes precedence, which board member feels that they have ownership of which part of the history; these were all elements that needed to be explored through our discussions.

Another element that became clear as we worked through our memories was the different possibilities of interpretation of each event. This was often dependent upon one's role and representation in the system. Was a particular action a serious threat or was it just intent on making contact? Were we in trouble at one moment or was that a moment of breakthrough? The discussions served to show the depth and kaleidoscopic nature of the views that can emerge within an organisation at times of transition and, most likely, at other times as well. It brought out some of the internal issues of competition and envy that may have been apparent due to our other relations, for example, to the founders or former members of the board. The possibility to discuss these issues brought out a more multi-layered view of the actual transition and put in perspective the multiplicity of experience as we moved through tradition and creativity within this process of succession. Interestingly, sometimes different members saw the same experience as part of a creative new force and as a pull to tradition. This brought to light some of the feelings of competition and of animosity that had been present at different moments of the transition over the years. It also brought to light the difficulty in truly understanding one another and the effort needed to do this.

In light of this it seems appropriate to comment on the container that we created to carry out our discussions. When the sole "authority" in the name of the "father or mother", or the heir to knowledge and power, is no longer present in one person, the need for some holding structure increases. When there is one perceived authority figure the dynamics of discussions about history seem to end up revolving around who gets to say what was "the reality" of what happened. This can lead to competition, whereby the "head of the family" is able to mete out his or her decision on reality, triggering the envy to go back into the rivalry of those discussing the topic. But when there is no overarching authority figure the question of how to make sense of the competing views can get even more contentious. We did not think about this, at least not explicitly when we decided on our method of writing; however we think it bears mentioning that the structure that emerged contributed to the ability to bridge these complex topics.

Our way of working was to have a number of meetings, separated from board meetings, and to let the stories and discussions emerge instead of fixing themes in advance. The chair of the board took notes, thus performing the role of scribe. This way of working provided a contained space in which various threads of the story emerged seemingly without much linear logic to the discussions.

At the point of writing Pim Stafleu, the person asked to present the paper, compiled his notes and wrote out the threads with minimum interpretation. On the basis of this document we discussed together, came up with a structure, and drafted the text as a joint effort. In this way the paper and its title served as a catalyst, and writing it pushed us to look differently at succession and to move "beyond".

Succession revisited

Referring to Siv Boalt Boëthius, succession is a process which is found everywhere in organisational life. The scope runs from small family businesses—where a successor as a member of the family might be informed about the business since birth, before taking over—to the succession of a chair of a board of a multi-national company, who is externally sought and found, and where the one succeeding may come from a totally different organisation, country, culture, and line of business. It may vary in its level of control from being extremely thoroughly planned and prepared—for example, as it is done in a monarchy—to instantly required succession due to the sudden and unexpected death of a leader or key figure of the organisation. It is necessary and inevitable for the survival of any organisation and involves strong conscious and unconscious feelings of competition and rivalry, loss and gain, fear of failure and losing (Boalt Boëthius, 2007).

According to the Oxford English Dictionary, "succession" means: "a number of people or things following one after the other", which refers to something of the not-deviating character of succession, and the expression is, for example, used for ships sailing in succession as in convoy. A second meaning is: "the action, process or right of inheriting an office". Such a sterile description does not do justice to the unavoidable dynamics involved and to how much has been physically and mentally invested over the years into establishing this "office". The process of succession is both filled with fears, projections, and fantasies of desire, and burdened with memory; from founders, predecessor(s), successor(s), and from the wider system in which the organisation is embedded.

The paradigm underlying the concept of succession, especially in group relations institutions, seems to be informed by Freud's idea that the family group provides the basic pattern for all groups. As such it becomes a personal succession from father to son or mother to daughter, a hierarchical succession at the top from a singleton to another singleton, at best supported with great loyalty and containable rivalry from the other family members. This results in a new head of the family who is in possession of those required genes required genes only present in members of the family. Succession from this point of view is narrowed down to a "copy-paste" of the role of the one leaving onto the one coming, with the fantasy that if the new person is capable and has "what it takes", nothing needs to change and the organisation will survive. What was idealised in the predecessor is now projected into the successor as idealised hope. According to Amy Fraher this may become "an overwhelming preoccupation where successors feel as if they have inherited the family business, but have been asked simply to maintain what the older generation originated" (Fraher, 2004).

In our search we discovered how the thinking about succession in Group Relations Nederland has traditionally been magical: as if the qualities of a predecessor could be transferred by "contamination", emerging in the successor through mere proximity over sufficient time. As a voluntary organisation without members it was always hard to find new members for the board, which in all these years was seldom larger than five. Board members were recruited from the earlier-mentioned courses or an attended conference, and selection into the board took place on the basis of expected qualities and generally considered loyalty.

We now think this unconscious belief in succession being "magical" was part of a defence against creating verifiable practices to be recorded and transferred by conventional means that can be tested in reality. A belief belonging to an organisation as a temporary organisation rather than a permanent one. A defence serving against the difficult and anxious questions that we found needed to be re-addressed in any transition: What has been achieved so far? What should be maintained? What are our aims? And what tasks, resources and leadership will be required to achieve them?

Group Relations Nederland was typically "held by a person". Although structurally a foundation, the locus of power in the institute was clear; as a very appreciated and respected authority, Erika Stern held the roles of founder, chair of the board, and director of its group relations conferences for many years. Most of the international relations were maintained through her extensive personal network, where boundaries between the various roles were not always easy to distinguish. Although as a board and as a community we owe a great debt to her engagement, in such a climate—according to Susan Long—the general body of people aggregating in and around the institute easily place the leaders as role models, where they become idealised. The leader represents the ideal and becomes the internalised parental authority with the inevitable accompanying underlying dynamic of dependency. This dependency can occur for many reasons. It may be that the leader(s) carry most of the work, hold most of the power, or dominate for other reasons, or the group is fearful of the authority of the leader(s), or members are unwilling to take up authority (Long, 2008).

That this was the case in Group Relations Nederland appeared in the general denial of the fact that Erika Stern had already left the board in 2004, had been succeeded as chair one and a half years prior to that, and had vacated the role of conference director before symptoms of her illness appeared. Even so, after she passed away several institutions said they did not perceive having institutional relationships with our institution, but just personal ones with her. With others, institutional relationships or partnerships were no longer as evident as they were before. Even the current chair, being the *third* chair in a row, was asked several times whether he had been appointed by her personally as her successor.

In this sense, all conditions were present to collude with succession as a paradigm of personal, hierarchical succession at the top of a family-system, full of expectations, idealised hope, anxieties, and envy from predecessors and successors. At the same time the system had become more and more dependent on its leader.

What was never properly addressed, and was perhaps denied, was the fact that a voluntary organisation like Group Relations Nederland could never continue to be run as it had been before. This denial inevitably sets a successor up for failure when taking up the role (as expected, desired, fantasised), unless he or she is also willing to merge it into their life's work in total service of the institution, as was a matter of course until 2005. According to the described paradigm, failure cannot be understood other than as personal incompetence, a failure of the person taking up the role, since all of the accountability lies with one person. With all the projections and introjections involved, the risk is that this belief of personal success or failure becomes the pivot in the succession, compromising the primary task, in the end putting the institution and its aim at risk.

Transitions: from a "recurring temporary organisation" to a permanent one

In 2005 the board started investigating how other group relations institutions were organised and what could be learned from them. With hindsight it can be argued that there was a growing awareness of the risk of an unsustainable institution and that Group Relations Nederland had become a closed system. Innovation and creativity appeared in the temporary organisation of the conferences, in its innovative designs and daring staff compositions. But innovation and creativity seemed to be lacking in the permanent organisation. The institution still had no space or provisions for members, its community merely represented by a database of addresses of people who had been to one of its conferences or shown interest of a kind. Innovation from within could hardly occur, the board being occupied by matters of its own continuation. Nevertheless, first attempts to establish a so-called "specific"s working conference (Sher, 2009) were made ("Colonialism, migration and society, on being a citizen in Europe and the world") using group relations methodology to make a contribution to society. Also, forms of a membership organisation started to be explored in an attempt to making the boundaries of the institution more permeable.

From the end of 2005 a number of disruptive events followed one after the other. Within one month the chair of the board, who had served on the board for many years, together with another board member, left abruptly. No process of succession was in place. Two months later the board was confronted with the news that Erika Stern had been diagnosed with an incurable illness. The news was not only devastating to all who knew her, but brought a number of succession related issues to the fore.

The need to prove to be good heirs and a responsible board, capable of functioning through the unplanned succession process, had an overwhelming and almost paralysing effect on the board. The difficulty and initial reluctance to take responsibility for cancelling the conference of 2007 is an example of this condition.

The complicated issues connected with the succession, either real or imagined, slowly emerged and were faced initially with great difficulty. The basic assumption fight/flight was in full motion during this period; expectations on the board's leadership from various stakeholders in and around the institution on "how things should be done and run" resulted in a number of conflicts. While still having difficulties in understanding and accepting the heritage, the board was met with criticism by key figures it needed support from. The process was painful and left the board feeling increasingly unauthorised and under attack. In retrospect, the board may have had a need to feel attacked to mobilise its energy to create and secure its identity, where others seemed to have a need to feel excluded in order to form theirs. Initiatives to organise events were tainted by this state of mind. Reaching out for support or cooperation was often impulsive and ill-defined, which in some cases resulted in disturbed relations, and left the board feeling even more under attack.

Despite this period of struggle we managed to continue the work, focusing gradually more on the task. In this period we owe thanks to the support received through our strong international links: older ones with The Grubb Institute and the various Tavistocks, AGSLO from Sweden, and some personal contacts from India, Germany, Australia, and France; newer ones like OFEK from Israel, several AKRI affiliates from the USA, and especially INNOVA from Barcelona who, over the last five years, provided major encouragement and was actively involved in several of our events. It was important that the long-lasting collaboration with Utrecht School of Governance, and the place of our international conference in their curriculum, continued. However, it was not until the board organised consultation that the patterns mentioned above were faced. The discovery of the possibility of allowing us to enrich and work *with* the inheritance, instead of being mere guardians, was an important discovery for taking the role of successor.

We realise that in this period we fell back on the support of another founder, Karien van Lohuizen, who was one of the consultants working with the board[2]. By then the board had already started to address its fundamental questions: What to promote? Are these activities still relevant? What is the primary task? What kind of leadership and organisation are needed?

From 2007, after cancelling the annual conference, we started to discuss mid-term policy. A number of procedures and structures were put in place and leadership and accountability more distributed. In the meantime a number of new activities were tried out in which cooperation was also sought with other institutions: for instance, in February 2007, Group Relations Nederland offered a listening post in cooperation with RINO Noord Holland (an institute for the ongoing education of psychotherapists). In May 2007 a workshop named "Consulting to the System as a Whole" was conducted, together with the Center for the Study of Groups and Social Systems and INNOVA. In the summer of 2007 the decision was taken to invite two male directors for the GRN conference, organised in collaboration with the Utrecht School of Governance (USG) that successfully took place in January 2008. In September 2008, an institutional event was held which provided significant data for understanding the relatedness between the board and others. In November 2008, an exploration day was organised together with INNOVA in Barcelona. In 2008 we also changed the policy of holding the conference on leadership, engagement, and accountability from being an annual to being a biannual event, opening up the opportunity to alternate it with a shorter and more specific event. In January 2009, the first such event, called "Exploring the Lived Experience of The Netherlands", was offered in cooperation with Group Relations International.

The growing awareness that Group Relations Nederland was a closed system led to the organisation of the earlier mentioned institutional event in which Dutch former staff members to group relations conferences were invited to work together with the board on the issue of relatedness to the institution. The event surfaced how closed the system was in which the board operated. The event led to changing the institute's charter, opening the institution up by founding a constitutional body of associates. Whether the associates will take up authority to co-create valuable activities within the realm of group relations will be an important question for the sustainability of Group Relations Nederland. Having experienced its spirited start, we are positively optimistic about the associates' contribution to the furtherance of our joint work.

Another transition is that for the first time in its history there appeared to be space for male leadership. In 2006, Pim Stafleu became the first male chair. The board also decided to invite two male directors for its conferences of 2008 and again for 2010, experimenting with distributed leadership and authority in its temporary institution too.

Beyond succession?

"Beyond succession" may suggest that it is possible to define the state and process that allows the before and beyond to be decided. Succession is more apparent when it takes place in a closed (family) system and gives the illusion of being transparent to all who are connected with, but have no part in, the succession. To them it leaves space for projections, envy, and denying the reality of the new situation, which may lead to undermining the process of succession and successor(s) to doubt their right to succeed and consequently to resort to an even more closed and secured system.

"Beyond" may also suggest the authors believe the process is over and that succession in Group Relations Nederland has been completed and dealt with in a "mature" way. On the contrary, through the process of writing this chapter, this board has learned and discovered from sometimes painful experience that succession is an ongoing process, which should be continued to be worked with and managed, and is inherent in the desire to be the board of a healthy and living institution. The transition from personal leadership to a form of shared and/or distributed leadership in function of the task held by an institution, causes issues of succession to occur in the process of being a board, to be considered as part of the task, in order to enable the continuity, growth, and development of an institution. It is highly important to explore and work through issues of envy and rivalry within this context.

This continuing process of managing succession requires, and allows for, an approach to succession which is less based in the personal/family pattern and, rather, puts a board in touch with its institutional role of succeeding and being succeeded, in service of the ideals and aim of the permanent institution.

References

Armstrong, D. (2005). *Organization in the Mind: Psychoanalysis, Group Relations and Organizational Consultancy* (ed. Robert French). London: Karnac.

Boalt Boëthius, S. (2007). Succession and managing the transition from predecessor to successor. In: C. Einarsson, E. Hammar Chiriac, G. Jedeskog, T. Lindberg & M. Samuelsson (Eds.), *Det enkla är det sköna. En vänbok till Kjell Granström*. Linköping: Skapande Vetande.

Fraher, A. L. (2004). *A History of Group Study and Psychodynamic Organizations*. London: Free Association Books.

Long, S. (2008). *The Perverse Organisation and its Deadly Sins*. London: Karnac.

Sher, M. (2009). Splits, extrusion and integration: The impact of "potential space" for group relations and sponsoring institutions. *Organisational and Social Dynamics, An International Journal for the Integration of Psychoanalytic Systemic and Group Relations Perspectives, 9*: 138–154.

Notes

1. At the time of writing this chapter the board of Group Relations Nederland consisted of the four authors.
2. We also explored with her the option of taking up the role of director for the next conference and she agreed to represent Group Relations Nederland as a convener of the memorial event for Erika Stern.

CHAPTER TEN

Leadership and innovation in management and consultancy

Mónica Velarde Lazarte

Introduction

This paper aims to share a story of the group relations network in Peru. In part it is my story, and I would like to introduce it with the voice of Pablo Neruda. "And something started in my soul, fever or forgotten wings, and I made my own way, deciphering that fire, and I wrote the first faint line, faint, without substance, pure nonsense, pure wisdom of someone who knows nothing, and I suddenly saw the heavens unfastened and open".

I will start by describing my story in the network of group relations (GR) and the context in which I started directing GR conference applications in Lima, Peru. Then I will describe a group relations conference application designed by T-Consult[1] for Esan business school and later adapted for the Peruvian Government. I will explore how the design of the conference reflects the interaction between various elements in the context, including my short experience of the group relations network and my personal story as a Peruvian consultant. I will describe what informed the design, both consciously and unconsciously, looking at how tradition, creativity, and succession are linked with my experience and conference designs. Finally I will be offering some conclusions of my experience as a member of the group relations network.

My story in the group relations network

With some hesitance I am inviting you into my personal story of professional development as a young, South American consultant finding her way in the group relations (GR) network. It is a story of passion, joy, and sadness, my struggle with tradition, creativity, and succession, and how that brought me to who I am as a person-in-role today. I believe that in my life I have been blessed by meeting the right people at the right time. Looking back, my own journey and reflections contribute to a deeper understanding of my approach and my yearning to make a difference through this work in my country.

In 2003, I was in charge of the leadership development plan of a large division of an important bank in Peru and was encouraged to attend the first conference co-organised by IFSI[2] and InnovAccion[3] in Peru. At the time, I went quite naively to that conference, without any sense of how it would change my life. Soon I started applying my learning from the conference to all the programmes I designed in the bank, and the results (measured by key performance indicators such as job satisfaction and quality of service) attracted the attention of the bank's top management, who then asked me to be trained in the GR method as quickly as possible, in order to be able to apply this as a possible methodology for change in the banking system. So here I was at twenty three years of age, going from one conference to another, using the bank as an interesting playground for application of all my learning and, at the same time, frightening some consultants in the field with my speed. Six months after my first conference, I attended the French training group, and within a year I started implementing change programmes within the bank, both in Peru and Panama, while also joining international conference staff in Peru and France.

At the time, I held a role in the cultural transformation task force of the bank and I was asked to search for a provider for our cultural transformation programme. I invited proposals from every organisation I had encountered in the group relations network, and this resulted in an incredible number of responses from the potential providers, who were interpreting my invitation to them in unexpected ways but not necessarily responding to me as a client. For instance, on one occasion I received a range of emails asking whether I was "playing" the network ... if only they had known that, as a manager in an open market, I had invited proposals from entirely different organisations such as the Hay Group, Inmark, and Union Fenosa. Their responses alerted me to inter-institutional tension linked with succession and competition, which I could not internalise at the time. In the end a provider was selected and a programme was developed for the bank led by a French provider, IFSI, and Praxis International. As project manager, it was an enormous experience to be growing in this field of work and in my knowledge of becoming an internal consultant. So much so that, after nine months, I was invited to join their office, learning about consultancy in Paris while I also enrolled in the leading consultation postgraduate programme.

While living and working in France, I had a difficult time adjusting to the new culture, country, and language. It was a time of accelerated personal growth, and professionally I was transitioning from the client role to that of the provider. Not entirely intentionally, I learned by experience about the dynamics of tradition, creativity, and succession. Looking back, it is clear that I learned much of what I know now from that experience, and for that I am grateful.

At the age of twenty-seven I decided to go back to Peru and was invited to inspire (co-direct) the first FLAM International conference in Peru, which was my first experience as a director and marked the end of my relationships with both IFSI and InnovAccion. In my role as inspirer, I invited new elements to the conference design that had been built by IFSI; I introduced a musician and a dancer onto the staff, which opened up another layer of conference work. I learned, through experience, about rivalry concerning dynamics of succession, cruelty in intergenerational dynamics, and difficulties of accepting new ways of working when tradition is idealised and robbed of its embedded creativity. I also learned how my enthusiasm blinded me to these dynamics before the conference and how pre-conference processes of authorisation are key to our work.

Within the staff, a national colleague expressed her envy, as I understood it, towards me as "this young consultant arriving from Paris", becoming the first Peruvian to direct a conference in an institution she had built. Despite, or even because of, all these dynamics, the conference in itself generated useful learning for members and staff.

A former member of this conference then requested me to direct a group relations programmme in Esan Business School[4], helping me find my own way in this field, first through T-Consult—my own practice—and now in my role as senior consultant at the Tavistock Institute of Human Relations.

At the time, I wanted to develop an approach taking into account my experience in a national and international context. My journey from the banking sector into Group relations organisational consultancy had enabled me to challenge the assumptions I held of both worlds, while also searching for a common arena in which to ground my work. I hoped to mobilise my experience as a client as well as a provider of different in-house group relations applications, in order to design a new application that would best fit the market's needs.

On this journey, I was soon accompanied by Liliana Galvan[5], a board member of InnovAccion and former staff member of the first FLAM Peru. She resigned from InnovAccion and joined me in our shared dream to build a different container for Peruvian group relations conferences, with the collaboration of The Grubb Institute and the Tavistock Institute. Liliana has accompanied me in many ways (especially with, as we would say in Peru, "the wisdom of life experience"). We understood the relevance of a constructive intergenerational dynamic in order to provide a safe container for young students to learn through gGroup relations methodology at Universidad Peruana de Ciencias Aplicadas[6], where we have introduced a four-year group relations programme.

It is interesting how, at the same time, the bank reconsidered their consultancy contract and decided on a new leadership strategy. They offered me a consultancy assignment which included travelling around the world interviewing *Fortune* magazine's 2007 top ten leadership development and organisational consultancy practitioners. The task was to provide insights and an approach for how the value of group relations could be integrated with contemporary management practice and adapted to their organisational needs. At my request, the Tavistock Institute was added to the list, and with this assignment a new stage of my professional life had started.

What became clear was that I needed to develop a better understanding of market behaviour and its needs in order to design interventions that would fit. What I learned is that the unconscious was sometimes perceived in the business world as a mythic entity that must be protected with data, norms, and processes. For instance, some clients experienced group relations in-house interventions as time-consuming, over-expensive, and detached from the core business. Others constantly asked for evaluation and new ways to measure leadership development within group relations in-house applications. The practitioner's language was perceived as over-psychological, inducing a resentment of clients towards the development of a "culture within a culture", which often resulted in creating divisions with the rest of the organisation.

I understood the challenge that globalisation and technological development presented for the exploration and understanding of contemporary organisations. Take-overs, mergers and acquisitions, partnerships, and new technological developments, were just a few of the dynamics that shaped the market's state of mind.

The contemporary organisation's drive for tangible results, production, and profit created tension with the desire to have space for reflection on the organisation's life. The networked nature of organisations required a different understanding of boundaries and therefore of containment (Cooper & Dartington, 2004). The structural changes and pressure to perform impacted the organisational well-being and sustainability in the ecosystem in which they operate. As much as this was relevant then, you may find some of these trends still relevant.

From my experience in the business world, there was a high degree of market competitiveness and consumption while watching the world economical model crash and contribute to several ecological catastrophes. The market was overcrowded, in constant change, and seemed to require new ways of understanding the socio-psychological, socio-technical, and socio-ecological dynamics within.

The group relations network that I had known was, of course, not so different; inter-generational and inter-institutional dynamics on the process of succession drained the purpose of our work. I wanted to work with colleagues that could join me in an approach, finding a market niche, which was aimed to serve society. Mainly, I wanted to develop designs that could address our context in a different way, working with artists as part of the conference staff to introduce different ways of communication (dance, music, videos) and paying attention to the role of marketing and branding as components of the aesthetic dimension of a conference's organisational life. My rationale for this approach was that I believe organisations invited us to work within a context of interdependence, dealing with uncertainty and confronting human systems with the illusion of separateness. The interconnected nature of networks and organisations made evident the impossibility of "standing alone" in organisational positions. There is a call to work from paradigms of co-creation and collaboration, making a dynamic containment for sustainability, and this is what I believe in.

Weaving a conference design

What do I mean by weaving a conference design? I believe that my story, my working experience and findings, every staff and every member who joins a conference and its context, contribute to the pattern of this design.

In this context, a new five-day non-residential group relations application was created. The primary task[7] of the series of conferences was to provide opportunities to exercise leadership and authority in order to transform and innovate the praxis of management and consultancy, learning from the experience of taking roles in purposeful systems that aim to promote sustainable institutions engaged with global well-being

This section describes the new conferences:

> **Plenary sessions**, during the beginning and towards the end of the conference, offer opportunities to reflect on the process of crossing the boundaries between the conference and daily life. In this space members and staff reflect on expectations, experiences, and learning. The final plenary provides a way to explore the emotional state and collective learning of the participants, providing continued opportunities to study the process of closure without ending the learning.
>
> **A social matrix (SM)**, built as a "here-and-now" event, takes the shape of a large group event, consulted to by the director and two or three consultants. The event also explores the way dreams, reveries, feelings, free associations, myths, and physical sensations reveal the unconscious "collective system in the mind".
>
> **Dialogue of purpose and interconnectedness (DPI)**, offering opportunities for dialogue, which generates an understanding of inter-group and inter-organisational dynamics in the conference membership. Members are invited to form five small groups of equal number by self-selection. They explore their deeper purpose, their interconnectedness

with other groups, the integration of their experience, and their presence in others. After the first session, one member of each small group is offered the option to visit a different group and later go back to report before the end of the session. This event allows members to exercise authority and representation while working with other groups in the exploration of their deeper purpose. Such exploration on occasion reveals a sense of interconnection. During this event, the staff consulted to the different groups, offering their perceptions of what emerged. In addition, consultants rotate taking meditation roles during each session.

Blue ocean event (BOE), developed as a creative chaos container, is specifically designed as space for innovation and potential prototyping. In this space different sources of expression and creation are explored. Music, movement, dance, and visual arts create a space in which to mobilise the collective potential for innovation and intrapreneurship, encouraging self and collective authority. It is strategically positioned in the conference and constitutes a great energy resource for creativity.

1.1 **The sustainable market event (SME)** works across the boundary of the conference and continues to have a life beyond. It is located in the place of the traditional institutional event, combining both "here-and-now" experiential learning and action learning principles. Members of the conference create and establish the basis for the implementation of a transformative organisation (a project of company design, product, or service) in connection with the conference's primary task. Focused on purposeful leadership, the event is grounded by the belief in the infinite possibilities of human potential. The event is an invitation to test the boundaries of "what is known" by mobilising and challenging all available resources in order to make a real difference in the system's context. The work mobilises intrapreneurship and networking skills, while being able to keep back-home organisations in mind, as well as the state, local institutions, and native communities where possible. The main preparation of the project is done during the conference itself under the leadership of an elected "SME management". The "SME management" designs an organisational structure and inspires the different working teams to achieve their chosen task, engaging their wider networks with their emergent organisational purpose. Members often work extra hours in order to get invitation brochures and advertisement material, such as banners and displays, ready to invite a wider audience into the conference for a public launch of the organisational project, which is a next event called the generativity event.

Generativity event (GE) carries the name of one of Erikson's (1963) stages of human development and presents both the potential for productivity and creativity and the competing danger of stagnation. The event is designed to be led by the "SME management" who has to engage the new membership with the conference process and learning so far. It is my experience in this type of event that participants share how the conference so far has impacted the way they take up leadership and authority roles within and across organisations while opening a space for reflection on the nature and design of their emergent organisation's viability and sustainability in the larger system. In this event staff members generally struggle to take up their roles. Staff members carry the anxiety of entering into an unknown space.

Application and role transformation events (ARTE) provide members opportunities to review and reflect on the meaning of their experiences of the various roles they took or found within the conference. In application mode, members have opportunities to relate these experiences to the roles they are to resume in their professional, organisational, and personal lives outside the temporary conference institution.

Meditation. The conference process as a whole was accompanied by meditation sessions. The primary task is to co-create a diverse space for contemplation, to access deep purpose and meaningful reflection on the personal and collective experience. As conference director, I lead the first session, and once the sustainable market event has started the leadership of the sessions is opened for co-creation between members and staff.

Rationale of the design

Central to my work is the clarification of the organisation's essential purpose[8] and its alignment with the organisation's primary task. The conference invites individuals and organisations to expand their conscious awareness of the organisation's meaning and its psychological, social, spiritual, political, and ecological impact. This exploration aims to promote the "spirit of enquiry"[9] of the organisation and the search for the organisational well-being and sustainability in relation to its context.

The conference container took a different shape because of the location of the SME at the heart of the conference design. This event is led by conference members elected by the whole membership. They engage in the creation of a sustainable product or service that is introduced into the market on the last day of the conference. In this last event, members present their new products or services to a subsystem of guests, activated through the networks of conference participants. Members/participants invite/recruit these guests as a representation of the market place. By doing so, a new membership (generation) arrives, which implies the expansion of the conference container by opening its boundary to the outside world.

As a director, one of my tasks is to facilitate an optimum space for learning. Especially in this event, it becomes challenging because it requires staff to be present with, and work at, many different layers to build a dynamic conference container, which holds the future needs to react to a changing environment, in which the whole concept of boundaries and ecology is constantly confronted by technology, globalisation, and science.

During the conferences, members and staff work collectively to surface possibilities for real co-creation and innovation as opposed to focusing attention on rival dynamics of a market in competition. The described design intends to move from competing against others towards finding, making, and creating a new and collective space for serving a larger system. Contemporary organisations' dynamics, structures, and boundaries are reflected by the introduction of networking within the conference, which brings an additional layer of containment.

From my experience, this leads to more anxiety for staff members than for participant members, as we all need to "let go" of our familiar ways of exercising management and consultancy in a GR Conference.

Holding the boundary of this conference design as director includes working with a paradox of "within and outside", as members work across the boundary of the temporary institution when they start relating with outside organisations. This is also reflected in the various consultancy services, including process consultancy in group dynamics; product consultancy; technological consultancy; product conceptualisation; and communications. In addition the consultant staff works with various spiritual frameworks, including meditation practices, to understand and mobilise "energy" within the conference. I have also included in the design different methods of evaluation and research incorporating The Leadership Circle Culture Survey® (TLCS)10.

I believe that one of the key aspects of my approach to group eelations is entrepreneurship. I have found that conferences can support the development of intrapreneurs, defined as dreamers who do—those individuals who take hands-on responsibility for creating innovation of any kind within an organisation. They may be creators or inventors and are always the dreamers who are skilled in turning an idea into a profitable reality. They take risks and operate with willingness to pursue opportunities that have reasonable likelihood of producing losses or significant performance discrepancies " (Pinchot, 1985). For this reason I applied Morris and Kuratko's (2002) and Nielson, Peters, and Hisrich's (1985) approach for intrapreneurship development by enabling, within the large organisation of the conference, "the emergence of internal markets and relatively small and independent units designed to create, internally test-market, and expand improved and/or innovative services, technologies, or methods". The SME and the GE are designed to work towards this specific aim.

Another specific design component I introduced is to invite artists as conference staff and to challenge staff-as-a-whole to notice, and offer for study, different ways of communication and expression. In different conferences, musicians, dancers, painters, and audiovisual artists become integrated into the conference staff. This integration is made explicit also by appointing a GR consultant in the role of convenor, which contributes to the exploration of unconscious processes and allows spirit to thrive beyond the verbal psychoanalytic lens. Working with artists within a GR conference has opened up a multitude of resources for the conference experience. However, it meant attending to some design challenges. For instance, artists work only in "system-as-a-whole" sessions up until the start of the SME, in which their role is publicly negotiated and contracted between members and staff. In my experience, this is still a learning process and has therefore become one of my main areas of interest. In general, as staff members, they will also respond to members' requests in the "here-and-now", following their participant experience by making use of their different processes of transference and countertransference.

The design, as described above, is inspired by the Tavistock Model (Miller, 1989), and particularly founded by two main practices/perspectives; open systems theory (Von Bertalanffy, 1950; Emery, 1969, 1981) and systems psychodynamics (Rice, 1958, 1963, 1965; Miller & Rice, 1967; Miller, 1997b). I also welcome Jungian analytic theory, as reflecting on dreams, mythology, and archetypal data is integral to my use of GR methodology, to the extent that it influences understanding of the collective unconscious. In addition to the above, I integrated elements of theory U (Scharmer, 2007), talent management approach of Wharton University (Capelli, 2008) and blue ocean strategy (Kim & Mauborgne, 2005) into the described design.

Theory U informs the DPI[11] event and refers to the individual and collective capacity to sense and bring into the present one's highest future potential by following five movements of co-initiating, co-sensing, co-inspiring, co-creating, and co-evolving. Another key concept in this design is talent management, and in particular Wharton University's approach, as this considers that talent problems of employers, employees, and the broader society are intertwined (Capelli, 2008) and involve risks. Part of managing the risk is then understood as managing the costs associated with events that are uncertain or at least difficult to predict. The approach aims to find balance between internal development and outside hiring, between the interests of the employee and those of the organisation, in a context of uncertainty. In my words, it then means finding balance between one's inner world and the outer world of the conference. This approach is of particular importance for the SME[12] and the GE[13].

As mentioned before, the concept of innovation incubators is core to the work at the BOE[14]. This event is based on blue ocean strategy, an approach designed to create uncontested market spaces and make competition an irrelevant concept. The BOE invites learning about strategies that can shape the structure to create a new market space. The focus is on how to re-construct industry boundaries, centring on organisational purpose rather than finances. It looks beyond the existing demand in order to pursue cost-effective differentiation, building profitable business models to succeed in new market spaces (Kim & Mauborgne, 2005).

Finally, many previous experiences have challenged me to explore the subject of evaluation within group relations conferences. My approach is to explore the value of the organisational talent and its efficiency in the specific organisational design created to develop the requisite competencies. For this purpose, I have worked with researchers who apply qualitative methodologies within the conference boundaries. The research indicates that the improvement of organisational dynamics, along with the development of leadership capacity, contributes to building a culture of innovation and new business development.

For this reason, the evaluation component in the conferences was then supported by the application of The Leadership Circle Culture Survey® (TLCS), a tool that I found particularly compatible with our GR work. All of these components work as an invitation to engage in a research spirit, observing the available resources and co-creating something through them in order to contribute (intervene) to the understanding of the system. We also evaluate the creation of a safe space for members, to learn while designing a purposeful organisation.

In the first conference edition, the co-creative process of members and staff translated into the creation of a start-up organisation dedicated to promoting GR methodology within the Esan business school. Participants designed an event to integrate their conference learning with their experience of market needs. They recruited ninety guests to the launch event for which they sold tickets. As a result, sufficient financial sustainability was developed for future GR conferences. Other outcomes are in the creation of two other sustainable projects: "Manos Limpias", a group dedicated to fighting corruption in the health sector, and "Leading with purpose developing Peru", a group that promotes tripartite dialogue between the government, private sector, and native communities in the Peruvian energy sector. This last project then developed into a new professional opportunity to work with the Peruvian government to design and direct a conference aimed at providing containment and resilience in a time of crisis and recovering from the national corruption case known as "petrogate scandal"[15] that came to light in October 2008.

Learning from the experience of directing these conferences within the group relations network, explaining how tradition, creativity, and succession are linked to the conference design

In my presentation in Belgirate, I also presented a set of videos. One of my challenges is to put these experiences into a readable text, and many times other media seem a more powerful reflection of experience. The first video I used is called "Tradition is the base for innovation"[16] and it links different moments in history with the development of the Tavistock tradition. With this video I tried to emphasise how I understand GR methodology to be a way to listen to the (system's) environment and to mobilise the system's talent to engage with the challenges of the context.

The second video presented is called "A story within the group relations network—an invitation to co-creation instead of ownership". It provides an invitation through the images of many people, who generously agreed to participate in the presentation, to see that we as Peruvians are touched by the group relations network. It is, even more, a personal acknowledgement of the various colleagues who have deeply touched my journey and who helped to make the work in Peru possible. The video shows snapshots of my short story in our network, with the metaphor of a DNA chain and a woman in gestation that refers to the different conferences in which I participated as member or staff until early 2009. On this journey, I have met colleagues who have become very close and others, with whom I sadly do not keep in touch, particularly because of the jagged journey between tradition and creativity in a network needing and resisting constant succession and renewal.

I have tried to express with images and sounds the fact that for me every conference design takes life and becomes lived as the result of the co-creation of human inter-connections, reaching beyond the members and staff that participated in these conferences between 2007 and 2010. I vividly remember one colleague's advice before I directed my first conference. She said that someone in the network told her, when she was going to start directing, to consider inviting consultants with directorship experience to the staff, as they would be very competitive, but in the end they would support her and the work. Whoever suggested that to her, it was indeed wise advice, and it was clearly reflected in my experience. The experienced directors I invited were certainly very competitive but they did support the work and my role.

My picture in the mind of our network is "un intercambio de regalos"—an exchange of gifts. Learning, advice, and experiences travel through generations for a bigger purpose. Many started at the Tavistock and travelled around the world. From time to time some of us get greedy and try to collect the gifts instead of exchanging them. We try to own "innovations", so we fight, we split, we hurt, we wound, and, fortunately, we heal. I wonder why we do this? Perhaps we are afraid of our potential if we really join together and work for a collective dream.

When I spoke of intrapreneurship earlier, of course, I also spoke of myself. My dream is to expand our work to less privileged areas of my country, to work on issues of corporate social responsibility and ecological sustainability. To allow the exchange of gifts to flow, bringing hope to those who most need it, while developing a safe container for inter-generational social transformation.

A colleague once smiled at me and said, "I wondered where the youth was in our network, and when I came to Peru I found it. You have developed a very special kindergarten". Although it is not actually a kindergarten, we do receive people in our programmes who are eighteen years old and who successfully graduate four years later. Working with them has been a gift, and I see them as co-creators of our work. Their generosity in sharing their learning with those who are less privileged, and the way they work, makes me hopeful and mindful of the beauty of our network. All the consultants that came to my country to help build our dream were co-creating a succession process of methodology in a new country without any colonising "owning" approach. They welcomed the creativity and different interpretation of their tradition, engaging with it in generosity.

Creativity might offer a particular mix in a specific time, but it is our life and context that defines how we apply our tradition, and design the containers in which we work. When I close my eyes and think of the number of lives that we continue to touch around the world, I just feel my soul open with wonder. For me our role is to be transformative agents of a more sustainable world, and as a network, that is our exchange of gifts.

Conclusion

When I submitted the first draft of this paper, I think I almost killed our dear editors with my Latin American thoughts in English words. The beauty of our network generosity offered me a Dutch proof reader, Marjoleine Hulshof. She has helped me through the pain of making this a readable text. I hope we have succeeded in this task after several extensions from our patient editors. I don't know if there is a conclusion for this paper, as it is a story, and a set of challenges, that continues.

I could conclude that a conference design is brought to life by a co-creative process that includes all members and staff but that is deeply impacted by the history of our network. I could also argue that our understanding of group relations conferences needs to adapt to the network and globalised world including the impact of new technologies. I would emphasise that intergenerational dynamics are core to the sustainability of our work and that GR sucession is not held from one person to another but in how our method adapts and works with contemporary challenges again and again. Therefore my main conclusion is gratitude towards this work and our network, and hope that the story will continue in a healthy way.

References

Aram, E. (2012). "Climbing fast up the ladder?!" The lived experience of directing. In: E. Aram, R. Baxter & A. Nutkevitch (Eds.), *Tradition, Creativity and Succession in the Global Group Relations Network*. London: Karnac.

Bertalanffy, L. von (1950). *An outline of general system theory, British Journal for the Philosophy of Science,. 1.*

Cappelli, P. (2008). *Talent on Demand: Managing Talent in an Age of Uncertainty.* Harvard: Harvard Business Press.

Chan, K. & Mauborgne R. (2005). *Blue Ocean Strategy: How to Create Uncontested Market Space and Make Competition Irrelevant.* Harvard: Harvard Business Press.

Cooper & Dartington (2004). The vanishing organization: Organizational containment in a networked world. In: Huffington et al. (Eds.), *Working Below The Surface: The Emotional Life of Contemporary Organizations.* London: Karnac.

Emery, F. E., (Ed.). (1969). *Systems Thinking.* Harmondsworth: Penguin.

Erikson, E. (1963). *Childhood and Society (Second Edition).* New York: Norton.

Miller, E. (1990b). Experiential learning in groups II: Recent developments in dissemination and application. In: E. Trist & H. Murray (Eds.), *The Social Engagement of Social Science. A Tavistock Anthology. Vol. I: The Socio-psychological Perspective* (pp. 186–198). London: Free Association Books–.

Miller, E. J. (1989). *The "Leicester" Model: Experiential Study of Group and Organizational Processes* (Occasional Papers *10*). London: The Tavistock Institute of Human Relations.

Miller, E. J. (1997). Effecting organisational change in large systems: a collaborative consultancy approach. In: J. Neumann, K. Kellner & A. Dawson-Shepherd (Eds.), *Developing Organisational Consultancy*. London: Routledge.

Miller, E. J. & Rice, A. K. (1967). *Systems of Organization*. London: Tavistock Press.

Morris, M. H. & Kuratko, D. F. (2002). *Corporate Entrepreneurship*. New York: Harcout College Publishers.

Nielson, R. P., Perters, M. P. & Hisrich, R. D. (1985). Entrepreneurship strategy for internal markets-corporate, non-profit and government institution cases. *Strategic Management Journal, 6*: 181–189.

Ostroff, S. (2006). Whispers of the whole: Tending to the system by the system for the system. In: A. N. Mathur (Ed.), *Dare to Think the Unthought Known?* Tampere: Aivoairut Oy.

Pinchott, G. P. (1985). *Intrapreneuring: Why You Don't Have to Leave the Corporation to Become an Entrepreneur*. New York: Harper & Row.

Rice, A. K. (1958). *Productivity and Social Organization: The Ahmedabad Experiment*. London: Tavistock Publications. (Reissued 1987, New York: Garland).

Rice, A. K. (1963). *The Enterprise and its Environment*. London: Tavistock Publications.

Rice, A. K. (1965). *Learning for Leadership: Interpersonal and Intergroup Relations*. London: Karnac.

Scharmer, C. O. (2007). *Theory U: Leading from the Future as it Emerges*. Cambridge, MA: The Society for Organizational Learning.

Velarde, M. (2009). Tradition is the base for innovation. http://www.youtube.com/watch?v=JRTrBR1xYvo&edit=ev&feature=uenh

Notes

1. T-Consult was founded in 2007 and works with the Tavistock tradition in Peru enabling spaces for the exploration and understanding of roles in organisational contexts with the purpose of contributing to sustainable development by adding spirit and meaning to organisational systems. (www.t-consult.biz)

2. The International Forum for Social Innovation, IFSI was founded in 1978 and continues the group relations tradition founded, amongst others, by W. R. Bion, Isabelle Menzies, A. K. Rice, and P. Turquet, and inspired by open systems and psychoanalytic theories. IFSI adds to this the societal dimension and the approach known as Institutional Transformation (IT) that is the fruit of its work with economic, political, and social milieus. (www.ifsi-fiis-conferences.com)
3. InnovAcción, a not-for-profit oriented to leadership development and institutional transformation process. (www.innovaccion-grupo.com)
4. ESAN was the first academic institution specialised in business administration for graduate students to be created in the Spanish speaking world. It was founded on 25 July 1963, under an agreement between the governments of Peru and the United States of America. Its organisation and implementation was entrusted to the Graduate School of Business of Stanford University, California.
5. Dean of the Faculty of Human Sciences at Universidad Peruana de Ciencias Aplicadas.
6. Founded in 1994 as an institution based on creativity and innovation to form future change agents. Since its establishment, UPC has been recognised for its innovation and academic excellence. The university has near to thirty careers in the faculties of administration, business, architecture, contemporary arts, health science, human science, communications, law, economy, business and engineering, tourism and hospitality services. The school's web site can be found at www.upc.edu.pe.
7. The concept of primary task was defined by Ken Rice as "the task that must be performed for an institution to survive." See A. K. Rice (1963). *The Enterprise and its Environment: a System Theory of Management Organisation.* London: Tavistock Publications (pp. 13–14), and E. J. Miller and A. K. Rice (1967). *Systems of Organisation: The Control of Task and Sentient Boundaries.*—London: Tavistock Publications.
8. "... The term "essential purpose" refers to a unique gift/, that every being has, It is the being life path to uncover and manifest it connection to the whole. It has implications for the way in which we conceive of leadership. From this perspective, leadership is not located in any one person but in every part of the system. This perspective expands the concept of primary task and reflects the relationship between the manifestation and evolution of the essence of an individual or collective, and the purpose of unfolding or expressing the unique essence in service of the larger system" (Ostroff, 2006) in Whispers of the whole: tending to the system by the system for the system.

9. Spirit of enquiry understood as joint creation "melacha". Encouraging the openness to what emerges and remaining curious to the experience without pre-judgment. (Aram, 2009), "Climbing fast up the ladder?!"- The lived experience of directing. Published in this book.
10. The Leadership Culture Survey™ (TLCS) highlights the potential within the conference as an organisation by drawing a map of its culture and the way it affects organisational engagement, performance and wellbeing. It reveals valuable data around the perception of the organisations current leadership culture, showing the gap between the actual culture and the one that is desired, making evident the resources that can be drawn on in order to make the changes required. This tool differentiates between relevant organisational levels of accountability.
11. Dialogue of purpose and interconnectedness.
12. Sustainable market event.
13. Generativity event.
14. Blue oceanevent.
15. The local Mafia conducted widespread surveillance and illegal phone tapping of rival politicians, journalists, business executives, government ministers, and judges. The scandal led the government to suspend five joint exploration and development contracts recently awarded. The information gathered was sold to the mass media and led to the resignation of the whole cabinet. As a consequence there was a lack of trust in leadership and experiences of corruption, finger-pointing, blaming, and separation. The private and public sectors were divided in maintaining complex relationships with native communities in the land where they needed to operate. What could have been understood as common goals were perceived as competing aims.
16. http://www.youtube.com/watch?v=JRTrBR1xYvo&edit=ev&feature=uenh

SECTION IV

POST-CONFERENCE REFLECTIONS

We are always particularly pleased with this section, which signifies for us what this project called Belgirate is all about. As said in the introduction, we were inundated with post-conference reflections this time, and the choice was hard, but we decided to accommodate as many as possible, as they are all thoughtful and moving, expanding the exploration of the conference themes and papers, furthering the opportunities for learning, continuing the quest and the inquiry—all without closing down the learning. For us, this is what group relations in practice is all about.

CHAPTER ELEVEN

A church with no followers: a split of knowledge and power in the group relations community

Daphna Bahat

In the "Introductions in Groups" event at the beginning of the conference the Quaker church was mentioned. A participant explained that the Quaker church has no priests; the church believes the Bible was not given by God only to priests, that everyone has a relation to God, hence this relation does not need to be mediated by priests. Thus knowledge could potentially be accessed by anyone.

I took note for myself, and then said in the group that the community of group relations is a church with no followers, only priests.

During the open plenary I wrote to myself only two notes of things that were said and thoughts that went through my head:

> "The founders are not here."
> "The word 'succession' appears for the first time in the title of Belgirate conferences."

In this chapter I will propose a hypothesis about the cultural nature of the community of group relations. I suggest that a split regarding knowledge and power exists within this organisational culture. This split is attached to the fear of learning and changing and is related to stagnation of learning from experience. The split is characterised by a division between a subgroup of informal, "as if" consultants that possess all the knowledge, and another sub-group that includes those who don't know or understand the process and are mobilised into feeling and acting. Everybody wishes to belong to the first sub-group.

It is the beginning of the exploratory event in Belgirate III. I have to join one of the groups. I find no passion within me. I don't feel like joining either of the groups. It seems as if nothing interests me. No subject which is being offered during the groups formation lures me. "OK" I say to myself, "sometimes you just follow people you want to be with." At this stage I find no one like that. It feels like a desert.

Finally I go to a group because somebody there says something that I like. I now cannot remember what it was.

I enter a room. About twenty people sit in a circle. Some women, rather young and attractive, are moving or dancing. There are some candles and music. It looks to me as if they are trying to appear sensual, sexy and unique, free yet sophisticated.

Dancing is an important part of my life. I could easily be one of them. Had I done that I would probably have felt somewhat pathetic, trying too hard. The group almost ignores their movements. They try harder. Members of the group are talking, trying to create something meaningful, but after a while the group splits into two groups with a feeling of frustration. It seems to me that these women are somehow exploited by the whole group, being pushed into the role of "feeling" and "living" as opposed to "thinking", "understanding", and "interpreting".

I leave the room and wander around through the whole exploratory event. I don't find myself. I don't find my voice, nor my capacity to think and understand.

As I mentioned, I love dancing. I lead workshops for women that explore the feminine experience through belly dancing, among other techniques. I have noticed that often during OFEK's exploratory activities I have an urge to move my body, to dance. I have also noticed that frequently it happens when I feel that my head is empty of thoughts, when I don't understand what is going on systemically or when I feel that there is falseness in the group activity. Throughout the years it has become a kind of a signal for me that something might be dead, within me or within the group.

I now understand my critical attitude during the exploratory event as a representation of my reluctance to be mobilised into one of two positions. The first is that of a wise interpreting consultant who sees the system at any time as a whole and understands what is going on, and the second is that of a body which only feels and acts. I have to admit that I cannot always be mobilised into the first position, as I sometimes feel very dumb, with no real thoughts or understanding. I think this is probably how I felt most of the time at Belgirate III.

It felt strange to me because in the first Belgirate conference I was in the role of administrator, I was rather new to the community of Group Relations, and I hadn't yet filled any role in a group relations conference except that of a member. Yet, at Belgirate I, I felt I saw much more than in the two others I attended. Among other things, I remember that I then keenly felt the inter-organisational succession issue, specifically in the competition between organisations over succession to the Tavistock Institute, over being the chosen progeny. I will get back to the issue of choice later.

Did I understand better because I was in role? Was it because in a way I was still an outsider? Was it just "beginners luck"?

My role in Belgirate I was not one of a consultant. There are no assigned consultants in Belgirate, or at least no formal ones. Yet sometimes I felt there were lots of consultants in Belgirate, or in other exploratory events in the group relations community, where there are no pre-assigned consultants. In fact, I believe that on these occasions the group splits into two main sub-groups: one is the group of as-if consultants, who mainly interpret, and who are usually the more senior persons in the group relations community. The other group is composed mainly of younger people with no roles in the global network, the people who don't see the system, who "don't understand" what is going on. One might say that it's a matter of competency and wisdom. It may even be true. However, I believe that many times there is a false process of group thinking. There cannot be real thinking when people are stuck in pre-known positions or roles, there cannot be real thinking when too many things are known in advance, there cannot be real thinking when "there is none of the painful bringing together of initiated and uninitiated, primitive and sophisticated, that is the essence of the developmental conflict" (Bion, 1961, p. 127). The group "… also avoids the painful bringing together of the new idea and the primitive state" (ibid).

If the "veterans" or "seniors" always "know", then their knowledge is false; if the "young people" always "don't know" than I am not sure I believe their "feelings" (or dancing). I think that the two groups are pushed into two poles and the learning from experience is blocked.

It sometimes appears as a Babylon tower of interpretations with no ground of data holding it, like a tower children make of hands being put one on the other until it becomes a tower of hands in the air. This is a different situation to the one in which there is a group of people whose formal role is that of consultant, because the formal role may enable a kind of potential space for the consultant himself or herself, and for the group as a whole. If the consultant does not have "to know" all the time, he or she has the freedom to learn. However, if he or she is pushed by a group to a position of omniscience, there may be false learning. The consultant does not hold "the knowledge", rather, his role is to enable learning. All this is very different from the situation in meetings like the Belgirate conferences because in them there is an unconscious process in which people take informal roles, according to their valency, and remain there without a lot of thinking and changing.

During the morning reflections and associations the chairperson of my organisation says that she doesn't feel sexy. I sit behind her and thank her because it enables me to say that I feel nothing but my sensuality. Strangely enough, apart from being embarrassed I don't feel alive with those feelings. I now think we were both mobilised to these polarities and were stuck there.

Bion wrote about the hatred of learning by experience:

> There is a hatred of having to learn by experience at all, and lack of faith in the worth of such a kind of learning ... In the group it becomes very clear that this longed-for alternative to the group procedure is really something like arriving fully equipped as an adult fitted by instinct to know without training or development exactly how to live and move and have his being in a group. (1961, p. 88)

The moment in which one learns something new, one meets and recognises what was not known until that very moment. Following that, there is a painful recognition of not being omnipotent and perfect.

I believe that the split described here between the interpreters, the "knowers", and those who are "blind", paralysed and can only act and feel, is in the service of the hatred of learning by experience. In conferences like Belgirate, where no consultants are assigned, and since the community is still under basic assumption dependency, there might be a fear of not knowing and being "blind". Attached to it is the fear of learning new things and being exposed as not being an omnipotent community. The split described serves as a defence against these fears as it assures that there will be no real movement and hence no new learning.

This situation resembles what Bion (1961, Ch. 7) describes as a split between the majority of a group which prefers to remain "ignorant" and the minority which acts as if it promotes the learning but, by making it too hard to follow, actually colludes with the minority so that the whole group does not advance.

During the same exploratory event a man visits the "women directors" group. After a few moments a woman says to him that he is sexy, and he leaves the room. At the closing plenary of the exploratory event there is a stormy exchange between the woman in the management team of Belgirate III, who is also the Tavistock director, and a woman-participant. It seems that the argument is related to the wish for approval and the participant's feeling that there is an attack on her liveliness, on authentic and innovative aspects of her actions.

I want to suggest that the dynamic of the relations between the two sub-groups of the split is characterised by exploitation. It seems that there is a collusion in which the "knowing" part exploits the "blind" one. The exploitation is expressed by the use of "youth spirit", the vitality and the willingness to play in order to gain power and status, as in the citation from the Bible: "Let the young men arise and compete before us." (2 Samuel: 14). To a certain extent this also represents an intergenerational conflict.

It could be said that the "knowing" part keeps its knowing position, which also includes power over the "blind" and "feeling" part. I suggest that the knowing part encourages the blind to sacrifice its sensuality and authenticity on the altar of as-if learning in return for the promise of recognition. Added to this is the culture of "waiting to be chosen" that characterises our community. This gives the seniors power of omniscience and omnipotence and the status of setting the tone. Their position is always desired, as is their approval, since in this community everyone aspires to be a wise consultant, or, as the title of this chapter suggests, a revered priest. Could it be one of the reasons for the difficulty of recruiting participants for group relations conferences around the world? Could it be that the community is so busy with its clear hierarchical structure that it inhibits true learning and development and has hardly managed to find any followers to its church in recent years?

I think that the community of group relations fears going through the succession process and that, because the dynamic is one of exploitation, the sensuality as well as the learning is inauthentic.

A fascinating paper was presented in Belgirate III by Brigid Nossal and Susan Long entitled: "Group relations in Australia: Exploring intergenerational dynamics in the field and their implications for group relations praxis". Since it is published in this book I will only mention that it explores the limiting and also the destructive aspects of familial and generational identifications when they are transposed into organisational contexts. While chairing this presentation, I was aware of a lot of comments which held identification and sympathy with those ideas.

Another interesting piece of evidence for that dynamic can also be found in an illuminating chapter in the post conference reflections section in the book based on Belgirate II (Aram, Baxter, & Nutkevitch, 2009). Green and Papadopoulos (2009) describe their walking out of the closing exploratory event plenary towards its end. They write that they left after a female member of their group "spoke with passion and tears about the shadow side of group relations life; the threats, attack, and violence that too often characterised our conferences and our work with each other". Later in the chapter they interpret their walking out as an attack by them, on behalf of the participants, on Eliat Aram as the "named director of the Leicester conference", where resides the authority for group relations. The authors understand their act as one they were "sent" to do by the whole group:

> We were chosen to launch the attack, ironically because we were relatively safe repositories for the unconscious, unexpressed primitive rage at the appointment of this particular director—a young Jewish immigrant in Europe, an unwelcome and certainly illegitimate interloper into a privileged place others had worked for years to earn. As younger and more polymorphous men of this "skipped" middle age, more likely to be allies with the new director, our attack would not be seen to be as brutal as that of older men who had already earlier questioned whether women could indeed be conference directors. We also served as a convenient mask for the fury of the women directors, with whom our group allied in

> the exploratory event. Surely any one of them would have been a more suitable choice than the Chosen One. When their most senior woman walked out, it was not seen as an attack, but a personal choice by a seasoned director. Similarly when she was proceeded by the previous director of the Leicester conference on account of illness, only concern for his well-being could be observed and expressed, not the symbolic meaning of his abandonment of his chosen successor.
>
> We were the fellow émigrés, willing foils to hold projections that could not and were not made available at any time in any public forum at Belgirate. The collective mourning was for the lost opportunity that now could not be realized. Death had come so soon and without notice while so many believed themselves to be alive. (Aram, Baxter, & Nutkevitch, 2009)

It seems that since the expression was projected into the "youngers", their act was dismissed as an acting out (something young people usually do), and the group could easily avoid integrating it into owning and learning. It is possible that had this work been done, the theme which evoked this move, the dark side of group relations, could have been thought about and not enacted.

To conclude, it may be said that the two sides of the coin of basic assumption dependency, which may be described as the impotent "We know nothing and hence are in a needy position" and its omnipotent denial by "We know everything and hence need no one" (or ba fight/flight) are being expressed through a split between sub-groups and are a hindrance to the group relations community.

References

Aram, E., Baxter, R. & Nutkevitch, A. (2009). *Adaptation and Innovation: Theory, Design and Role-Taking in Group Relations Conferences and their Applications.* London: Karnac.

Bion, W. R. (1961). *Experiences in Groups and Other Papers.* London: Tavistock Publications.

Green, Z. G., & Papadopoulos, N. (2009). A walk out before mourning dawn: Reflections on innovations and adaptations at the boundary. In: E. Aram, R. Baxter & A. Nutkevitch (Eds.), *Adaptation and Innovation: Theory, Design and Role-Taking in Group Relations Conferences and their Applications.* London: Karnac.

CHAPTER TWELVE

Intimacy and detachment: working relationships in a temporary institution

Angela Eden and David Sierra Lozano

Background

At Belgirate III there was an opportunity to form small groups, and we both joined one of the self-selected groups called "creativity". The group started well, and we felt comfortable being together, maybe because there was a match of expectations and skills in the group, which confirmed the choice we made in moving from the large group.

We played with ideas and acts of creativity which proved to be a satisfying experience. At the end of the conference, as we were saying goodbye and thinking about detaching from the intimacy of the conference, we were musing on the power of GR events. These are places where strangers join together, share experiences, often become quite close, and then say goodbye. Often the closeness is not continued, or it is renewed at another conference. It felt strange to be in such intensity of relationships and then let the contact evaporate. As we thought about this phenomena, so many other associations came to mind about our work in organizations, and we coined a phrase—"working intimacy".

The invitation to contribute to a book enlivened the idea and we have developed a virtual working intimacy in the hope that this idea will have some currency in other settings. Consequently we wrote this chapter as a direct experience of working together at Belgirate. It was a joint project, written from two different countries, using the internet, Skype, and emails. It was a great challenge to maintain the intimacy and create an elegant chapter; we hope for generosity and creativity in reading this collation of our two different experiences, cultures, and language.

Introduction

In the design of GR events there are moments of choice: Which group to join? Which role to take? Where to invest time, energy and relatedness? The stakes, in the moment, feel fraught with implications of power and personal authority. This becomes especially significant in a peer group or a network of potential colleagues. Why a group forms and how it develops, how it is lead, what roles people take, have been discussed in numerous publications. Here we look at how the intimacy appears and why some of the relationships in GR events become so potent.

We took our own experience at Belgirate III as a source of inspiration and analysis. There's no doubt that in relation to any other GR Conference, a meeting of peer practitioners has more facets. In Belgirate, many people have earlier personal or institutional relationships, so the question of "intimacy" is camouflaged among multiple implications. There is an additional complexity when we thought about the apparent knowing one another. (We say "apparent" as there are no criteria for the depth of knowing, from superficial acquaintance to deep and long relatedness, and intimacy.)

The form that "working intimacy" has taken for the authors of this chapter has also been the subject of exploration during this writing process. In order to maintain our connection we used Google to establish a conversation about our experience, which we include here as an example:

Angela: Tell me David, what made you choose the creativity group?

David: My feeling is that the group choose me. I felt the creativity when you took the leadership in this proposal, both in what you said and how you expressed it ... I am always very interested in exploring new ways to enrich the GR approach to organisations, other complementarities, new perspectives ... and of course it needs some kind of pairing assumption that I think the group of creativity that was forming represented. What made you make this proposal?

A: I remember the moment that I offered the idea of creativity. I remember the energy, but I did not think it would resonate with other people. It was in the hope that I could have fun and not be in an intellectual group. I do too much thinking, and wanted a different experience. I also felt that this was a place I could play.

D: Apart from a coffee we took together, I think there is a moment that you contributed to the creation of working intimacy in the creativity group. It was when you openly shared with us a personal dilemma outside the conference. A question out of the task but it worried you in that moment ... What do you think?

A: Yes I agree, bringing something personal opened a new door to trust. The way the group responded so warmly made me feel an insider, part of the group. Usually I feel a visitor in other people's work.

D: For me it was not only something personal, but a working issue because it affected the internal process of the group. By the way, Angela, what makes you feel connected to people at work?

A. Apart from connecting through a shared task, it is a shared sense of the humour, or informal exchanges that seem to have a deeper resonance than task relationship; and you?

D: To share perspectives and world visions with my colleagues. Although that does not ensure the creation of a working intimacy, it is a previous condition. For example, a significant experience in Belgirate was being in contact with other colleagues of GR Netherland with whom I occasionally work. This contributed to my understanding of what similarities/differences there are in our perspectives, and what we have in common.

A: How have you found this virtual working intimacy that we are trying to create while writing the chapter?

D: Sincerely, my feeling is that being in a virtual relationship diminishes the intensity of working intimacy. It is not easy and requires more persistence. And you?

A: Yes, it has been hard to manage a connection through distance and time. I feel we had to struggle, but when we did connect through Skype it came alive.

D: Yes, I agree.

Some thoughts about intimacy

"Intimacy" is one of those words that practical experience and definitions are hard to pin down. Even so, the concept has been incorporated naturally into our everyday language and we associate it vaguely with "private", "personal", "close", "family", "near", etc. Etymologically it comes from the Latin *"intimus"*, referring to something very (*"-mus"*) internal (*"inti-"*).

There are many theories, and much research, which discuss the need to create and maintain interpersonal relationships. Freud, Maslow, Bowlby, and other authors have studied, through various prisms and in depth, the empirical evidence in this field (Baumeister & Leary, 1995; Hazan & Shaver, 1994a; Reis, 1990). They all note that humans, as eminently social beings, have for various reasons a need and desire to form social bonds and that intimacy is a characteristic attribute of these close relationships.

The concept of "intimacy" strongly suggests a movement into the private terrain. Many intimate issues are naturally associated as private, but at the moment we share them with other people they become more public, though they can still remain intimate. At this point, private or public is a better description, and the amount of privacy depends on the amount of inclusion that others are allowed. The grade of intimacy grows according to the emotional value it has in relation to the sight of others. For example, I can have some pictures of mine that are private and intimate, but at the moment I publish them on the internet they become public, although they still remain intimate. Anyway, in both cases intimacy or privacy cannot be conceived without the presence of an "other", so it is a social phenomenon.

In most of the theories, we see that the creation of relationships of intimacy is associated with satisfactory states of happiness and personal well-being (McAdams & Bryant, 1987). We appreciate that these investigations have principally examined "intimacy" from the domain of relationships between "persons", avoiding the perspective of the role as a construct. This mediates between the person and the principal task of the system. We think that this ambiguity has brought with it confusion and difficulties in daily organisational management.

Our perspective: working intimacy

Dealing with any human working system starts from the premise that relationships of intimacy among its members can be both a favourable factor and a difficulty in achieving the task. We understand that relationships of intimacy become favourable when the role relationships and the interests of the shared main task take pre-eminence. For this reason we have chosen to refer to "working intimacy" or "inter-role intimacy". In later sections we shall describe a plausible definition of this term and the conditions which could facilitate its appearance.

However, relationships of intimacy may also represent a distorting factor for the fulfilment of the task. This condition can be found in two possible scenarios:

1. When the relationships cause great conflict between the various members of a work unit, making it plausible that the style of attachment—anxious-ambivalent or avoidant—may be a factor participating in this process (Bowlby, 1969).
2. When the type of attachment among the members of the work unit is felt from the personal perspective as being very positive, although playing, all unawares, a role contrary to the development of the task.

In both cases, whether in detachment or attachment, our understanding is that there is a very strong relationship of personal intimacy (but not "working intimacy").

In any case, the greater the contact between members of a human work system increases the probability that relationships of intimacy will be generated. The tendency is to pigeon—hole the other into one's valency, in roles of repetition and in imago-affective representations (Roma, 2007).

We might define "working intimacy" as a relationship that furthers and improves the work and completing the task. It has a sense of co-operation/collaboration and exists in a culture of shared values and shared understanding of the primary task.

Of course, there is also a shadow side of this "working intimacy". We mean a kind of basic assumption or "as if", when apparently we are on "working intimacy" but we are not. It is as if pairing turns to baF/F or ba P. It is the "fake intimacy" (Roma, 2007). There are socially accepted patterns stereotypically, where everybody says together, but in reality the apparent intimacy is a defence. This emerges in organisations but also is socially accepted: for example, in the gossip magazines it is as though everybody already has an intimacy with all those famous people, with the king, with this soccer player, etc.

Some hypotheses from the experience

As stated above, when we reflected on how we joined the small group we also became interested in the element of choice and unconscious valency. At this point emerged two complementary hypotheses that we have described as:

Hypothesis One

If one can *choose* whom to work with, then the wish to relate and have a "working intimacy" has a stronger motivation than when there is an imposed instruction to relate

and/or

Hypothesis Two

Due to the unconscious and social dynamics, we make choices that are less free than we would like to imagine.

GR conferences make a contribution to this debate in that it helps people to understand that they cannot make such individual decisions. If you cannot choose your working group, are there some guidelines that facilitate enough intimacy for the work to flourish?

Hypothesis Three

"Working intimacy" incorporates the "other" in its multiplicity of facets and dimensions.

Our third hypothesis aims to contribute to the creation of these types of conditions. Contrary to what one might think, establishing a working intimacy with another member does not involve knowing her/his more private side (e.g., gossip events from his/her history), but rather in discovering complexity and being able to identify more shades which enrich the relationship in order to achieve the task. So we pass from a partial view to a more complex perspective.

This complexity might emerge when people involved in a system explore the elements that do not strictly form a part of the principal task to be processed, but underlie it and affect it, namely psychic, social, political, transcendent, or contextual dimensions. For example, this exploration connects with the sense of the morning reflections and associations events in Belgirate.

In our experience, more and more executives are introducing a space for "exploration of the state of the system" before starting the meetings. This has very satisfactory results. In short, these mark the boundary of transition to the main task and invite the construction of working intimacy on the basis of sharing these physical, emotional, and contextual states ... which in some way are present through each one of the members.

At another level of analysis, from our perspective "working intimacy" is a living process and may change over time. One of the outcomes of a group relations conference is the very tight link which many participants end up enjoying. There are not many studies on this aspect, but the recurring experience is that there is a greater intensity in relationships when the conference ends. With the support of new technology, this can be extended for a period until it is eventually weakened by time. However there are cases where very strong and creative relationships have been maintained in the form of projects and very productive business enterprises. It is not unusual, therefore, that among members, the experience of intimacy in the relationships established is an aspect which helps to make this type of seminar a very powerful experience. In addition, we need to recognise the death of the intimacy. The moment a project group or team has completed the task, the process of mourning and loss is in the air. Saying goodbye in Belgirate was tempered with the sense of the tribe meeting again soon at another event. However, that experience was finished, and though we learn to forge relationships we have also learnt to drop them without too much pain. We learn as organisation travellers to pick up and build intimacy appropriate for the task.

Hypothesis Four

There is a skill in creating, transforming, and closing working intimacy that should be recognised and appreciated.

Our experience in organisations, as working managers, is that we constantly build and change our relationships in teams, projects, and groups. These are often temporary but with fixed boundaries of role and task. In efficient organisations the project or product has a set time-frame, clear authority, and allocated resources. We have to create and maintain relationships, sometimes intense and under pressure to deliver results. People are put together like an "arranged marriage" and we have to learn how to build working relationships.

Implications for our work in group relations conferences and organisations

From this perspective, there are some inferences, both from group relations experience and from the theory. Working as a consultant or a manager in organisations means we have to pay attention to the formation of groups. The relationship needs to be "healthy", contributing to the task. We need to gauge the tone of this working intimacy to ensure it does not disintegrate to BaP, or BaF/F, or BaD. We have to find ways to develop the connections to speed up the work without forcing people into superficial intimacy. The memory of team games and "icebreakers" makes people averse to enforced bonding.

We also experience that managers are losing a lot of energy trying to build this working intimacy or repairing the detachment processes that sometimes happen in these working teams. We know many cases where these managers understand that they need more personal intimacy and mistakenly invest a considerable sum of money in an outdoor activity or in "team-building". But in general, if people don't understand the differentiation between "role" and "person", then the differentiation between "intimacy" and "working intimacy" cannot be built correctly. There is a phantasy that short-term intimacy in these team-building events will be a permanent mode in the team. However, if the real dynamics (role/authority/power) are not addressed, we know that the previous types of partial relationship can re-emerge with more virulence and destructive potential.

In family business organisations, intimacy can be fundamentally confused, particularly in processes of succession. The excess of interpersonal intimacy, throughout the family history, is so strongly consolidated that the creation of working intimacy can be difficult. More privacy is sometimes connected with a diminished sense of working intimacy.

At the other extreme in larger organisations, the working process and necessary intimacy between colleagues/departments/projects are sabotaged by online communication, via email (even two feet away!). This is an example of technology that can speed communication but avoids working intimacy.

The message which all this conveys is clear. Group relations conferences offer conditions in which, in an existential and intense way, areas of working intimacy are created, completed, and transformed.

Learning the mechanisms of GR—for example, the drive to make contributions and have influence—is a meaningful experience. It is this which can be transferred to the external professional situation. It supports the argument of seeing GR conferences as a valuable place when various members of the same work unit attend together.

Our point is that distinguishing and examining the processes in relationships of intimacy, fake intimacy, and working intimacy is, without doubt, among the themes which must be considered by any institution. Even the Belgirate experience, with experienced participants, can include a phantasy of intimacy.

Conclusions

Building intimacy in a work setting is not often a conscious, defined task. It moves under the radar as a valuable function of team and project work. In exploring this concept, we have alluded to emotional intelligence and a maturity of relatedness. We hope this stimulates a wider debate and more working intimacy in the GR network.

References

Baumeister, R. F. & Leary, M. R. (1995). The need to belong: Desire for interpersonal attachments as a fundamental human motivation. *Psychological Bulleting*, *117*: 497–529.

Bowlby, J. (1969). *Attachment and Loss: Attachment*. New York: Basic Books.

Freud, S. (1930). *Civilization and its discontents* (J. Riviere, Trans.). London: Hogarth Press.

Hazan, C. & Shaver, P. R. (1994a). Attachment as an organizational framework for research on close relationships. *Psychological Inquiry*, *5*: 1–22.

Maslow, A. H. (1968). *Toward a Psychology of Being*. New York: Van Nostrand.

McAdams, D. P. & Bryant, F. B. (1987). Intimacy motivation and subjective mental health in a nationwide sample. *Journal of Personality*, *55*: 395–415.

Reis, H. T. (1990). The role of intimacy in interpersonal relations. *Journal of Social and Clinical Psychology*, *9*: 15–30.

Roma Vergés, J. (2007). *Blasfemias empresariales*. Innova Associació.

CHAPTER THIRTEEN

Belgirate as the crossroads: discovering the essence of the work elsewhere

Vivian Gold and Siv Boalt Boëthius

Introduction

An experiential international meeting can provide the opportunity to meet new people in the work, and to meet people we have known before in a new context. It also allows us to reflect upon where we have come from, as people dedicated enough to group relations work to spend time together, while on a beautiful lake in Italy, with fog and sun dancing on the lake. It encourages us to explore where we have come from in the work, where we are now, and where we are going. This particular chapter is based on the experience and reflections of two senior women, and their experiences of a very special, somewhat large subgroup, which formed itself during Belgirate III. Our focus will be on the importance of affect and bonding in all group relations experiences and on developing the tradition. We believe that our encounter reflects the importance of the personal to the collective experience in groups.

The Belgirate present

We will focus on our experience in one particular sector of the Belgirate meeting.

This exercise was similar to intergroup events in conferences. It was called "The Exploratory Event", and consisted of five sessions plus a plenary session, each session one and a half hours long. During this event the task was to explore (1) tradition, (2) creativity, and (3) succession. We could divide up and explore this in whatever ways we wished. We were approximately eighty members from seventeen countries. Many of us had attended one or both of the prior Belgirate conferences, or other similar international group relations events.

Vivian's experience

A woman from India said, as I remember, that she wanted to explore the work in less developed parts of the world, looking at the development of group relations globally, especially from the point of view of people with fewer resources. I followed this group, pulled by my 1964–1966 experiences in the Peace Corps, as well as my interest in the work of A. K. Rice and Eric Miller in India.

I did not go to the women directors' meeting. I had been at such subgroups in national and international conferences starting in the 1970s in Texas, and including a group in Oxford in the 1980s. I have directed five conferences, and feel that my strengths and limitations as a director are not due to gender issues, since many women directors have thrived doing this work. I was more interested in learning how to make group relations work relevant to global issues.

When we were together in our sector, I discovered that we were actually two groups. One subgroup was composed of those wanting to explore the application of group relations work globally, especially in under-developed places. The other subgroup was led by a woman from Europe who wanted to explore the death of tradition, mourning who and what have been lost. We were a group with two separate agendas, in some ways opposite agendas. What would we do? Would we divide again?

A man in the group suggested that we were together for a purpose, perhaps an unconscious purpose; we stayed together, struggling with the issues that arose. I definitely felt the non-linear process of a group which is self-organising. There was a profound impact, as we stayed with the tension of being in the room with people from multiple countries, and with multiple agendas.

As we stayed together, I found myself being drawn to Siv, curious as to why she was here, rather than in the group of women directors. I saw Siv as someone who is a very competent woman director, accepted by all as a leader of group relations. I was very curious.

A critical incident

During a break, Siv shared with me hurt feelings that she had experienced during a previous international meeting. She had approached the women's group at that time, and the door was closed in her face by the women in the room, who were from the United States and wanted to stay only with women from the United States. I had been in that room, although I had been working and living at that time in Israel. I had not realised that she had been turned away. I was very surprised. Instead of analysing the "why" of the closed door, I felt empathy for her. One of the most successful women warriors on the path of creating this work has had doors closed in her face, and yet gone on to lead the development of the work in Sweden, in the other Scandinavian countries, and globally. I saw the scars that we acquire on the road, as we take up leadership in this work, or in any work.

Later, after we had bonded, Siv suggested that we write about the development of this work as we see it, from our different perspectives. This writing fulfills that impulse to express what was important to each of us at Belgirate, what traditions had led to Belgirate, and what is happening in terms of succession at home.

I learned a great deal exploring the two subgroups coming together. The group I had initially joined had the overt task of exploring the difficulties in application globally. We discussed non-profits in India and elsewhere. Also, during the breaks and at meals, I spoke with members of other groups, such as a man from Catalonia, Spain who was applying group relations work in Peru and Cuba.

Members of the second subgroup prevented us from escaping the issues of our past, and what we had lost. The combined group joined together in a ritual of mourning for, and appreciation of, those people whose ideas form the basis of our work, who united us in the past, and whom we will not see again. This internal work of mourning and appreciation, held together with the exploration of where we are going, gave this group its special dynamic. We were holding together, and working on opposite impulses, desires, and passions about the work. This capacity led us to build a container for our exploration of tradition, creativity, and succession. After considerable struggle, we were able to hear each other and to learn from the experiences of others.

At Belgirate, deep feelings of connection (or disconnection) with other people emerge. We are also able to process our internal, deep struggles with the work. Belgirate was a crossroads, where we could sort out the burdens and the benefits of the work.

Siv's view of the "present" at Belgirate

When I sat in the large group, and various themes were suggested, I stayed in the room fairly long before I decided where to go. I felt the need to connect with people who worked with the application and development of group relations approaches in new directions. Like Vivian, I didn´t want to join the women directors' group. I had joined such a group during the first Belgirate conference. It had been a very positive experience positive experience, but this time I had other needs. I was occupied by a wish to get a more thorough understanding of how this theoretical frame of reference and its various applications could be developed. When the theme of application in developing countries was suggested, I was interested, but still hesitant. Then another woman proposed a theme that I resonated to how to relate the past to the present; and how to deal with the fear of the death of a tradition, and mourning what had been lost, in order to find new ways. I found myself following this small group of people.

When the groups combined, it felt very large at first. We were approximately sixteen members, probably the largest sub-group in that event. However, somehow, the dynamics in the group made the group feel alive in spite of its size. It was at times very intense and at times quite difficult, but we seemed to be able to stay with some of the difficulties. The sincerity of the people who had joined felt very real, and we actually took the time to listen to each other. The exchange of views and of personal experiences engendered a feeling of trust. I felt that many of us could talk about personal things that mattered to us.

I remember that we didn't appoint a leader, which is quite interesting considering the size of the group. Or, if we did for short periods of time, it went with the flow in a way that was helpful. Some people went out and came back after having met other groups as well as the management; somebody left and came back after a number of sessions.

In contrast to prior experiences of group relations conferences, I didn't feel the need to go out. When I ask myself why, it felt like being part of a flow of thoughts and ideas. I think it had to do with the process of trying to link ideas about what had been lost in the tradition—perhaps about what had died—and the appreciation of what had been learned, and the need to let go, in order to be able to go on, with hope and curiosity.

At the same time, I experienced important personal links. I have known some of the members for a long time and have worked with them in group relations conferences in different countries with their different cultures, languages, and nationalities. Others, like Vivian, I had met elsewhere in the group relations world, but we had so far not worked together on a common task. I was also curious about her and wanted to get to know her a bit more. The opportunity to do something together occurred to me when we spoke about our different experiences, and I felt that we might represent a generation who took over after the first generation, and created our own tradition. A succession process, with a younger generation wanting to do things their own way, was very clear in this conference as a whole, but interestingly enough, in our subgroup, this process felt more integrated compared to how it felt in the conference as a whole.

Our past, before Belgirate

Vivian's view of the tradition

No one at the conference was one of the founders of the tradition. Eric Miller would turn over in his grave to hear me call it the "Tavistock" tradition, but this is how it has become known globally, despite many variations which may be viewed either as "innovations" or "deviations". In my view, all of us who build conferences which allow people to explore, in depth, experiential learning and unconscious factors in groups, are continuing a precious tradition.

Our tradition was not developed by one set of leaders. Charla Hayden, at a conference at UCLA years ago, spoke of underground streams, of people who had learned together from the same mentors, the same sources, and with them had experienced and treasured in-depth learning. I have been privileged to swim in many streams, and to experience many leaders creating opportunities for this in-depth learning. One mentor I have shared with Siv was Lars Löfgren, who was my associate director when I directed my first conference in the 1970s. My experience of him was of solid competence, wisdom, and humor about groups.

In Israel, in the 1980s, I was one of the founding members of OFEK, and was privileged to work with the Israeli founders, such as Jona Rosenfeld, Eric Miller from the Tavistock Institute, and other eminent leaders in the field.

Since then, I have worked with three women who were instrumental in developing the work on the West Coast of the United States. Faith Gabelnick and Kathryn West have passed away. The third is Charla Hayden. These three were not alone in weaving the work in the West. However, without these three women the organisations which carry on the work would not have survived.

Siv's view of the tradition and building the work in Sweden

As mentioned by Vivian, Lars Löfgren introduced group relations conferences in Sweden. AGSLO was founded in 1974 by a number of people engaged in working with groups in industry, psychiatry, social administration, and with research, among them Britta Högberg, myself, and, later, Stefan Jern. Our first conferences were in English, and the staff members from abroad were Margaret Rioch, Garrett O´Connor, Kathryn West, and Dick Herrick. After some years I became the chairperson of AGSLO and I directed many conferences, both residential and non-residential, in Sweden and also in Norway and Finland.

After having been to a training group in Leicester, I was invited to work in France, which I did for many years, and also in Germany, Israel, and the USA. I was asked to direct group relations conferences in the Netherlands, and later, as a consultant, also in the UK, Spain, and Denmark. I had a fairly long period in my working life that was very tough, and the intense work in many group relations conferences really helped me to find new solutions to many of the problems I faced. I still feel grateful for these experiences and the unique opportunities for friendship that the conferences have given me. In all the conferences there have been people I have liked a lot and learned a great deal from. Faith Gablenick, Erika Stern, and Karien van Lohuizen have died, but most of the others from my generation are quite active, doing interesting things which I perceive as creative ways of developing group relations thinking.

The incident Vivian mentioned above occurred during the Oxford conference, where I had presented a case study of a symphony orchestra. During one event there was an invitation to join a group of women directors. I knocked on the door with a sign "Women Directors" and was told that this group was only for US women. I left and felt shut out, but it was also a valuable experience as I learned not to take things too personally. At that time there were few women directors and women who chaired group relations organisations. I remember sitting at the high table in the traditional old dining hall at the university, being the only woman in the group of presidents of national group relations organisations. It was exposing and symbolic, in a strange way.

During the first Belgirate conference, I joined a small group of women directors together with Johanna Crafoord, who is now the chairperson of AGSLO. It was a lot of fun, and we worked mainly with questions about succession and about how different group relations organisations have dealt with this issue. An important learning experience from that conference was to take responsibility for and test the reality of what you have been told, and to try to find out the facts behind specific rumours.

Over the years AGSLO has developed very well and for many years we had more than twice as many applications than we could accept. But times changed, and during the last years AGSLO has had difficulties with recruiting. These difficulties have also affected the succession process. The transition from the founding generation to the next generation has involved a lot of work, but it seems now as if AGSLO will survive, even if it will take time to find new ways of working.

The future—coming home from Belgirate

We have had a year since the conference before finalising this chapter. What have we experienced, and does our work look any different, having been in Belgirate?

Vivian

One week after the Belgirate conference, Shahin Sakhi, MD, directed a conference in Los Angeles after a two-year hiatus. It was amazing for me to witness him, an Iranian psychiatrist who had become passionately involved in this work while a resident at the UCLA psychiatry training programme, take up his first role as director. He had resurrected the conference developed by Kathryn West and others at UCLA, and put his own spin on the work. He has witnessed the struggles of large group and intergroup relations in his younger days in Iran, and he sees the current struggles in Iran through a group relations lens. He also brings an egalitarian view of authorisation. Between Belgirate and the

Los Angeles conference in a two-week period, I felt a rekindling of my passion for the work.

Before the finalisation of this writing, I was the associate director of a conference directed by Jeffrey Roth on addiction, combining group relations and twelve step processes. Dining with Jeffrey at Belgirate many times helped us develop the relationship which led to the collaboration in Chicago at his conference. The innovative aspect of his conference was not only the work on addiction, but also having a conference in which specific application was embedded throughout the process.

In addition, a second conference was directed by Shahin Sakhi at UCLA in January 2011.

A colleague brought in a newspaper article from the Los Angeles Times about me and other women engaged in interfaith activities, Muslim and Jewish women worshiping together. I enjoyed the synchronicity of seeing the article on "intergroup" in the middle of our group relations conference. My group relations work continues to permeate my activities in intergroup work across boundaries representing huge international conflicts.

Siv

One of my main concerns today is to find ways of integrating and developing this type of theoretical thinking with other aspects of work psychology, and to do this together with a group of experienced consultants and managers. I came to Belgirate this time because I was going to start a two-year masters programme in organisational psychology at Stockholm University. It had been accepted by the faculty a year before the Belgirate conference, but at a later faculty meeting many protests were raised, and the person who had been appointed as my associate was forced to resign. One reason for this was that the programme is based on systemic and psychodynamic theory; another that it includes workshops based on a group relations approach. Both these aspects were seen as very controversial, and negative rumours about group relations work were spread, but died eventually when about one hundred people expressed their interest in taking part. It was evident that the programme had attracted a large number of very qualified people. The general attitude towards the programme today is quite positive, and I think my experiences in Belgirate have been very useful in working both with the resistance to the programme and with the programme itself.

Discussion

What are some implications that can be gleaned from our group's experience at Belgirate? Here are some reflections.

When the merger of two groups representing two different agendas became apparent, there was a period of tension about what to do. When the member suggested that there might be an unconscious reason the two groups were together, there was a settling down in the group, a feeling of containment. The experience was one of *synchronicity*, the Jungian concept in which there appears to be a mystical, magical occurrence, not by chance, in which the gestalt of the group is much more than the individuals meeting together. The groups represented, in a simplified way, the past and the future coming together in the present. One of the pleasures of group relations conferences is to experience, in the absence of other agendas, this in-depth self-organising principle, or clarity emerging from chaos.

How was our subgroup related to the leadership of Belgirate? Our subgroup was a microcosm of the total system. The leadership team, consisting of Robert Baxter and Anne-Marie Kirkpatrick from the United States, Avi Nutkevitch from Israel, and Eliat Aram from England, provided the leadership and containment of Belgirate that allowed the themes of tradition, creativity, and succession to be explored. Our subgroup, in its graphic split of those who wanted to explore and metabolise the past, and those who wanted to stretch the boundaries of where our methodology can be applied, was able to sit together in a way that enabled the participants to see the importance of both agendas in order to integrate our tradition with the passion for carrying the work forward.

What characterised the process of our subgroup during the exploratory event? The authors did not experience the work primarily as "mourning", although this was definitely one important aspect present in the room. Instead, we felt we were reconnecting with the past, not only with people no longer among us, but also with those aspects of ourselves that know this dance, with people we have met before at similar dances, and with strangers who are doing exciting work elsewhere, and who are creating new dances.

There has been much past work about the "task" systems and the "sentient" systems as they contribute to the work (Miller & Rice, 1990). In 1991, Siv and Vivian each presented papers at the 10th Scientific Meeting of the A.K. Rice Institute, Siv on work in Europe (Boalt Boethus,

1993) and Vivian on her work in Israel (Gold, 1993). We met several times over the years. In Belgirate, we struggled with the confluence of sentience and task. When Siv suggested to Viv that we write together about our past experiences, we formed a bond that was actualised in the work that became this paper.

Conclusions

The Belgirate conference was a crossroads, an opportunity to meet those people who are carrying on the tradition of this work, and creating innovations for today. It is clear that the relevance of this work is as strong today as ever. It developed after WWII to help people understand the horrors and potentials of groups. This chapter gives a perspective about the meeting in Belgirate, acknowledging and mourning together those who were not present with us, digesting and metabolising a wide range of our previous experiences, hearing the Belgirate presentations of those at the cutting edge of this work, and energising us in doing group relations back home, wherever that is. It became clearer to us that our passion for this work lies in the potential to give others the opportunity to learn from their own experiences, and to become authorised to work together to tackle important social and organisational issues. Our sector at Belgirate, working on both mourning and applications, provided a space and opportunities for searching deeply into our connections with the work and with each other.

References

Boalt Boethius, S. (1993). Report on what consultants can gain from sharing experiences. In: S. Cytrynbaum & S. Lee (Eds.), *Transformations in Global and Organizational Systems: Changing Boundaries in the 90s*. Washington, DC: A. K. Rice Institute Publications.

Gold, V. (1993). Intergroup issues in a center of global conflict: The development of Tavistock group relations work in Israel. In: S. Cytrynbaum & S. Lee (Eds.), *Transformations in Global and Organizational Systems: Changing Boundaries in the 90s*. Washington, DC: A. K. Rice Institute Publications.

Miller, E. J. & Rice, A. K. (1990). Task and sentient systems and their boundary controls. In: E. Trist & H. Murray (Eds.), *The Social Engagement of Social Science: A Tavistock Anthology, Vol. 1, The Socio-psychological Perspective* (pp. 259–271). Philadelphia: University of Pennsylvania Press.

CHAPTER FOURTEEN

Manliness in the era of female leadership

Yermi Harel

I worked with Freud in Vienna. We broke over the concept of penis envy. He thought it should be limited to women.

—Woody Allen, *Zelig*, 1983

The Scottish sociologist John MacInnes, in his book The *End of Masculinity: The Confusion of Sexual Genesis and Sexual Difference in Modern Society*, concluded that it is impossible to define "masculinity" because "no such thing exists". He claims that one cannot say merely that masculinity is now in crisis, because "the briefest historical survey will show that masculinity has always been in one crisis or another" (MacInnes, 1998, p. 11).

"Man lost? Dialogue between masculinity and femininity in second-millennium organizations" was the subject of an OFEK event, and the subject of female leadership and feminisation of group relations organisations throughout the world was the main topic of the latest issue (January 2010) of *Kav-Ofek*.

In Belgirate III, as well as in Belgirate II, during the exploratory event there formed a female leadership group. By definition this title did not exclude men from being members of that group, but as it turned out, it was mostly women who were interested in the topic. A lot of feelings, associations, and thoughts arose in me as a participant in that experience, and these were the inspiration for this article.

Short description of the group and its formation

The group consisted of twelve women and two men, representing nine countries. For me, there are, as far as I am aware, two threads of motives to participating in this kind of a group; one intellectual and the other more sensual. The first episode occurred when the group gathered in a room that was in use at that time by the management of the event (minus one woman). Members from the group asked the management to leave the room because they chose it as their own in the plenary. The management accepted this claim. By leaving the room physically, they left the group with two narratives; one narrative was about aggressive occupation and banishment and the other narrative was about assertiveness, the claiming of the right to a space/territory.

From those first moments I wondered, as an observer and as a participant simultaneously, if the events were connecting to my male gender in a "female space". To my understanding, the way the group was formed also influenced the culture of the group, which was very belligerent, interested mostly in its internal dynamics and less in the relationship and relatedness to the organisation. There was much rivalry, and there were many alliances, queens, princesses, and admirers. I was swamped with feelings of excitement, being ignored, taking offense, voyeurism, and guilt. When I spoke I felt as if I was in a large group; I felt invisible and that nobody paid attention to my presence. I also noticed that the other man was quiet, and we didn't form a partnership between us. There was a lack of tenderness and generosity. In this respect, Bion, in his definition of arrogance, wrote: "The meaning with which I wish to invest the term 'arrogance' may be indicated by supposing that in the personality where life instincts predominate pride becomes self respect, where death instincts predominate, pride becomes arrogance" (Bion, 1958). These contradicting processes in relation to female leadership will be the centre of this paper.

As to the presence of men in the female leadership group, two men joined from the beginning. Two additional men joined in the second session; one was invited, and the other was "kidnapped". Both of them experienced, at different time points, disrespect and sexual discomfort.

In the mythology, men are always kidnapping women. The symbolic meaning of "kidnapping" a man by a woman, and "forcing him" to come to the group, can be seen as the little girl's wish to have a phallus of her own. Near the end of the last session, one man declared he felt offended about his erection going unnoticed by the women. This last moment event was a kind of snapshot representing the group; the ignoring and disregarding of masculinity within it. It is interesting to think about this scene with regard to the title of this chapter—"manliness in the era of female leadership".

Male, female, and succession

The primary task of the Belgirate III conference, with its theme "Tradition, creativity, and succession in the global group relations network", was to provide opportunities to learn about, and explore, the roles of tradition, creativity, and succession in the global group relations network. In practice, much emphasis was put on the succession processes.

Succession (according to Wikipedia) is the act or process of following in order or sequence. It may further refer to many fields, such as politics, business, law, religion, and urban renewal. In ecology and biology it includes generation and decay processes.

I found myself pondering the "old stereotype"; "males are for fighting wars" and "females are for upbringing children". I had thoughts and associations about female as passive, receptive, and humble and male as active, penetrating, and dominant. I also felt admiration and attraction for some women, letting myself play and be in relationship with them.

Participating in the group gave me the opportunity to open up my thinking, disassemble some representation into its fragments, and explore it at a deeper level. All this has a network of interrelated connections and disconnections. I looked at the unthinkable elements and fragments as the essence of preconception and multiple representations of female and male. As strange as it may be, I found that biology gave me the basis and the advantage for opening the concepts and thinking; the biology narrative of conception, the order of reproduction, and the corresponding psychological attitudes and feelings. These are not metaphors, for they are about embodiment processes that are located in our cells, body, and mind and are the basic experiences of the self.

Where did it all begin?
We can start at birth, where the baby's body is revealed to the world marked by the genitals of a boy or a girl, and then the process of choosing the name.

Or it is possible to start earlier from the place where sperm and egg create together the magical fertilisation, and then implantation in the womb, and then growth.

Or maybe earlier, at the times where the parents were raised and matured, and personal and family histories were transferred through the memory of the cell.

Close and far-away worlds, feelings, sensations, images, almost all human development is in one assemblage, between the biology and the mind.

Where did it all begin?
We can start with the name, or from the moment, in the plenary, when two senior experienced women suggested the group and another less experienced woman joined them, or from the place where the group of female leadership gathered and claimed the space, confronting the management of the event.

Or earlier, in Eliat Aram's lecture, which gave a fresh and inspiring look at the thinking and creativity of women's leadership in organisations. This kind of female leadership was the object of idealisation and envy.

Or perhaps in the beginning when there were two men, representing just two organisations, who formulated the idea of this conference and planned it, and then the joining of a third man, and then the first woman. This dynasty was described associatively in the conference (by a woman) as the legacy of King Arthur and Queen Guinevere.

Or perhaps in the connections between previous Belgirate conferences, with the establishment of a women's leadership group, and the last three years concurrently, which saw the empowerment of women directors in group relation conferences around the world.

We ask about the past in the light of the future. Can female leadership be a process of creation, full of growth and potential, as pregnancy and birth are symbols of progress and life? Or will it lead to the archetype of the possessing mother, the blurring boundary and destructiveness that is marked by jealousy and paralysis of transformation. This mode of thinking leads the subject of female leadership not as a contrast with male leadership. It is also not about attempting to explore the sameness and otherness, or the wish and need to be in a process of fertilisation with male leadership. That locates the exploration in the unconscious elements of male and female in men and women and to the developmental processes that mark life or death, Eros or Thanatos.

In the group I wondered if my presence disturbed the development of a space where only women could explore male and female elements. Maybe my feelings as an intruder were a projection of the women's disappointment in not creating this kind of "safe" space. These observations facilitate thinking about the quality and characteristics of male and female elements. There are two kinds of journey archetypes; the first one is the sperm's journey and the second one is that of the egg.

Embodyment of male and female elements

Big sperm race (Terry, 2002)

Of the approximately 250 million human sperm cells that enter the vagina, just a few thousand are able to enter the fallopian tubes, and only one will fertilise the egg. There are many obstacles sperm cells must overcome to reach their destination. These include: the acidic atmosphere of the vagina; the mucus of the cervix; the narrowness of the uterus-tubal junction (the entrance to the cervix); the white blood cells of the immune system, which see the sperm as a pathogenic "foreign invader" which needs to be destroyed; and what scientists think is a molecular screening process at the final checkpoint that allows only some sperm through.

The nature of the sperm competition is a race. In every ejaculation the participants undergo change. All of them, all 6,000,000 sperms, except for one, are going to die by the end of the race. (The obliteration phase aroused in me the association of "the holocaust"). During the conception phase the chosen sperm has two major tasks; the first is to lose its tail (castration) and the other is to dissolve its head and merge into the egg (surrender).

The sperm originate in the male body and stay there for a short while (three months). Then, during the ejaculation, they leave together with strong energetic forward movement. The life cycle of the sperm is characterised by being task-oriented, without fears and with a small shared past. The competition is started without selection, but the journey ends in the success of one. These qualities colour the nature of this competition.

Karl Figlio (2010) wrote about seminal masculinity, which would include the capacity to withstand and repair the corruption that undermines it: something inherent in seminal capacity, as opposed to phallic power. In seminal masculinity, the focus of ambivalence shifts from phallic dominance, which is paranoid–schizoid in organisation, to seminal, which is depressive in organisation. Phallic ambivalence is a conflict between pleasure-giving penetration and attacking penetration, fearing retaliation by loss of the penis. Seminal ambivalence is a conflict between generosity in giving semen in order to nourish, repair, and procreate, and injecting semen to pollute, with the fear of contamination or retaliation against the insides of the body, specifically the internal genitals, leaving them bad, desolate, depleted of life.

In the egg colony—inside the ovary (Terry, 2005)

The eggs' journey is very different from the sperm competition. The eggs have been present in the ovary of the woman since she was in her mother's womb. There are 20,000 eggs in every ovary. Just 200 (one percent) will mature for fertilisation. The eggs reside together and struggle for their chance. There is a place just for one. If one wins the others lose. For more than thirty years, each month, the same participants, the same processes, the same competition.

The competition of the eggs is ruthless, uncompromising, and intransigent. The winner of the ovulation phase grows significantly (thirty fold) in a short time and then separates from her sister eggs to start the journey. The egg that was selected must leave. After so many years, it is all alone. This process carries the roots and preconceptions of being with siblings, the ability to transform, separate and mourn without guilt or regret, and the ability to move and fulfill the essence of your being—to create life. The ability to separate from the old and familiar and to move on is in confrontation with these qualities of competition, envy, guilt, and melancholia. Most of the time the journey ends in death, and only a few eggs will have the opportunity to participate in a fertilisation process.

When the fetus is growing, its gender is being determined. Anatomy is destiny (Freud, 1924). The merging of these archaic pre-conceptions: competition, separation, and mourning, the aggressive force forward, the other as welcome and not as intruder, the facilitating environment, all these become unified and consolidate into a body-mind that is gendered, to be a man or a woman. The general narrative is embodied differently between individuals; a personal structure is built. This is the destiny of the personal body-mind. Everyone has male and female elements (Winnicott, 1956).

The integration of the male and the female elements is the prerequisite to creativity. There is a narrow divide between creativity and destructiveness, and it is connected to the denial of bisexuality. The main thesis of Winnicott's comments on male and female elements is that the sense of self depends on a marriage of both these elements emerging at appropriate developmental phases (Abram, 1997, p. 127).

Tango in the mind

"Learning by stealing" was one of the other themes during the conference. Many associations and dreams referred to this subject. In the group, the act of kidnapping one male figure was a significant event. It was a manifestation of the will to have something and to take it. This can be viewed as a repetition, the act over the man and the struggle over the room in the beginning of the group. Both were an act of using force. A kind of stealing.

Stealing, according to Winnicott's theory, is one of the threads of the antisocial tendency, which manifests itself in "two trends" (Winnicott, 1956, p. 125), hope versus destructiveness. But what motivates the child to steal? Winnicott asserts that the stolen object is not important. What matters is the object it stands for, the mother from whom the child at an earlier period of his life had "a right to steal", a right for something he creates in his mind. But the key here is that stealing, as "the center of the antisocial tendency", is a sign of hope. "Lack of hope is the basic feature of the deprived child" (Winnicott, 1956, p. 123), and in that way it can enable a bridge for the future.

In Belgirate III, it was cynically implied that the conference is a "convention of thieves". It is intriguing to think about what the object of stealing was in the group of female leadership, and where we should search for hope.

Destructiveness and envy between men, and repair by the women, are the essence of the old Egyptian myth; the story of Osiris and Isis. Osiris was killed by his brother Set, who was jealous of Osiris's position as king. Set took his body, and dismembered him into thirteen parts, scattering them across the land of Egypt. Each part represented one of the thirteen full moons (each year has twelve or thirteen full moons). Isis, Osiris's wife, searched for the pieces and was able to find and put together twelve of the thirteen parts. The thirteenth part, the penis, was eaten by Set. Isis fashioned a phallus out of gold and sang a song around the body of Osiris until he came back to life. Isis then conceived Horus, their son. Due to this experience, Osiris became lord of the dead and of the afterlife.

The myth also implies the act of being turned into pieces and the transformation of the body under the process of destructiveness and hope. The two journeys I described before, those of the sperm and the egg, terminate in the woman's body. There are biological systems which enable this to happen. The immune system identifies the sperm as a non-intruder, allowing it to progress towards the womb while suspending the normal defence mechanisms. This constructing of boundaries is essential for biology as it is essential for psychology. This "magical" phenomenon of suspending the immune system in order to create space for the creation of life corresponds to the ability to move between a paranoid and a depressive organisation, which may enable the development of thinking. This is also how mothers suspend their regular body-mind organisation and create a facilitating environment for the forthcoming baby, for which Winnicott coined the term "primary maternal preoccupation". In relation to this, was the group of female leadership of Belgirate III like a woman's body, which can suspend the immunity and enable the foreigner to germinate and create new life, or was it a space that could not use its internal masculinity resources, idealised phallic narcissistic elements which could not be objects for fertilisation, leading to the devaluation of the seminal masculinity within? This process leaves the group with blurred boundaries and traces of meaningless.

In Belgirate III, the story of the global group relations network is recounted. The succession is already being acted; the "castle is being conquered" by female leadership. In the central stage, the elected egg is already fertilised and she is "climbing fast up the ladder". In the back yard all the others are left with idealisation and envy.

A wish which I experienced during the group was for a "tango in the mind". In retrospect, I can add to the idea of integrating male and female elements, the necessity of music, synchronicity, pleasure, passion, and movement.

References

Abram, J. (1997). *The Language of Winnicott: A Dictionary and Guide to Understanding His Work*. Lanham, MA: Jason Aronson.

Bion, W. R. (1958). On arrogance. *Int. J. Psycho-Anal.*, *39*: 144–146.

Figlio, K. (2010). Phallic and seminal masculinity: A theoretical and clinical confusion. *Int. J. Psycho-Anal.*, *91*: 119–139.

Freud, S. (1924). The Dissolution of the Oedipus Complex. S.E. 19: 171–180.

Harel, Y. (2010). Man lost? Dialogue between masculinity and femininity in second-millennium organizations. *Kav-Ofek, 10*.

MacInnes, J. (1998). *The End of Masculinity: The Confusion of Sexual Genesis and Sexual Difference in Modern Society*. Buckingham: Open University Press.

Terry, K. (2002). The sperm journey: five biological stages and some psychological correlates. Institute for pre and perinatal education Publications.

Terry, K. (2005). The egg journey: biological stages and some psychological correlates. Institute for pre and perinatal education Publications.

Winnicott, D. W. (1956). The antisocial tendency. In: *Through Pediatrics to Psychoanalysis: Collected Papers*. London: Karnac.

CHAPTER FIFTEEN

The chains of tradition: escaping, endorsing, or exploring?

Britta Högberg and Magnus Larsson

Introduction

Contemporary society is characterised by fundamental changes[1] posing serious challenges to the intellectual and practical tradition of group relations work; challenges that concern the assumptions of what constitutes a social system, as well as how the dynamics of these systems can be understood. Within the group relations tradition (GRT), a number of creative attempts to engage with these changes have emerged. The Belgirate III conference, organised around the themes of tradition, creativity, and succession, could be seen as an attempt of this kind.

We believe, however, that these changes have also affected the self-understanding and structure of the GRT, in ways that are yet to be acknowledged, described, and explored. Based on our experiences of Belgirate III, we will reflect on this by focusing on one of the three themes: tradition. In this contribution we will argue that the ways in which tradition was perceived and related to during the conference reveal important aspects of the impact of these societal changes on the GRT.

More precisely, during the conference the perception of tradition as a prison emerged. The notion of tradition evoked feelings of being imprisoned and of losing vitality and creativity. Indeed, there were moments during the conference when we shared these feelings. In order to make sense of our experiences, we linked the notion of prison to the relation between GRT and contemporary society. In our post-conference reflections, we will argue that the perception of tradition as a prison can be understood both as a defence against the threat posed by societal changes and, at the same time, as an expression of how contemporary society at the unconscious level has shaped GRT.

First, we will describe how the notion of tradition as a prison came to our attention and our exploration of this notion during the exploratory event of the conference. Secondly, we will draw on Kristeva's (1995) and Amado's (2009) discussions of psychic imprisonment to explore this further.

The exploratory event

The primary task of the exploratory event was given in the brochure:

> The task of this event will be to explore conscious and unconscious forces and meanings underlying the conference and its themes of tradition, creativity and succession.
>
> (Belgirate III, Brochure, p. 3)

Thus the primary task comprises both the conference as a whole and its specific themes.

The event started with a plenary session in which the management stated the task of the event and clarified the territorial resources. The management announced that they considered themselves as one group among others and in which room they would work, whereupon they left. The event was thus opened in the well-known fashion of an institutional event, with the exception that the management took a different role. Embedded in this role is, as we see it, the assumption that the event did not need any managerial function or that it was to be managed collectively.

The group formation progressed by themes being proposed, groups forming and, at times, leaving the room. However, none of the suggested themes resonated with our concerns and we both lingered in the room. Gradually we became aware that tradition was not mentioned in the proposed themes. Looking back, Magnus reflects:

> A number of themes were suggested, and groups formed all around us; however a significant amount of people were still not very active. I did not feel particularly engaged in the themes that were proposed, instead I found myself somewhat disengaged and lost. Slowly, I became occupied with a feeling that much seemed to focus on trying to escape this room (as usual in an institutional event), but also that many themes seemed to struggle with doing new things and being creative. Many themes (but not all) related to two of the words in the conference theme, namely creativity and succession. I slowly became aware of the third theme, tradition, and that this seemed to be the least attractive of the three themes. This was interesting! How come? I realized that this is really what I am curious about right now—what is this thing called tradition, and what does it mean to us?

Magnus announced his curiosity and that he wanted to explore what tradition means in GRT. Quickly, a few others gathered around the project. After a few minutes a group was formed, consisting of seven members of different nationalities and experiences of working with Group Relations. We left the room and began our work.

Working with tradition in the exploratory event

We started out exploring the composition of our group. It turned out that the group consisted of pairs from three countries: Sweden, UK, and Finland;, and a single member from India. All three pairs comprised one person with very long experience of GRT and one person belonging to a later generation. Hence the theme of succession was embedded in the relations between the group members. Our subsequent explorations of the theme of tradition included reflecting on how the group was formed and on our experiences in the here-and-now and actively exploring the system that emerged during the exploratory event.

When exploring the connotations of the notion of tradition, held by ourselves and others, we found links to founding fathers and mothers, rituals and rites. For example, designing a group relations conference was perceived as something to be done "as always done", that is, it emerged as something of a ritual.[2] As our data accumulated, tradition appeared more and more as a hindrance to creative collaboration. This was reflected in expressions like "breaking free of tradition", looking upon tradition as a prison and being imprisoned by it. Tradition was also associated with orthodoxy.

Our work started in a spirit of curiosity and engaged collaboration. We enjoyed our explorations within the group as well as our contacts with other groups. However, as the event progressed we lost our energy and felt imprisoned. From being a group exploring tradition, we now experienced ourselves as transformed into tradition, not quite knowing whether we were perceived as a dragon in its cave or a pitiful fossil.

Eventually we were revived by a number of visitors. These rapprochements provided us with new material for our understanding of why tradition was experienced as a prison. One theme was the indigestible tradition, enacted when different visitors ended up in the bathroom[3] on their way out. This was interpreted as: interaction with traditions was simply indigestible and had to be evacuated immediately.

Another theme was: to sacrifice to tradition. This was enacted by younger women who approached one of the senior male members of the group with seductive charm, thus placing tradition between the "king" and the "princess". Britta reflected that the roles left to senior female members seemed to be that of "the wicked stepmother" or "the dragon in the cave". Indeed, when visiting the group of female directors, she witnessed how a male visitor was rebuked and forced to leave the room, as in the fairytale when the dragon spat fire on the challenging prince. By conflating gender and generation, tradition could be split into a good and bad part. The good part could be preserved by putting the future of GRT in the combination of younger women and senior men while the bad parts were to be harboured in the group of senior women. When looking back, Britta concludes:

> For me as a senior female member, I felt that my genuine concern for the younger generation was perverted. I felt that I either had to accept the role as a bitter and envious old lady or warble along in the idealization of the "princesses" that at times were produced by the conference. The only other option was to withdraw and

> disclaim my experience and desire to contribute, and that made me feel imprisoned, indeed.

Tradition as a prison

As described above, our work during the exploratory event provided us with rather rich material on how tradition was experienced as a prison and seen as an obstacle to creativity and succession. To further analyse this, we will use the notion of psychic imprisonment, as described Kristeva (1995) and Amado (2009).

Kristeva (1995) conceives the psyche as an open system, where the body interacts with culture and language. If this interaction fails, the psychic space might collapse or become imprisoned, meaning that the psyche becomes closed and turns on itself. She further emphasises the role of language, arguing that verbal expression is a necessary link between "psychological rumination" (Kristeva, 1995, p. 29) and the cultural environment. Without possibilities for this linguistic interaction, the psyche becomes imprisoned and left to its own ruminations, losing vitality and generative capacity.

While Kristeva focuses on the individual in relation to the cultural environment, Amado (2009) focuses on contemporary tendencies to create imprisonment in organisations. He argues that imprisonment is related to reduction of otherness, and that the impulse to imprison emerges from a wish to annihilate differences. Through closing the psychic system from creative interactions with the environment, the potential pain of differentiation is avoided and otherness reduced, at the price of loss of desire, generativity, and creativity. Amado further outlines how psychic imprisonment is created in social systems by describing seven traps, commonly found in contemporary organisations[4]:

1. A "collaborationist" form of participation
2. The attack on professions
3. The hypomania for individualised assessment
4. The ideological alibis that people internalise
5. The stimulation of the ego ideal
6. The scrapping of conflict
7. The capture of the imaginary through stories.

This outline might help us in exploring how GRT was turned into a prison. In order to do so, we need to look at the conference as a whole.

We have identified three major ways of relating to tradition: escaping, endorsing, and exploring.

Escaping tradition

Within the Belgirate III conference, we found elements of escape from imprisonment in initiatives that were labeled "creative" or "fostering innovation". During the exploratory event, this was evidenced through expressions like "wish to break out of the verbal prison" as well as through the enactment of this wish in non-verbal activities, such as dance, music, sculptures, and craftwork. Surely, non-verbal activities may very well be a vehicle for learning, but here during the exploratory event we experienced an escapist quality in them.

Further, the escape of tradition emerged in keynote and paper presentations. Innovations, such as introducing music and yoga as conference events were presented as challenges to GRT. However, we failed to recognise how such events would promote the study of social and organisational systems; they seemed to be more oriented towards the intrapsychic world of conference members and to facilitate individual learning rather than deeper understanding of the social context. To us, innovations like these, as discussed during the conference, reflected a wish to escape from traditional parts of GRT, its theoretical foundation as well as its practice of using words in the exploration of roles and systems.

Such inward tendencies may have contributed to the imprisonment and can be seen as a "psychologization" of the social that Amado finds inherent in psychic imprisonment (Amado, 2009, p. 10). Further, avoiding the mobilisation of skills and intellectual resources, that is inherent in GRT, could be interpreted as an attack on professions, as the attempts at professional and personal differentiations were harassed.

Traditional conferences are firmly anchored in reality through the transparency of authority, roles, and boundaries. This anchorage is a central element in GRT, seen as a necessity for the exploration of unconscious processes in social systems. The design of the Belgirate conference, on the other hand, made the structure quite obscure. What was visible in the opening of the exploratory event applies to the conference as a whole, in which the authority embedded in defined roles such as management, convenor, and chair seemed to be jettisoned.

Avoiding differentiation and disclaiming authority contributed to Amado's first trap, a "collaborationist" form of participation.

As a consequence, the boundary between the inner and outer world was blurred, which constitutes, as we see it, one of the mechanisms behind endorsing tradition as prison.

Endorsing imprisonment

Another way of relating to tradition was to perceive it as a place providing safety against a chaotic environment, and as such it was endorsed and applauded.

One form of endorsement was reflected in the way "traditional scientific papers" were organised. Neither abstracts nor text were available beforehand, as is customary in academic settings. This limited the distance necessary for reflective engagement with the content. Further, the content of the papers was mainly about personal or group experience, without the necessary analysis to make them into case studies. Emphasising the emotional appeal of narrative form did not facilitate conceptual and theoretical clarification, critique, and development. Labeling this format "scientific" seemed to us to be mimicry of the academic world, which resonates with Amado's traps "scrapping of conflict" and "the use of narratives". The format of "the scientific papers" endorsed the urge to close off the contemporary cultural and intellectual environment, and thus jumble subjective experiences and academic authority.

Further, in various plenaries we often shared an experience of having become part of a revivalist movement. Under the notion of "we who do this work", we saw members indulge in the desire to bring salvation to the world. Changes in society were often addressed in a negative, almost repulsive tone. Clearly, we were in the grip of a basic assumption mode. The prevailing mode, we suggest, is that of BaOne. Turkey (1974) characterises this as joining in a powerful union with omnipotent and unobtainable forces, and to surrender self for passive participation and thereby feel existence, wellbeing, and wholeness.

In line with how Bion discussed societal institutions as embodying basic assumptions, Krantz (2009) suggests that the modal institution for BaO in contemporary society is fundamentalism, of which he sees reflections throughout society. BaO emerged in what we experienced as group relations fundamentalism. Here tradition emerged as a "received truth", not to be re-interpreted or critically engaged with. In fundamentalism, interpretative meaning and nuanced conversations are turned into numbing stereotypes, reminiscent of Kristeva's (1995) description of "psychic ruminations". Such cultural homogenisation and scripted language is, according to Kranz, accompanied with rigid prohibitions against reflecting on experiences and exploring prescriptive approaches to human interaction. One such prohibition is challenging the conviction that senior GRT consultants are inoculated against the forces of basic assumptions. Strauss (2007) observed this phenomenon at the previous Beligrate conferences as well.

Exploring imprisonment

In this contribution we have explored our experiences of the dominating meaning of tradition in the GRT Network. Through the theoretical lenses of Kristeva and Amado we have explored the prison metaphor and the experience of imprisonment further. We suggest that two different strategies can be identified in relating to and enacting the chains of tradition: either escaping or endorsing them. As enactment, both strategies tend to empty crucial elements of group relations work, such as task, role, and authorisation, of their meaning.

Further exploration would include trying to understand the underlying dynamics contributing to the notion of tradition as a prison. Here we will briefly indicate a few possible directions.

First, one important aspect of contemporary societal changes is that the network has emerged as a new social form. By definition, a network has no centre and, dynamically, it operates on the binary logic of inclusion/exclusion. Castells argues that networks are value-free and neutral: "they can equally kill or kiss: nothing is personal" (Castells, 2000, p. 16). Thus, inherent in network dynamics is the lack of recognition of the Other that transforms the most basic element of GRT—that of relations. It seems that what was experienced in Belgirate was a forceful superimposition of the network as social form over the more hierarchical form inherent in GRT.

Second, we would suggest that GRT suffers from a lack of engagement with the intellectual environment, evidenced in the general scarcity of engagement with social science and organisational literature evidenced in papers and discussions. The inability to mobilise the intellectual resources for engagement with contemporary organisational and social phenomena could be related to idealisation of psychoanalysis with its tendency to interpret such phenomena as pathological, to be treated in the same way as individual pathology. This therapeutic approach is in line with the neutral and value-free stand embedded in the network as a social form. Thus the lack of engagement could be related to forces wanting to preserve the psychoanalytic doxa and personal identities stemming from this doxa.

Third, the critique of the "therapeutic culture" (Illouz, 2008) has made the societal relevance of GRT more problematic. In his exploration of this, Sher (2009) observes that GRT does not fit into any of the social domains it is linked to nor does it constitute a domain of its own. What emerges is a rather ambiguous societal position of GRT, and along with the aforementioned changes in society, this ambiguity is growing more problematic. This problematic position, with its pertaining problem with the legitimacy of GRT, was, as we see it, denied during the Belgirate conference and projected into the notion of tradition as prison, enacted in the mimicry of academia and in the group relation fundamentalism.

GRT's position has always been problematic, but now it faces the risk of being expelled from contemporary society. Like the spaceship Aniara in Martinsson's poem (Martinsson, 1963), GRT seems to float away in space with no destination and no control over its course. Facing the threat of losing its fragile link to society, the inhabitants of the spaceship tend to turn inwards and idealise the vessel that was turned into prison, denying the need for connection with the external and quickly changing society. In closure, it is our firm conviction that there are a lot of useful and valuable tools in the attic of tradition that could vitalise the exploration of the relation between GRT and the societal context of today.

References

Amado, G. (2009). Psychic imprisonment and its release within organizations and working relationships (Opus Conference, London 21–22 November). *Organisational and Social Dynamics, 9*: 1–20.

Barker, J. (1993). Tightening the iron cage: Concertive control in self-mamaging teams. *Administrative Science Quarterly, 38*: 408–437.

Castells, M. (2000). Materials for an exploratory theory of the network society. *Britsh Journal of Sociology, 51*: 5–24.

Foucault, M. (1980). *Power and Knowledge*. Brighton: Harvester.

Geertz, C. (1973). *The Interpretations of Cultures. Selected Essays*. New York: Basic Books.

Illouz, E. (2008). *Saving the Modern Soul. Therapy, Emotions and the Culture of Selfhelp*. Berkley: University of California Press.

Jermier, J., Knights, D. & Nord, W. (1994). *Resistances and Power in Organizations*. London: Routledge.

Krantz, J. (2009). The evolution of basic assumptions in twenty-first organizations. *Socio-Analysis, 11*: 1–15.

Kristeva, J. (1995). *New Maladies of the Soul*. New York: Columbia University Press.

Martinson, H. (1963). *Aniara: A Review of Man in Time and Space*. London: Knopf.

McKinlay, A. & Starkey, K. (1994). *Foucault, Management and Organization Theory: From Panopticon to Technologies of the Self*. London: Sage.

Sher, M. (2009). Splits, extrusion and integration: The impact of "potential space" for group relations and sponsoring institutions. *Organisational and Social Dynamics, 9*: 138–154.

Strauss, G. (2007). Learning from experience: The two international group relations meetings in Belgirate. In: E. B. Aram & R; Nutkevitch, (Eds.), *Adaptation and Innovation: Theory, Design and Role-taking in Group Relations Conferences and their Applications*. London: Karnac.

Townley, B. (2004). Managerial technologies, ethics, and managing. *Journal of Management Studies, 41*: 425–445.

Turquet, P. M. (1974). Leadership: The individual and the group. In: G. S. Gibbard et al. (Eds.), *The Large Group: Therapy and Dynamics*. San Francisco: Jossey-Bass.

Notes

1. See Castells (2000).
2. A ritual is here understood in line with Geertz (1973) as an action motivated by symbolic or mythological meanings attributed to it, rather than by instrumental objectives.
3. Our room was in the hotel part of the premises, equipped with bathroom and foldaway bed.
4. It might be noted that Amado's elaboration of psychic prison is very akin to discussions in the organisational literature about symbolic control (Jermier, Knights & Nord, 1994), concertive control (Barker, 1993), and construction of subjectivity (Foucault, 1980; McKinlay & Starkey, 1994; Townley, 2004). However, Amado does not link to this field.

CHAPTER SIXTEEN

How envy, fear of envy, and manipulation of envy can paralyse healthy competition and healthy succession

Lilian Hupkens

Is envy allowed to see the daylight?

This reflection absolutely refused to be written. It seemed as if the whole cosmos collaborated into its neither seeing daylight nor being born. When I promised a reflection about envy and succession, and this was accepted by the editors early in 2010, I had more than enough time in which to write it.

Then health issues, international travel, volcanoes and ash clouds, hurricanes, and death of a close family member intervened and took up so much time that this reflection almost stayed unformed in the mind and thus unborn.

However, there is also an inner world. I realised that if I wanted to make my point clear, to base my thinking on evidence seen and experienced in the conference, I would have to name individuals. In such a small community this could be problematic because people tend not to read what is written but to read what they think is there. On the other hand, not naming individuals can create a rarefied atmosphere which leaves much space for phantasies and speculation. Vagueness, however politely meant—and hoping readers will understand what you mean to say—can lead to feeling that there is a "group of insiders" of those who know and a "group of outsiders" who don't know.

I had to find a balance between using names and describing in a more circumspect way. When I found the balance, I could write. My decision was to name only those people who had formal and public roles in the conference.

In retrospect, envy is such a difficult emotion to feel and to bear that I should not have been surprised that a reflecton on envy was difficult to produce.

Why envy?

An idea germinates

During the opening plenary, the management team (MT) of three and the administrator sat in front of the membership opposite to them and introduced themselves as being representatives of the three joint sponsors: group relations programme of the Tavistock Institute in London, OFEK in Israel, and AKRI in the United States. They spoke of, amongst other subjects, developments in the field and the sometimes fragility of the institutes. It would seem they were representatives from three different countries. Actually what was visible, from the "audience", were two Americans and two Israelis. England, with the Tavistock Institute as original designer and intellectual owner of the group relations conference model, seemed not represented. So my first question was "Where are the English?"

Later, I was told by a UK member that at that moment, sitting in the back row, a senior English person in this field had said to his neighbour "Here we are, in the back".

There was a great deal of confusion, both in professional identities and in nationalities. Eliat Aram was in the MT as representative of the group relations programme of the Tavistock, when in fact Mannie Sher is the director of that programme and was a conference member. Eliat Aram had two other roles—director of the Tavistock Institute as a whole and, in recent years, director of the Leicester conference. From which role was she speaking and in which role was she seen?

This links to the question of Eliat being, at least originally, from Israel and also an OFEK member, and Mannie Sher being originally South African. This led to a string of thoughts at that moment:

- Why is there no English-born successor?
- Has no one else stepped up?
- What role has envy played in subduing competition?
- Or, have Eliat and Mannie been set up by the English? For success or for failure: "let a foreigner do the dirty work".
- But what then is the "dirty work"?
- Is this the "glass cliff" phenomenon?

These thoughts stayed with me during the next event.

Exploratory event

Opening plenary exploratory event

Space to investigate these thoughts further became available in the exploratory event.

> "The task of this event will be to explore conscious and unconscious forces and meaning underlying the conference and its themes of tradition, creativity and succession. The event will open in a plenary session and, after five sessions, conclude in a plenary discussion."

In the opening plenary session I put an embryonic thought into words and that was that "envy and fear of envy inhibit succession". This led to reactions of interest and expression of recognition. Geographically, quite a large group formed but as other more attractive subjects came up the initial group of more than ten dwindled into three. It seemed as if the subject was "too hot to handle". Group members were Frans Cilliers from South Africa, myself from the Netherlands, and Mario Perini from Italy.

Later we found out that we were the smallest group in this conference. The other groups had been quite large, between ten and fifteen persons each.

Looking back, we think that our group worked efficiently, intuitively, and went into great depth. Our work took place in the following phases:

1. first internal exploration
2. formulation hypothesis number one

3. testing of hypothesis, each member visited one or more other groups
4. internal discussion
5. formulation hypothesis number two
6. testing of hypothesis by visiting other groups as a whole group
7. internal discussion again before plenary
8. plenary.

First phase, internal work

We started our group work by using ourselves as resources. We identified who we were, our experience in the field of group relations, and our own experiences around envy. Mario Perini was one of the two founders of Italian group relations work. Frans Cilliers was a pioneer in taking group relations work into organisations within South Africa and helped design the Robben Island diversity experience.

The author has been active in the group relations field from 1993, first as a member and later as a staff member of conferences in Netherlands, France, England, Germany, and Turkey. My role has been more like a "midwife", helping other colleagues develop their own conferences.

Our first hypothesis was that envy paralyses successful succession because the fear of envy stopped people from openly showing their competencies and prevented open competition and succession processes. "If I stick my neck out, they will kill me".

Discussing envy within a group relations institute, we identified several types of envy, namely between founders, between followers, and between those groups. Put into a table, we have the following:

Type of Envy	TOP	DOWN
TOP	1. Envy between founders/seniors	3. Younger colleagues envy founders or seniors
DOWN	2. Seniors envy younger colleagues	4. Envy between younger/followers of founders

1. Top—Top: envy and competition between founders
2. Top—Down: founders envious of colleagues who come later

3. Down—Top: newer and younger colleagues envious of position, status of founders
4. Down—Down: between newer and younger members: sibling rivalry and envy.

Envy types one and three make abdication difficult for senior members or founders. "I am not going to give up my position if a fellow founder stays in place", and "If I have something others envy, I won't let go of it". This is often expressed as "The younger generation just isn't good enough."

Envy types two and four generate a fear of being envied, fear of standing out, so younger people stay low profile and hide their skills.

In our subgroup on envy and succession, we then worked on the question of how to survive envy. As resources we again used our own experiences; we had all experienced envy in its different forms, including the pains of envy and of envious attacks. We identified the following valuable lessons:

A. Don't be afraid of envy, but realise it's there and accept it.
B. Don't go for a low profile, but keep your high profile.
C. Realise you are carrying the projections of many others, be prepared to carry them and to tolerate them.

Why is envy so difficult to bear?

Envy is a difficult subject, and in large parts of psychoanalytic theory and literature it simply does not exist. For example, an article about envy in the Netherlands Journal for Psychoanalysis in the late 1990s stated that for nearly fifty years that word had not appeared in Dutch psychoanalytic literature. Envy is one of the greatest taboos, even from Biblical times. After all, the second story in the Old Testament is about Cain murdering his brother Abel—rivalry and envy.

Melanie Klein is the first psychoanalyst to give it a place in psychoanalysis. Kleinians and object relations-oriented thinkers use this term and the term "envious attack". An envious attack is difficult to recognise, and even when recognised it is difficult to bear. In June 1995, Brenda Dean, who directed a non-residential conference in the Netherlands, said with great feeling, "OK, so you recognise envy and you know what it is, but does it hurt any the less? Does it help you bear the pain? I find it doesn't help me at all, it still hurts me."

Melanie Klein and others explain how the baby, envious of mother's breast and lovely milk, wants to destroy the mother and the breast by invading it, to poison the milk. In an envious attack a person feels physically attacked and invaded. It goes further than feeling someone wants to take something away from you. Like Cain's attack on Abel, an envious attack feels like a murderous attack; the other wants to annihilate you, to make you cease existing.

Our subgroup then asked the question, "Can envy be useful? Can we identify any positive aspects?" We differentiated between envy and emulation. Emulation makes you admire the Other and instead of wanting to destroy the Other, it stimulates you to develop, to try to be as good as the Other.

Envy is based on the assumption that there is only one good object. Emulation is based on the assumption that there are two good objects. The Other is good and I can work to become just as good. Then emulation can lead to generativity, as Erickson calls it, and to generosity, passing on knowledge and position to the next generation.

Second and third phase, hypothesis, and contacting other groups

We formulated a hypothesis remembered as "Fear of envy leads to people not daring to show their qualities and avoiding competition; this make a healthy succession process difficult".

The next phase was to visit the other groups. We agreed to share our hypothesis with the visited groups and to report back with our findings, our experiences, our observations and thoughts. These observations and thoughts are described here very briefly in outlines, as well as the images we came back with.

A group calling itself "Creativity" sat around on the floor and on chairs, playing with string, twigs, and flowers from outside, weaving something. The atmosphere was felt to be 1970s, a hippie kind of feeling to the room, a very relaxed attitude, everything was OK. Almost as though everyone had smoked pot/marijuana.

The group calling itself "Management Team" seemed to have no inner differentiation; the differentiation in roles described in the brochure were not visible, all were equal. We did not know in which room they were. They had not chosen a room beforehand and Eliat Aram, who stayed a little longer, told Avi Nutkevic to just go and take any room. On entering that room, the discussion going on with another visitor was around the issue of whether there was going to be a fourth Belgirate conference at all. This led to anxiety with the visitors. To them it seemed as if "all power and authority had been abdicated", "that there was no leadership, as if that function was vacant". The opinion of the MT was that this "abdication" was a good thing and should be stimulating to the membership. Our hypothesis was listened to respectfully and appreciatively.

One other group seemed at that moment not to really know yet what they were doing, did not have a name yet, and discussed breaking up into sub-subgroups.

In the group "Tradition", the reception was courteous and the image of the process going on at that moment was "older people are talking the most and explaining to others who listened respectfully".

We came back to our working room to share the experiences, observations, thoughts, and impressions. This led to an image of the whole conference being in flight-mode, in denial. It was not working to the task at hand "to explore conscious and unconscious forces and meaning underlying the conference and its themes of tradition, creativity and succession". The groups had an "as if" quality, going through the motions but not really addressing any of the issues or their relatedness.

As a way of surviving envy we had come up with the guideline, "Realise you are carrying the projections of many others, be prepared to carry them and to tolerate them". Implementing this guideline, we decided to use our counter-transferences as a resource in studying the dynamics of the whole conference. We decided to take a good look at our own feelings and to explore them. We expressed feeling personal pain and loneliness, feeling not being seen, being excluded, not being recognised, as having no part in the international group relations scene. Because this subjectivity did not fit into external reality, a further development of the hypothesis was that it was envy itself that was being denied, that had no place in the conference, and that by making us feel excluded as a group, the envy could be pushed out of the conference. More or less like the scapegoat phenomenon.

This hypothesis seemed to be confirmed when at that very same moment several people rushed into our room without knocking, convinced our room was an empty space designated for a meeting, to discuss what to do when members left the conference. Our existence as a group was denied and our working space could be appropriated for any other purposes, for example, deciding on how to spend a free afternoon.

Fourth and fifth phase, hypothesis number two, and testing it

After a break we formulated a second version of the hypothesis along the lines of "The conference is in flight mode with all subgroups denying envy and competition. This denial has a dampening effect on the dynamics within each group". To test this second version we went to all other groups, together as one group. Here follows a brief description of the different subgroups, what their reactions were, and how we experienced and processed the interaction. We had decided beforehand to stay for fifteen minutes and to then move on.

The group "Creativity" sat around a piece of weaving, on chairs or on the ground. They were very proud of it and proud of having improvised, using material from the garden and the hotel. They appeared friendly and interested and in retrospect seemed vitalised by our visit.

Altogether opposite to the prevailing relaxed atmosphere, an older woman from Scandinavia questioned us in a criticising and interrogating manner, in a quasi-consultative stance, saying we were just describing ourselves. We overstayed our fifteen minutes, staying longer out of politeness. When we did leave, the same Scandinavian woman attacked us, questioned our leaving and suggested we found her questions too difficult. Her behaviour was that of a small group consultant in a consulting role.

"Guru" group. A group downstairs in a room next to the management team contained many of the "gurus" of the group relations network. We found it was a large group, with people hanging around rather than sitting in their chairs. The discussion seemed dispirited and went round and round in circles; we could not discern a clear subject. One of us found himself falling asleep sitting there. Our impression was that they were bored, and as a group we found them boring also.

The group "Tradition" was in a small room, and with so many people in it, it was a very full room. The group members were mostly middle-aged or older. During our first visit a senior member from the UK had patiently explained past history with colleagues listening politely and almost admiringly. Now in the second visit they seemed very "busy" in a work-like mode that seemed attractive to us. They were interested in our work and made a meaningful connection with us.

"Group Left in Plenary Room". The large room that had actually been designated for intergroup meetings was occupied by people who had remained there after the opening plenary session. It was an extremely relaxed group and they seemed extremely satisfied with themselves. A senior member from the USA (over seventy) applauded their attitude of "taking it slow and easy", saying it had been a conscious decision and it was a very good thing because it was new and different. They did not agree with our hypotheses and criticised us for doing it the "old way"; according to them we were far too active and just stuck in a traditional "intergroup activity".

Sixth phase, internal discussion before plenary

After all our visits, we reflected and felt that the interactions confirmed our hypothesis, that the groups were denying competition and envy, and that bringing in the "envy" group seemed to bring life to the subgroups. The whole conference seemed to be so overly relaxed, detached, and disengaged that we had images of a "retirement village", a holiday settlement like Club Med or *pensionados* on a cruise ship. Perhaps the underlying assumption was "Make love, not war", banning "war" by banning competition and envy.

Clearly in each group we had been lectured to, silenced, criticised, and attacked by people over seventy years of age, almost treated like stupid children. This observation made sense later in the plenary reflection that ended the exploratory event.

Seventh phase, exploratory event plenary

During the exploratory event closing plenary the people who spoke the most, and very confidently, were all members around or over seventy years old, as if from a comfortable armchair position, secure in the knowledge everyone was listening and that no one dared interrupt them. The question under discussion was "Is tradition impeding succession or creativity?". Yet, at the same time, there was an atmosphere of general discontent and disappointment.

Then the thought struck me that perhaps it was not tradition in a general sense stifling succession or creativity but people, individuals, who were. The evidence was that identifiable older members, who had been in the field for forty years or more, were speaking most, claiming air space, and literally not giving up their positions, but hanging on as long as possible.

More evidence was that for nearly each country, it was possible to identify two persons, one an elder person, around seventy or older, taking on a position and the other an identifiable younger person, in her/his fifties or sixties, who was waiting patiently on the sidelines. More evidence for this hypothesis was our experience of visiting the subgroups where in nearly each group someone of more than seventy years of age had lectured us, corrected us, questioned us, and treated us like delinquent or stupid children. Whilst in reality our ages were fifty-six, fifty-eight, and sixty-one respectively, and two group members were founders in their own country's tradition.

Parallels of this phenomenon can be found in the outside world, for example, the royal houses of the UK and the Netherlands. Queen Elizabeth in the UK is staying on in her eighties with Prince Charles over sixty, still not considered good enough to be King. The press says she is waiting for her grandson in his twenties to be the successor. Which leaves the question: is he being set up for success or for failure, or at least being impossible to compare with grandma who has more than sixty years of experience?

In the Netherlands the same thing is happening. Queen Beatrix, a widow, now over seventy years old, is still showing no signs of going into retirement, of abdicating. Her son, forty-five-year-old Crown Prince Willem-Alexander, is being "given space to raise a family" and to "develop wisdom".

Extra support for this hypothesis was the comment that the OFEK members seemed so much at ease. Not publicly, but personally, members from Israel said to me that it had been much easier for the "younger" generation, although nearly sixty years old, with Mira and Shmuel Erhlich not present as the "Father and Mother" of OFEK.

Succession, by birthright or appointment

In the final plenary, this issue of the absence of competition for succession came forward in a fairy tale told by a member from the USA. She spoke about the safety of the Tavistock tradition, of Leicester being like Avalon where Eric Miller and Olya Khalalee had ruled like King Arthur and Queen Guinevere. After King Arthur had died, Mannie Sher (in a role as Merlin?) had then gone to his home country and had brought back a princess, Eliat Aram, who was to rule from now on. This phantasy was admired, and there were angry reactions to bringing in reality elements, such as the fact that Mannie Sher is originally from South Africa, not Israel. Mannie Sher himself described the rigorous selection process where the board of trustees had decided Eliat was the best person for the job in a field of stiff competition.

The magical thinking described here demonstrates that competition is so dangerous in a succession situation that a successor must be appointed and anointed. If open competition is not possible, if there is no transparent succession process in place, then the solution is appointment, becoming a royal successor by birth-right, not by competency, and if not by birth then by adoption.

My understanding is that envy and fear of envy make open and transparent competition so dangerous that the competition is avoided. Exploiting this, older colleagues in the field hold on to their relatively powerful positions by manipulating envy and stimulating envy. They do this by way of their staff positions in group relations conferences. It is never clear why or how staff consultants are chosen and invited. Also it is my experience that, within conference staff, allusions are often made about consultants having different levels of experience and expertise. This makes people insecure and nervous about "upsetting the boat". The seniority which may be relevant within a conference staff is then taken into the outside world. In this conference, it was easy to identify two groups, the "have's" and the "have-nots". The have's were relaxing on a cruise and the have-nots were busy applying for jobs.

Further evidence that this last hypothesis about individuals blocking succession comes from an analysis of the title of the Belgirate III conference—"Tradition, creativity, and succession in the global group relations network".

The words "tradition, creativity, and succession" are general terms and the "global group relations network" is a virtual network, one that is not defined and has no clear boundaries. In this conference title, neither the individual nor the institutions are named.

My thought is that this hiding or masking has made it difficult, if not impossible, to deal with the real issues at stake. The issue is: how do individual persons become successors in their national institutions, each with their own tradition?

Later Reflection

Half a year after the Belgirate III conference, the three members of the original group "Envy and Succession"—Frans Cilliers, Mario Perini, and I—reflected back on our process by exchanging emails. We felt we had taken the work very seriously—working hard, staying in a lot of the time, thinking, and working on hypotheses. Our visits created anxiety for us—maybe we took on the performance anxiety while the other groups took on the denial of anxiety.

We had been a small group and the others larger—"the work gets done in small and serious pockets" versus "the laid-back atmosphere (holiday style) attracts large numbers".

We also felt isolated—as if the system rejected us and what we represented. There seemed to be ambiguity in the feelings other groups had about us, the "Envy" group. On the one hand, we were different, and therefore attracted "opposite projections", both envy and isolation. On the other hand, a group doing hard work and being busy with the task was experienced as attractive and meaningful, but it also created envy in the system.

The role our group played in the whole could be that the three of us had been "used" by many groups, and maybe by the whole conference, as a container of others' envious feelings, which were perceived as too dangerous within the succession process. The envy and the danger were therefore denied and projected onto us, a projective identification leading us to become or feel like an isolated, excluded, and envious/envied subgroup.

CHAPTER SEVENTEEN

Some reflections on the experience of Belgirate III: tradition, creativity, and succession in the global network from a lateral perspective

Jacqueline Sirota

This chapter is a reflection on some of the themes expressed in recurring words, images, activities, and concepts, including the geographical setting on the shores of Lake Maggiore in Italy. Given that so much of our thinking was about the meaning of networks and peer culture, I'm writing these reflections from a lateral/sibling perspective in relation to the vertical dynamics suggested by group relations tradition grounded in the psychoanalytic theory of Freud, Klein, and Bion, where interpretations are generally offered from vertical power relationships.

Themes include founding fathers and mothers, dynamics of succession, freedom, equality, and the desire for leaders to meet our fear of peers. These include creative pairings, (that is, generative), but also the "sibling" pairings that are more connected to the idea of "polymorphous perversity" curiosity, playfulness, aggression, and creativity as the result of unusual pairings (Koestler, 1964).

An opening dream seemed to present us with an uncomfortable picture of a dark aspect of power and the exercise of assumed rights. It suggested archetypal images of the "Primal Father", Kronos devouring his children and an image of a female "star" working to rescue them.

Belgirate III was the third conference for members who have taken formal roles in group relations conferences as directors, consultants, and administrators. My interest and investment in attending was to participate in, and learn from, the thinking that goes into the creation of conferences and the shaping of their future in a changing global scene.

I am writing as one not closely affiliated to any of the group relations organisations and therefore with no real knowledge of the workings of them. The thoughts and reflections come from personal experience of the Belgirate III conference and the fantasies and projections that inevitably accompany them.

These reflections attempt to pick up and invite associations to some of the fragments and strands that seemed to be weaving in and out of the conference. Central to these is a dream that arrived at the very beginning of the conference that seemed to run counter to the post-modern lateral nature of networks and matrices. It suggested something about what might be lying beneath the surface, an "old order" like monsters of the deep, emerging as a shocking image. This dream continued to occupy my thoughts beyond the ending of the conference, and informed these reflections.

I wondered about the function and price of leadership and succession with the implication that something inevitably has had to "die", be displaced or lost, and where "latent violence inherent in the trauma of displacement by another (person or idea) who is like oneself", but also other (Sirota 2005) in a network rather than a hierarchy that contains, as Juliet Mitchell (2000) proposed, murderous potential on the lateral plane. The group relations tradition is founded on the vertical axis of parent/child interpretations of classic psychoanalysis. My interest and writing has been to invite exploration of the lateral axis (Sirota, 2003) and how this dimension might contribute to the way GR Conferences are conceptualised (Armstrong, 2007; Huffington & Miller, 2008).

This was my second attendance at the Belgirate Conference so I already had a picture of the place, its setting, and memories of the last gathering. This time I had a room with a full length window looking across the lake. Afforded this beautiful view, I could sit back and observe the movement of the mist and cloud concealing and revealing the distant mountains. On reflection, it seemed to offer a metaphor for my conference experience in that sometimes it was impossible to see anything through the veil of mist, then, looking again, the mountains became visible, opening up a larger vista and a clearer view like the different configurations of formal and informal groupings, individual exchanges, dreams and associations, and often having a sense of not knowing or understanding the communications taking place all around.

I watched as torrential rain, like a scornful outpouring, drove arriving members inside the hotel, deterring any further exploration of the surroundings. Beneath the lake, like the surface exchanges of our gathering, the mountains, like the unconscious, disappeared into the depth, their shape lost to all except those whose work and interest take them beneath the surface, as, of course, we do in engaging with the exploration of human depth.

In this setting I found myself thinking about *The White Hotel* (Thomas, 1981), the novel based on one of Freud's analysands, which begins with the fantasy of an erotic encounter with his son on a train journey to a resort in the Alps. Much of the story was set in a lakeside hotel and illustrated a case of hysteria, weaving erotic fantasy, sibling betrayal, and murder in a world ravaged by the violence of war and the mass murder of fellow citizens identified as the 'threatening' other. The violence and passions were mirrored in natural disasters, storms, Leonid showers, and avalanches, while the hotel "flowed with milk and honey".

At the time of the conference the world was waking up to a global financial crisis and world leaders were meeting to work on what to do. These were people who needed "armed guards". We, clearly, did not.

The Hotel Villa Carlotta certainly kept us warm and well fed while outside a chill wind blew over the lake and cold autumn clouds released bursts of rain. The warmth and pleasure of reconnecting with old friends and colleagues, an easy journey, arriving relaxed and in good humour, gave way to the shocking dream that arrived on the first night.

The dream

What does an opening dream say about the unconscious of the group and its beneath-the-surface pre-occupations that often lie in opposition to the surface themes, here of tradition, creativity and succession in a global group relations network?

The warmth of the hugging and kissing at the start of the conference and the pleasure of reconnection, "sat with us at the table" while the shadow, containing all the hidden rivalries, hostilities, disappointments, and aggression "lay asleep on the bed" (Gibran, 1926).

It was difficult to voice this dream in the first morning reflection and association event. It felt as if its violence broke into a shared feeling of goodwill.

The dream was memorable because of its stark and horrible opening images and ideas. Waking up from it I hastily scribbled:

> At a gathering of male "elders", a boy is called in and his nipple is seasoned with salt and pepper. I know they are going to cut it off and pass it around as a delicacy. The women had to go where they couldn't see. We are on the stairs. I wait in dread to hear the screams. I see other boys with blood- stained faces and limbs and then see the boy being carried out into the garden, as yet unmutilated. The men are cheerful and in good humour as they do this. It is an accepted tradition and a good thing. News then comes that the actress Emma Thompson is campaigning on behalf of children trafficked as sex slaves who otherwise have little value and are therefore "ungrievable" (Butler 2004).

Was this a dream about the shadow of the "founding fathers"? In a conference whose title included "tradition" and "succession" this would not be surprising. Did this dream contain more than the dynamics of the present but also what was about to unfold in the conference?

The dream referred to "seasoning"; the need to add spice and flavour to something otherwise rather tasteless sounded strange, but why the nipples of little boys? Season is also a time of year: here it was autumn; then it could it be a reference to someone or something weathered by time and grown in experience. Was this referring to the group relations tradition?

The dream seemed to me to speak about an unquestioning acceptance of the assumptions of power and rights of "founding fathers". It rested uncomfortably with the notion of a peer organisation and brought to mind the domination of the "Primal Father" (Freud, 1921) who then had to be killed by the "brothers" and Kronos (time) who devoured his children. In the dream, though, the boys were mere tit bits to nibble and pass around.

What was the significance of Emma Thompson? She is a British actress who does not trade on sexual glamour in a profession that largely does. In life she works for refugees and asylum seekers. I wondered if she might represent a female "star" who might challenge the assumed rights of these "founding fathers".

Further, since Belgirate II, the Tavistock Institute had appointed a new, relatively young female director and was bringing about a new order. Did this changing dynamic affect, in different, possibly gendered and " sibling" ways, the "climate" present in Belgirate III? Did I sense it as paralleled in the play of mist and cloud revealing and concealing the lake and mountains?

In the dream the women removed themselves and turned a "blind eye". This seemed to link in my mind with the way the "women directors" took themselves off so immediately (as they did in Belgirate II) as if pre-arranged and as if removing themselves from the potential difficulties of choosing groups, a time of enormous anxiety and uncertainty, when the groups in the exploration event were in the process of forming. Was this "acting out" something, as in the demonstrations of knitting, like the "tricoteuses" of the French Revolution. They were the women who attended the executions of the nobility, not acting but yet complicit.

Sibling, lateral (global?) organisation

During the conference questions were posed about how we deal with succession in a "lateral" network. We talked much about networks and globalisation that seem to contain ideals of equality and freedom, openness and transparency. Images were presented of nets and webs, weaving and knitting perhaps demonstrating, something of the warp and weft of the vertical and the lateral dimensions of the relationships between conference members. This occurred especially in the creativity group which produced a piece of weaving and presented it with great ceremony as if to a queen, to Eliat Aram in the final plenary. This certainly revealed something of the fantasies around (female?) hierarchy.

Seniors (big beasts) and juniors (small fry), those closer to the founding fathers and mothers and those newer to GR were like younger siblings vying to find a place and to be among the favoured and chosen. As in Cain and Abel, Issac and Esau (Huffington & Miller, 2008), competition is introduced by the actions of a "parental" figure, the "Father" who possess the power and invites the brothers to compete for His favour. It is in the GR tradition that conference staff are chosen by the director, which may look like a similar dynamic.

In the group relations tradition, understanding unconscious processes has been based upon the vertical, parent/child, analyst/patient dimension. My interest has focused on the lateral, sibling dimension of groups and organisations from reading Bion's experiment with the "leaderless group" (Bion, 1961), to a brief paper about the renewal of hostilities between the countries released from Soviet rule (Žižek, 1999). A search for psychoanalytic literature on the lateral led to the discovery of Juliet Mitchell's works on siblings and to wondering how this new paradigm might contribute to the way we understand and interpret unconscious fantasies and the behaviour they give rise to in the context of group relations conferences. I see this dynamic at work especially in inter-group events where immediate and passionate bonds come into existence almost at the moment of group formation and are often closely followed by visceral hatred of and rivalry with other groups (Sirota, 2003). This is sibling stuff of worst enemies and best friends; it just does not fit with the vertical axis though it's strongly related to it.

Are peer relationships so difficult to think about and manage that we give ourselves, so readily, to a leader, or ideal, who will take the burden away and restore a feeling of omnipotence? The benefit to members is that they can surrender the need to think, take responsibility or be troubled by doubt (Sirota, 2003, p. 15).

So might we need to create leaders as an "upward displacement" (Armstrong, 2007) in order to alleviate the intense anxiety arising from the responsibility of our own unconscious wishes and actions, These wishes and actions are reactivated by the hidden trauma of displacement, replacement, and annihilation brought about by the advent of a new sibling (new idea, new colleague, new role, etc.). This raises the awful question "Who am I now that another is in my place?" (Mitchell, 2000). It is a dimension that harbours murderous and erotic wishes, love and hate, connected to survival, and a fratricidal taboo that gives rise to the traumas inherent when over-ridden by the "father's permission to kill our brothers. "Sibling" activity is more connected to polymorphous perversity, as Freud described it, and to curiosity, playfulness, aggression, and sexuality that does not lead to procreation.

We accept and internalise the dominance and authority of those who stand on the vertical line of parental tradition. It promises containment, guidance, learning, and growth. We know there is a natural order where they will grow old and we will replace them. Our peers are of a different order; they are our rivals, lovers, partners, colleagues, the enemy and the ally.

During the exploratory event my curiosity was aroused by some members saying they had been "imprisoned" and "captured" and

I wondered, as it was clear that there were no "prisons" and no-one was taking anyone prisoner. Could this be the expression of a hidden wish to be held, enclosed, and relieved of the responsibility for one's actions, of being exposed, "naked before one's peers" (Armstrong 2007) and, maybe, an avoidance of the inevitable conflicts inherent in "equality"? How might this link to a desire not only to be held safely but to create the conditions even of oppression within which the desire for freedom and creativity might be rekindled? And then, was the idea of imprisonment connected to a fear of being imprisoned by old "traditions" or even "captivated" by new ideas that might threaten to displace them?

Creativity

Arthur Koestler (1964), in his book *The Act of Creation* wrote about creativity arising from "unlikely pairings", conceptions within the pressure cooker of urgent need. The creativity that gives birth to the new and can change things forever often comes about under difficult circumstances, accidents, and often acute limitations. Sometimes the idea of being creative is expressed as a kind of pseudo playfulness, almost as if *saying* one was being creative was all that was required for it to be so. The knitting, weaving, dancing, howling, and jumbling up chairs in this conference could well be thought of as playful and "creative". It could also be seen as a regression to more childlike states and the "comfort" of old traditional crafts as well as the expression of a desire to "weave" something new and to "knit" together what has been broken. It could throw us into a lateral/sibling dynamic with its primitive excitements and anxieties of the playground, including that of displacement and annihilation. It was clear that, with succession came new thinking, and with it real displacements in the old order of things. Was this too terrifying to think about among peers in open forum and needed to be hidden in the "mists" of dreams and images? Who now does and does not get invited to staff membership? How does that impact on the unconscious of the peers? Who is now "in" and who "out"? Thus posing the question, "Who am I now that I'm not who I thought I was?" (Mitchell 2000).

One of the most obvious difficulties in global group relations seems to be recruitment of members for conferences and the limitations for many of potential members of time, travel, and cost. That the Belgirate conferences were so well subscribed was good evidence of the enthusiasm for the work and for taking staff roles in conferences. This gave rise to many thoughts, some of them voiced during the conference, about the possibilities of "virtual" conferences, imagining them, stimulated by a recently released film *Avatar* (a story exploring a virtual world notable for its technological accomplishment) and knowing that there were already web games where people could inhabit virtual forms (I supposed, all beautiful and sexy) to interact in eternal games of "sibling" competition, rivalry collaboration, and lust. I doubt many would choose to be "parental" avatars.

I didn't know until after the conference that a virtual large study group was already in the making until receiving an invitation to be "recruited" as a member.

Traditionally, in the vertical structures of patriarchy, succession is handed on from "parent" to "child" and, predominantly, to the first-born male. This dynamic remains in the unconscious of our culture and still operates in many societies.

The sibling/lateral dimension of peer relationship is becoming increasingly important and visible as more women take senior roles in the workplace. For me, and others (Visholm, 2007, quoted by Huffington and Miller (2008) and Sirota (2005)), the group relations conference, drawing on the vertical, Oedipal, axis has, as in the analytic literature, largely neglected the sibling/lateral dimension. When seen and acknowledged, how might it bring about changes and developments in our thinking about group relations? (Sirota, 2003). The sibling dimension brings to light other aspects of relationship where manifestations of envy, love and hate (Sirota, 2003), competition, and collaboration are seen to be different from the vertical hierarchies of the parent/child axis.

Competition on the vertical axis contains a sense of the natural order of things in that the young will inevitably replace the old. Lateral, sibling/peer competition is something that is more contentious. It's winnable, and to dispose of one's peer/sibling rival with or without collaboration, in gangs and teams and other affiliations, serves to increase one's own chance of gain and inheritance. This must hold true in families, societies, and organisations of all kinds.

This is not an argument to replace the vertical but to take on the complexity of the interplay of both.

We might also consider how birth order influences the way roles are, formally and informally, taken up in our organisations. Looking through a sibling lens could provide useful evidence about how we gravitate to certain roles/niches influenced by family birth order (Sulloway, 1996). Alfred Adler wrote extensively about the significance of birth order which might also contribute to thinking about our own roles and valencies within the group relations context.

In workshop and other settings with people engaged in psychoanalytically orientated work, I've found a high proportion of participants were either firstborn, or only, children. They seemed to take up authoritative roles with great ease while those born later tended to be more competitive and the youngest often the creative "innovator". According to Sulloway, later born children might take up a role or "niche" to diminish the competition by doing/being something different. Whenever the subject is raised I've found people keen to explore this dimension.

This is by no means a scientific study but my own experience and reading suggests that it might be something to take into account when reflecting on our own roles and the way in which we observe others.

Conclusion

If the sibling dimension is so strongly present could we mobilise it to add to the thinking in group relations. Belgirate might offer opportunities to experiment.

The Oedipal question of "what goes on behind closed doors?" became a frequent topic during parts of the conference. The hotel had private "closed" spaces into which we retreated into the "mist" to become private, invisible, to rest and to dream. The public spaces, formal and informal, provided the stage on which we could see and be seen, heard, and voice our contributions, conscious and unconscious. The dream became something sitting in the mind.

In the end we reach the boundary of the conference, disperse, and take away new and renewed alliances, "sibling" bonds, and creative pairings.

Prompted by the dream I've been attempting to look at Belgirate III and the group relations tradition through a lateral lens without losing sight of the vertical axis of the great minds of the founding fathers and mothers who, like the mountains, dominate our view at Belgirate. It's something that might add to the development of our thinking about conference design and some of the resistances to "lateral thinking".

References

Adler, A. (1928). Children characteristics of first, second and third child. *Children 3: 14–52* (Publisher unknown, quoted from Sulloway, 1996, *Born to Rebel.* London: Abacus.)

Adler, A. (1956). *The Individual Psychology of Alfred Adler: A systematic Presentation in Selections from his Writings* (Edited and annotated by H. L. Ansbacher & R. R. Ansbacher). New York: Basic Books.

Armstrong, D. (2007). The dynamics of lateral relations in changing organizational worlds. *Organisational and Social Dynamics, 7*: 193–210.

Bion, W. R. (1961). *Experiences in Groups.* London and New York: Routledge.

Butler, J. (2004). *Precarious Life*. London & New York: Verso.

Freud, S. (1921). Group psychology and the analysis of the Ego. *Civilization, Society and Religion* (Vol. 12) (1985). London: Penguin.

Gertler, B. & Izod, K. (2004). Modernism and postmodernism in group relations theory and practice: A confusion of tongues. In: D. Neumair & S. Cytrynbaum (Eds.) *Group Relations Reader 3: Group Dynamics, Organizational Irrationality and Social Complexity*. Washington: A. K. Rice Institute.

Gibran, K. (1926). *The Prophet*. London: Heineman.

Huffington, C. (2008). Where angels and mere mortals fear to tread: Exploring "sibling" relations in the workplace'. *Organisational and Social Dynamics, 8.*

Koestler, A. (1964). *The Act of Creation* London: Picador.

Mitchell, J. (2000). *Mad Men and Medusas*. New York: Basic Books.

Mitchell, J. (2004). *Siblings: Sex and Violence.* Oxford: Polity Press.

Sirota, J. (2003). The social and political expression of sibling relations'. Unpublished dissertation.

Sirota, J. (2005). Review of *Siblings: Sex and Violence* by Juliet Mitchell. *Organisational and Social Dynamics, 5.*

Sulloway, F. (1996). *Born to Rebel: Birth Order, Family Dynamics and Creative Lives* London: Abacus.

Thomas, D. M. (1981). *The White Hotel.* London: King Penguin.

Žižek, S. (1990). Eastern Europe's republics of Gilead. *New Left Review, 123.*

CHAPTER EIGHTEEN

Boundaries, connectedness, and networks: reflections from Belgirate III

Rina Tagore

> Strange, is it not? that of the myriads who
> Before us pass'd the door of Darkness through,
> Not one returns to tell us of the Road
> Which to discover we must travel too.
>
> —The Rubaiyat, *Omar Khayyam*, 1120 CE

Life journeys take place in and across many orbits. It is in these journeys that peoples' identities are shaped, collective forces formed, and spaces negotiated and shared. In the orbits travelled, the contacts, crossings, connections, and even collisions spark the pathways and networks that give meaning and hold potential for experiencing, movement and change.

This paper puts together my reflections stemming from joining the third Belgirate conference, "Tradition, Creativity, and Succession", November 2009. The reflections are not in isolation from my life journey. They are closely connected to who I am, including ongoing reflections on group relations work. The paper is a combination of vignettes from the conference and associated thoughts and concepts that I grapple with in life.

Finding drivers and joining the conference

At the outset, I start by saying that I had not known about the Belgirate Conferences until very recently. It was a fleeting invitation—"Rina, why don't you come to the Belgirate conference? There will be people you know, and Gouranga is giving the keynote address". That was the starting point, or a driver that made me enlist.

It felt ambitious at different levels; that I would have to travel literally half-way across the world, the resources involved, and, moreover, where do I fit in the glitterati of experienced group relations professionals?

Nevertheless, I wanted to join, and meet others. I had a longing to be part of the wider group relations network. I wanted to meet and talk to people who worked in this area, who believed in the approach and were in their own ways making a difference to organisations, structures, and systems.

My entry into group relations work was back in 2000 as a member in a group relations conference in Bangalore, India, with Gouranga Chattopadhyaya as director. In one little corner of my mind Gouranga represented the "guru", a part of the glitterati in relation to group relations work. I realised that another driver for me to sign-up was the awareness that he, would present a paper in Belgirate.

The process of de-bunking fantasies, myths, and challenging notions held in the mind has become more or less a part of my thinking. Having had exposure to group relations work. Well before setting off from New Zealand for travel to Belgirate I got the news that the "guru" was unable to join. The idea of tradition was, in my mind, held together in the cluster of the notions, including the notion of a "guru"—the knowledgeable and experienced teacher—and other ideas that I will touch upon later, such as rituals and legitimacy of expertise.

In Gouranga's absence, Ajeet Mathur presented the keynote address on the evening of the first day of the Conference: "Experiential learning: The Indian experience from the Proto-historic Period to the present" (Gouranga P. Chattopadyay and Ajeet N. Mathur, Keynote address, Tradition, Creativity and Succession, Belgirate III).

The words in the presentation that became relevant for me were as follows:

> The guru-disciple traditions in India need to be understood both as an enabling paradigm and a constraining one. The word guru consists of two syllables "gu" meaning darkness, ignorance and

> "ru" annihilation of darkness by illumination ... although the loose connotation is "teachers with great knowledge", a *sui generis* concept where the emphasis is on learning through introspection, meditation, questioning, and dialogue rather than teaching or being taught.

In stepping out of a stereotypical notion of "guru" or expertise held in a teacher, group relations conferences have time and again hammered home the need to break out of some of the traditional models of learning, which I have held. The theme of the conference—Tradition, Creativity, and Succession—was another such opportunity to explore these ideas.

In the absence of the notional guru, tradition was nevertheless present in the minds of members, and the conference provided the churning to discover and test the notions with reality. It was possible to test notions through experiences shared in the narratives of papers presented and the transactions in the conference events.

The de-construction of the word "guru" still lingered on my mind. That evening I made a call to Gouranga to find out about his well-being, as well as to acknowledge his contribution and convey that in his absence he still was present in the hearts and minds of people. A number of members had expressed this sentiment.

As noted in another set of reflections from the second Belgirate conference, "... the absence of these presenters did not mean that their thinking was not represented in and through the minds of those who were there" (Reekum & Gottlieb, in Aram, Baxter & Nutkevitch, 2009).

Connecting through shared identities

My joining experience revealed a few more drivers that led me to Belgirate. One of these was a part of my identity, that of being an Indian. I wanted to be part of the international gathering as one of the Indians who has experiences in group relations work. Further, I felt a sense of pride, as an "Indian" narrative around group relations was in the forefront. As a nation, India represents a land of ancient history and tradition and a place where tradition and modernity live side by side. I am not completely convinced if both sides are well integrated, but the paradoxes are fascinating nevertheless.

In arriving at the decision to travel to Belgirate, an added impetus was the possibility of re-connecting with two women friends from India. Of pertinence is to note that there was a feeling of being a part of an unspoken network. The elements of this network stemmed from many aspects of my identity—being Indian, being women, being professionals in a similar area of work, and as colleagues in the past, in group relations conferences in India.

Clearly, this was a layer of a network that prevailed, connected, and made itself present in the third Belgirate conference. Moreover, this layer represented, somewhere in the Indian context, breaking of tradition through the life journeys of these women, and succession in the context of group relations work.

For me, going to Belgirate stemmed from a search for a combination of experiences—to re-connect and connect with more than one network, whether loose, formal, or informal, and the joy of being part of the bigger whole. I believe that networks represent the multitude of layers, representing the many identities, peoples and groups carry. Over time, traditionally held boundaries have become increasingly permeable. We travel, literally and metaphorically, across several spaces with relative ease. Boundaries are more and more permeable and not necessarily restrictive. I will come back to identity and networks later.

Gaining space, voice, and legitimacy

The conference experience started with finding two persons from a recent Leicester conference, in the same train carriage to Belgirate. The joy was tempered with a humorous spar on being told, "But I did not see your name on the list of participants". So there, in the midst of hellos and hugs, I had to confirm that I was indeed a legitimate participant member, with a lingering curiosity as to what lay behind the obliteration.

In the packed room of about ninety people, true to the spirit of group relations conferences, the opening plenary held a feeling of anticipation, trepidation, and excitement. There was mutual comfort for two co-workers, including myself, from the recent Leicester conference, to sit together. As usual, finding my voice in a large, unfamiliar setting was disconcerting. The room was full in many ways. There was joy and excitement, of meeting friends and ex-colleagues. There was also the opportunity to re-acquaint with people, thoughts, and convictions. I did find my voice, to name myself and parts of my joining experience.

The full room, one large wall covered with a wallpaper ripped in many spots, seemed to be carrying a point of reference to those who had "been here before", the earlier Belgirate conferences. Many people spoke, but what struck me and another member later was that the three Indian women were the only ones to introduce themselves by including their names. What was happening then? The need to name and label seemed to be one means of gaining space and legitimacy. It could also be that the three women—Anuradha Prasad, Rosemary Viswanath, and Rina Tagore—were holding a small group identity that formed in Milan earlier. Naming ourselves was perhaps an affirmation of the group relations network in the subcontinent (I might add, that although I migrated to New Zealand from about seven years old, my "Indian" heritage is integral to who I am).

Of the many statements about joining, the one that struck me the most was the one that spoke about identities. That coming to Belgirate was like "joining my tribe", said one of the American participants. Identities find expression in many ways and clearly the conference was a gathering of the tribe. It gave a sense of wholeness, camaraderie, and solidarity. That may sound rather "happy", but happiness in this case comes from the churnings produced through group relations work. Tribes travel; their boundaries are not defined by bureaucratic or legal structures. Instead they connect, share, and reciprocate for life and livelihood. Joining the conference was as such about a desire to belong as it was about a longing "to be".

Identities as dynamic dimensions

Identities are multi-layered; they sit side by side and contain a repertoire of resources to help connect people and systems. The connectedness could stem from many reasons such as the desire "to be a part of", relatedness stemming from shared experiences, as well as a need to progress who "I" and "we" are, together in the group relations network. The conference space held for me the processes to contain the uniqueness of the different identities as much as to develop or strengthen the repertoire of resources held within it.

This brings me to the subject of migration, and the related sense of belonging. Migration became a reality for me less under a decade ago when I moved to New Zealand from India. I often say that in migrating I suddenly became "an Indian". Everyone surrounding me viewed me as "an Indian". I had to figure out not only what others held in mind, but also to figure out for myself what it meant to be an "Indian".

The experience is a doorway to discover what it is to be "the other", and to negotiate difference and perhaps a fluid sense of identity and belonging. In this fluidity, in my view, lies the strength, a repertoire of skills and capacities that enable movement across different identities. Facing "the other", and embracing difference, helps to permeate and expand boundaries.

Chimamanda Adichie (a Nigerian novelist) describes the "danger of a single story" and speaks of the risk of living with stereotypes (Adichie, C., TED.com, 2009). The message is that our lives, our cultures, are composed of many overlapping stories so that it is in the overlapping dimensions that the "other" is present; it is in there that tradition paves the way for newness, creativity, and renewal.

There is no single way to be "Indian", as that is indeed a static notion. Identities are dynamic, expanding, and growing. This dynamism stems from the "longing to be", in an existential sense, as well as from addressing to task. I use the term "task" with reference to groups, organisations, and entities that exist for a purpose.

In the world we live in today, we need to work with differences and understand identities in a deeper way, so that we can collectively shape the future. We live in spaces that are changing dramatically, through increased mobility of people, of human resources, of labour in the form of migration, and the like. Drawing from Leonie Sandercock, " 'national space' is an imaginary … embodied in the local spaces of one's street and city, where it is either reinforced or undermined. Fears are generated. Loss is experienced. 'The Other', the stranger, is thought to be taking over. Resentment builds …" (Sandercock, 2003). I relate this to the need to confront difference, to shed stereotypes, and understand the "other" in order to move beyond the superficial layers of transaction.

I was part of the Belgirate conference through my different identities and furthering my longing to be part of the wider group relations network.

A vignette from a small group event

Following the opening plenary, I found myself in a pre-determined group, where the purpose was to get to know each other. All faces, bar one, were unknown to me. In a way, that single face symbolised "tradition" as Mannie Sher represented the Tavistock Institute.

Anyhow, moving into the small group gave some comfort, as small groups invariably do to me. Reflecting on the conference theme, I shared with the group, memories of the time when my father died. A part of me holds a negative association with tradition as a source of control, power, and the many mechanistic rituals and ceremonies that tend to take away instead of give meaning. Often traditions and rituals are a shield from experiencing, reflecting, and making meaning. At this juncture, in dealing with grief, I realised that tradition and traditional practices played a role in paving the way, in holding together a space and enabling collective human expression.

This first group encounter held grief and loss, and recognition of possibilities of new pathways. Taking the point from the above illustration, our group connected with the idea that tradition and rituals need not necessarily be signs of stagnation but instead pave a way, providing grounding, anchoring, to enable risk-taking, learning, and an emerging newness. The Belgirate conferences are a space that allows for the confluence of the old and new, for them to relate to each other, to dialogue, and find common ground. The churnings of the players in their work in their places, and the collective churning in the conference space, has the potential to yield newness and new pathways.

I noted that it was Mannie Sher who managed the boundaries by closing the door after everyone in the group was seated and also kept the time boundary in the end of that first event. In a way, "tradition" was holding one set of boundaries at that moment.

Joining the network group

I have used the word "churning" with reference to group relations conferences, as they create or invoke a churning process. The churning is inside as much as it is outside of the individual and the group. A process of churning began around the task to form groups to explore the role of the conference theme—tradition, creativity, and succession in group relations network.

The exchanges in the large group felt random and a search for resonance had begun in the room. People spoke, glances and looks were exchanged, and physical movement ensued as the whiteboard and flip chart brought back memories of the institutional event. I continue to marvel at the feelings, and turmoil, that is produced in GRCs. The subgroup formation process is one such moment. The process experienced was of finding purpose, yet again rationalising the cognitive and emotive connection.

I was inclined to join the "social relevance" group, by virtue of its name, but held back as I was conscious that my two Indian women friends were in that group. In stepping away from the known there was a chance to relate with more than the known. Just then another member spoke of "hatchers" (referring to eggs hatching), young ones joining the conference and group relations network. That part of me that held a thought that I am a "newbie" among the "experts" in Belgirate, related to the idea. Considering myself as being on the edge of the wider network, there were many moments that I had to give legitimacy and authority to myself to be part of the larger group.

"Hatchers" did sound like "hackers", who enter a network with skill, stealth, and often break boundaries in virtual space by entering closely guarded knowledge and information. I believe the wider group relations network is finding its feet through the Belgirate conferences, as these are unique and are held together by a few institutions.

Finding sufficient resonance with one member's views about expatriates remaining tied to single networks, often unchanged and holding on to "tradition", a few members came together along with "newcomers/hatchers". Without too much ado, the small group came together. It was also of a need to claim a space in the event.

The energy level in the room had increased; there were people around the flip chart and whiteboard, bringing back images from group relations conferences. The groups coalesced around "social relevance", "women directors", "creativity", "tradition", "envy", "inter-wicked", and "network".

As it turned out the network group comprised six members of whom four had been connected by the recent Leicester conferences. The gender-balanced group of three women and three men reflected diversity in terms of gender, sexual orientation, faith, and of having crossed national boundaries through migration.

Our diverse group occupied a large room. The door to enter the room provided symbolic and literal amusement to those inside and to those who attempted to enter the network. Even though we wanted to keep the door open and welcome other members, it would not remain open. Once closed it was a challenge to push hard in order gain access to the room.

The group worked on whether or not the exploratory event was effectively an institutional event. The tension between tradition and creativity through change was reflected in this discussion. For some, the exploratory event was nothing but an institutional event and for others it was not. The shadow of Leicester was unique to the network group, as pointed out during a visit from the management and administration. There is a kind of "aura" about Leicester. No doubt it is to do with the Tavistock Institute's role as the home ground and place of seeding and growing group relations work. However, that the Leicester conference (through Tavistock) has seeded change and innovation is easily lost sight of (highlighted in the key note presentation by Eliat Aram at the conference).

The network group grappled with its own dynamics: of members desirous of leading, and related competition and aggression; of finding social relevance inside instead of seeking it through names of groups in the system; and of exploring contacts with other groups. My experience showed that there was an openness in giving and receiving. Members from the network group made contact with a few other groups; one member went and taught dance and in return received a token gift (twig of leaves). In many ways transactions were taking place across boundaries that were permeable. However, the connections possibly remained in a flux as proposed meetings to connect all the groups were abandoned and the closing plenary of the "IE-like" exploratory event felt palpable with a variety of emotions and unresolved thoughts. The experience in a way mirrored the life of networks.

Conclusion

> *And those who were dancing were thought to be insane by those who could not hear the music.*
>
> (Friedrich Wilhelm Nietzsche)

Experiences around group relations conferences do not lend themselves to conclusions very easily. Reflections and insights continue. And the third Belgirate conference was no different. I drew strength to bring my voice, through different aspects of my identity—derived from shared history, experience, and ongoing life journey. The conference was a means of making greater meaning through another shared experience and expanding the sense of connectedness to the group relations network.

There was a shift from a self-imposed boundary restriction that I held—that of a "newbie"—to discover many spaces to connect with others, to make and give meaning in the conference.

References

Adichie, C., The danger of a single story, TED.com: Recorded at TEDGlobal, July 2009, Oxford, UK, viewed 11 March 2010, <http://blog.ted.com/2009/10/07/the_danger_of_a/>.

Aram, E., Baxter, R. & Nutkevitch, A. (Eds.) (2009). *Adaptation and Innovation: Theory, Design and Role-Taking in Group Relations Conferences and their Applications* (Vol. II). London: Karnac.

Bromell, D. (2008). *Ethnicity, Identity and Public Policy: Critical Perspectives on Multiculturalism*. Wellington: Institute of Policy, Victoria University.

Khyyam, O., (1048-1131). The Rubaiyat, viewed 10 March 2010, <http://classics.mit.edu/Khayyam/rubaiyat.html>

Sandercock, L. (2003). *Cosmopolis II: Mongrel Cities in the 21st Century*. London and New York: Continuum.

CHAPTER NINETEEN

Remnants, Quakers, and group relations

Simon Western

Introduction

This chapter reflects on an experience at Belgirate 2009 where a number of individuals in the exploratory event remained *in situ* in the plenary venue and became the "Remnants", those that are left behind. The themes that arose within this remnant "collective" are explored in this chapter. I use the term "collective", as the word group carries with it specific connotations, boundaries, and expectations that we resisted for a long while. Bringing new theoretical and intellectual resources to our traditional framework of ideas (psychoanalytic and systemic) is a necessary way to open new thinking. There is a lack in group relations thinking; an absence of critical theory as a lens to question the very co-ordinates of our practice. To address this, the chapter meanders into theology and specifically draws on the religious movement of the Quakers, who considered themselves a remnant group, to shed new light from a critical perspective on group relations experience. Slavoj Žižek describes this process as *short-circuiting*, to bring new resources from different traditions in order to see something new or hidden:

> Is not short-circuiting, therefore, one of the best metaphors for a critical reading? Is not one of the most effective critical procedures to cross wires that do not usually touch: to take a major text and read it in a short-circuiting way, through the lens of a minor (marginalized) author, text or conceptual apparatus? ... such a procedure can lead to insights which completely shatter and undermine our common perceptions. ... The aim is to illuminate a standard text or ideological formation, making it readable in a totally new way. (Žižek, 2003, Foreword).

This chapter will begin with a brief description of my experience of the exploratory event, highlighting the main issues that were evoked in me and others. Reflecting on this "remnant experience" is to think about being still in an event full of movement. We worked emergently on our collective identity and what we were doing, given that our starting position differed from a starting at the conventional place of forming a named group around an idea and a working task.

The chapter will then explore the theological idea of a "remnant people" and take the Quaker movement as a case study. The early Quakers sat and waited for a direct experience of the divine: they experienced themselves as a remnant community and were an early influence on the group relations movement.[1] This reflection led me to wonder if group relations itself should become a remnant community or use this metaphor to regain its dynamic early influence.

The conclusion will play with themes that emerge from this short-circuiting of ideas and see if any new readings of group relations might emerge.

The emergence of a remnant group

This chapter reflects on a group relations experience where a number of individuals from an exploratory event remained *in situ*, observing as the plenary session dissipated into diverse themed groups, as is the consistent pattern in group relations events. We were sat individually around the plenary room, and slowly pairs emerged which became triads, and then we gathered in a loose collection of chairs to reflect on what this meant for us. We were initially united by an unspoken "resistance to repetition" as a defence against learning. The familiar process of becoming separate groups with themes—"the happy group", "the women's group", "the naughty group", etc.—and after a period of consolidating then visiting other groups in the system to see what they were doing, seemed a little rehearsed and contrite; it had been done a thousand times, it was too familiar and didn't present us with the learning opportunities we desired. Eric Miller warns against the institutionalisation of group relations conferences; he writes of the Leicester conference:

> The problems of institutionalization are more insidious than that. The model is in constant danger of becoming a movement. A movement is fed by and feeds ritual. There are quite subtle pressures on staff to become priests of the ritual. (Miller, 2010, p. 30)

Miller foresaw the situation in which we find ourselves, although I think the problem is less of something becoming a movement, for social movements are some of the most exciting innovators of change (as the Arab spring again reminds us). The danger is of it becoming a movement with fundamentalist tendencies (Western, 2005, 2008), one that looks back to an idealised past, to idealised figures in the past, repeating their sayings, and whereby conformity and institutionalisation outweigh innovation and desire.

This loose network of people, "the left-overs", coalesced over a period of time. Initially we were nameless and task-less; we had no theme to convene around and did not experience ourselves as a group. After a period of time we became a group to others, and later to ourselves. A name, "the Remnants", emerged through a process of being asked who we were by visitors. It is not clear whether our group formed and then took on a name, or whether the name we adopted for ourselves formed us as a group.

After a number of sessions, we slowly became a group with a formidable culture, although this was never explicitly planned or discussed. Our "groupishness" was brought into being by "the other" and by language. We "spoke ourselves into existence", to paraphrase Lacan. Visitors came to the room asking who we were. They came as emissaries from other groups with specific tasks/questions, usually "we are here to find out what your group name is and what task you are working on?" Initially we resisted visitors' attempts to name us, to order and categorise us. This was met with some aggression—"You must have a name/task?" The saying, "If all you have is a hammer, everything looks like a nail", is important here: "If the only lens you have to look at conferences is groups, roles, and tasks, then all you will find is groups, roles, and tasks". For group relations in the future this might be an important restriction on development, as we have to work beyond the boundaried idea of group and organisation and begin to grasp social networks and virtual corporate organisations, which operate more like rhizomes and brands, appearing everywhere but without clear boundaries, where roles are multiple and not fixed and where tasks are emergent as well as planned (see eco-leadership approaches: Western, 2008, 2010).

In our remnant group we found ourselves just being. To be and exist without a name or theme, we had no desire to be a task-orientated, functional group. No desire to explore what others in the system were doing at this stage. We began by wondering what to do, then we started to enjoy the experience of just being. We also quickly learnt that if you don't go exploring the system, it will come to you, and a particular type of systemic insight is gained.

We wanted to experience our experience fully. We collectively discussed our wish to experience what it was to discover our collective selves without jumping into pre-ordained categories. What did it mean to sit and wait? What did it mean to wait without a function or task? What, if anything, would emerge?

Which paradigm—modernity or post-modernity?

The external pressures to name and form us into a recognisable group felt like a battle between modernity and post-modernity. Modernity at work emerges from industrial manufacturing with clear structures, hierarchal constructs, division of labour, and clear tasks. This contrasts with post-industrial and post-modern work forms: digitalised economies, virtual and real, cognitive labour, and knowledge networks (Berardi, 2009). This tension exists in the workplace and is reflected here in our group relations work. Modernity is a force that rationalises, orders, codifies, separates, and categorises; it is based on empirical science and stems from the enlightenment idea that progress brings liberty through reason and knowledge. Whereas post-modernity experiences the world as fragmented, deconstructed, hybrid, and partial, claiming there is no grand narrative. In our remnant collective, we were experiencing ourselves in the post-modern, post-industrial sense, whilst others were experiencing us in the modernist sense, and this tension resided within us for the whole time of the exploratory sessions. The lack of a task/theme seemed to bother the "outsiders". To be without a function seemed to be without purpose, without meaning. It seemed annoying and threatening, and some became aggressive with us, as if we weren't playing the right game. Reason and functionality is the axis of modernity and it marginalises subjectivity, emotions, and the irrational. Socio-technical thinking has been strongly influenced by this modern environment, and group relations was born into this modernist mindset, drawing on science and its metaphors, and continues to use this "modernist paradigm" as its lens to study group relations. Eric Miller writes about the Leicester Conference:

> In the conference itself, staff are aspiring to use a version of the scientific method in the here and now: they are putting forward working hypotheses with evidence from their observations and internal feelings, and are inviting members to use their own evidence to verify or falsify the hypotheses. (Miller, 2010, p. 16)

However, the "empirical" scientific method as described by Eric Miller does not hold in the theoretical world where quantum physics, post-structuralism, and new understandings demonstrate that much of science itself is a construction rather than an absolute (Latour 2004; Law, 1993) and the idea of a neutral scientific observer is fantasy. Observation changes the object observed. In an enterprise like group relations, where we study the subjective truths of human relations, as in other "social sciences" the meaning of empirical is very loose. It might help us to review the methods we have of interpretation and hypothesis, from a critical perspective, analysing how power and elites reproduce results, how staff are selected to reproduce paradigms of form and structure that urgently need reviewing. Being in the remnant group at Belgirate in some way brought these issues into sharp focus.

The radicalism of sitting still

When there is chaos all around, the immediate reaction is to act. When faced with the emptiness of the void, where there is a space to think, flight also very quickly takes hold. A dash for the door, the grasping at a task, any task, as if it is a life-raft in a stormy sea. The intolerable thought of being still, of facing the silence and the stillness, the abyss of the void, creates tremendous fear and flight.

In this conference exploratory event, we collectively resisted forming a group with a name and a task, and instead used the psychoanalytic method that is in tension with the scientific method and with the project of modernity itself. The approach relates to the concept of contemplation, long known by religious and spiritual traditions, and what in psychoanalytic terms is known as "negative capability and not-knowing" (Bion, 1961; Bollas, 1987), drawing on John Keats' writing. Observing emergent phenomena we hoped to find a subjective truth, the truth of experience that could not be gained other than by being still and waiting, listening contemplatively to each others' experience. Doing this without "a persecutory consultant" in the mind offers a different kind of group experience from the small group that is filled with the basic assumption states, provoked by a culture of interpretations created by the object of a "sphinx" consultant (Bion, 1961, p. 162). Bion's insights into how groups reacted in a basic assumption manner did not pay enough attention to one vital point—him! He sat there as a powerful psychiatrist with a particular, formidable, intimidating, and withholding approach, counter cultural to the group participants' expectations and previous experience. This Tavistock approach invokes this nameless dread, and then interprets it as if it is a normative phenomenon. Nikolas Rose explains:

> If we look, for instance, at Bion's descriptions in *Experiences in Groups*, you can see the way in which, in the forced "hothouse" atmosphere of the groups that he deliberately produces, certain phenomena pertaining to the relations between individuals which are invisible in other situations are forced in to existence (Bion, 1961; c.f. Miller and Rose, 1994). They are rendered visible, thorough a kind of intensification of effects that is entirely analogous to that intensification that is deliberately produced in a scientific laboratory to make the invisible visible. This is why I think that therapeutic situations are like laboratories, they force certain things in to existence. And, in the same way as scientific experiments, they force those things into reality which have already been dreamed up in the minds of the therapists ... This is the way in which the "irreal" reality of the therapeutic encounter is produced ... Balint says that the Kleinians have developed "a very characteristic,

> though somewhat peculiar, 'mad' language, but nevertheless the patients learn to adopt this language if it is consistently applied". "As a result of the interaction between a consistent analyst and his conforming patient," Balint says, "an atmosphere is created in which certain events will inevitably happen". (Rose, 1991)

There are many other examples in groups where an inquiring consultant creates an atmosphere of engaged creative inquiry, by taking a different stance. Tavistock clinical group work fails to account for this phenomena adequately. This is the critical lack in the work of psychoanalysis. If you remove the "big other" of the omnipotent consultant on behalf of the authoritative system, the dynamics change. Of course, other forces can step into this space (lots of small brothers and sisters), but in contemporary society many examples exist of project groups and self-managed teams operating successfully. This is not to say that psychoanalytically informed group-work is wrong; it is extremely useful. They are like a hothouse, increasing certain phenomena that allow us to learn important things about ourselves as individuals, groups, and organisations. The mistake is to account for the phenomena that arise in them, and to universalise this to all groups and organisations. In the remnant group we found ourselves working in a context whereby the collective takes responsibility and acts with maturity, creating a greater possibility of non-persecutory and non-dependent, reflexive experience to occur. As a Quaker I experience this when worshiping, we call it a "gathered meeting". It is the contemplative experience of being still within a collective where group dynamics are minimised and creativity emerges due to a lack of anxiety. We created something of this in the remnant collective, without planning to do so.

As we settled into accepting and enjoying our collective experience, and we accepted the name of "the Remnants", I shared my thoughts that from the Judaic-Christian tradition a remnant community is one that survives a disaster holding onto the truth. It is the faithful remnant left over from the persecutory disaster. I explained how the early Quakers in the 1650s experienced themselves as a remnant community, faithfully waiting for inspiration and to discern their experience before acting.

The remnants spent the whole of the inter-group event together, sending no expeditions outside but feeling engaged in the system, welcoming visitors to hear their preoccupations and stories. We fell in love with ourselves a little, but this was mostly because our journey was with a fellow group of travellers, who were convivial; we liked each other, and we were all doing something new for ourselves and it was refreshing. Falling in love a little is an important aspect of community building. Remnant groups (as other groups) need to have love, hope, and faith if they are not to turn into fundamentalist aggressors. Each group requires some ego functioning, and a dollop of narcissism, and we had ours, but self-effacing humour was abundant, there were no flights into grandiose fantasy, and we didn't experience aggression to the outside but enjoyed our encounters with "the other" as they enriched us and reflected back to us our journey as we tried to explain ourselves to them. This is perhaps another learning for group relations, utilising the positive transference. Staff members at group relations conferences are often loved by the membership, but they go through a kind of perverse journey; withholding at first, making aggressive interventions and creating dependency and regression, before a kind word/smile is offered to the beleaguered group who at this stage are in awe of the consultants' power and grateful for the crumbs of kindness that are offered.

Being still, we became calm, a gentle humour and acceptance of difference occurred, and we shared previous group relations experiences of being very active and restless; contrasting this with our current state, most of us were previously often leaders of groups. (My particular default position is a restless "nomad" where I tend to lead from the boundary, wandering between groups). We shared here and now experience, too, all surprised at how much systemic experience we gained from being still at the centre. The remnants finished the exploratory event as we had started, together sitting contemplatively in the same space, having had a rich conference experience, a bonding experience and a thoughtful and creative experience.

I will now explore the meaning of a remnant community from theology and Quaker experience to shed new light on group relations experience.

Remnants and Quakers

Theological understandings of remnant communities

A remnant community is one that is left over after a catastrophe. It is those who have escaped a disaster and are able to continue community life (Porter, 1993) The catastrophe can be a natural disaster (Noah's flood) or caused by human conflict (the destruction of the temple and the exiled community). The catastrophe is usually interpreted as God's divine retribution for a community that has lived sinfully and unfaithfully. The remnants are saved by grace and carry the faith and hope for the future.

Some examples of remnants from theology are:

Noah and his family were a remnant of a divine judgment in the flood (Genesis 6: 5–8; Genesis 7: 1–23).

Lot was when Sodom was destroyed (Genesis 18: 17–33; Genesis 19: 1–29); Jacob's family in Egypt (Genesis 45:7); Elijah and the 7,000 faithful followers of the Lord (1 Kings 19: 17–18); and Israelites going into captivity (Ezekiel 12: 1–16). They were survivors because the Lord chose to show mercy to those who had believed steadfastly in Him and had been righteous in their lives.

Amos: About 750 BC the prophet Amos found that many people in Israel believed that God would protect all of them and their institutions. With strong language he tore down their mistaken ideas (Amos 3: 12–15; Amos 5: 2–3, Amos 5: 18–20; Amos 6: 1–7; Amos 9: 1–6). Divine judgment would be poured out on all Israel. He corrected the tenet that everyone would live happily and prosper (Amos 9:10) with the doctrine that only a few would survive and rebuild the nation (Amos 9: 8–9; Amos 9: 11–15). This new life could be realised if one and all would repent, turn to the Lord, and be saved (Amos 5: 4–6; Amos 5: 14–15).

Isaiah: The remnant doctrine was so important to Isaiah that he named one of his sons Shear-Jashub, meaning "a remnant shall return" (Isaiah 7:3). The faithful would survive the onslaughts of the Assyrian army (Isaiah 4: 2–6; Isaiah 12: 1–6) as illustrated by the remarkable deliverance of the few people in Jerusalem from the siege of the city by the Assyrians (Isaiah 36–38).

Cited from http://www.biblereferenceguide.com/keywords/remnant.html (accessed in July 2010).

In the post-exilic period, the Qumran community (and other dissidents) also saw themselves as the true remnant. In Christian theology, St Paul identified Jews who followed Christ as the remnant of Israel "chosen by grace" (Romans 11:15), and in Revelations a remnant is predicted to survive persecution and be taken to heaven (144,000 people).

To summarise: Theologically, a remnant community juxtaposes conflicting perspectives: mercy and hope versus punishment and despair. God has passed his judgment on a sinful people and, at the same time, shows his mercy, preserving a small faithful community as the hope for the future.

The remnant community is both a passive and active community. Passive in their obedience to a punitive God, waiting patiently, often under persecutory conditions, for a sign of redemption; and active as God's agents in the world. Their task is both to wait and to act, and they interpret the divine signs to know how to proceed in any given situation.

Those that have been saved by grace hold a continuity perspective. There is a backward view holding the best of tradition and also remembering the catastrophe and sin, and a forward trajectory of holding the hope for the future, their task to build the "New Jerusalem". Another important aspect of a remnant community is that God and truth sides with the minority over the majority. The remnant community represents the marginalised and "the exception".

From a Lacanian psychoanalytic perspective, a remnant can represent the truth that is unseeable, and found in the lack. Lacan's "object petit a" is the leftover, a surplus (that is always produced). This leftover, the remnant, represents an imaginary part-object external to ourselves (Lacan, 1964). As Žižek points out, the truth from this perspective is not found through excavating deep within ourselves; it is found outside of ourselves in the left- over surplus. It is the lack, the "object petit a", the unobtainable desire that we seek in the other, and it is here we find subjective truth (Žižek, 2003).

So a remnant from a Lacanian perspective represents the desire of the unknowable other (God, in the case of religious remnants), and to secular society it represents a truth effect, like an interpretation. A remnant sits outside, in its minority, often persecuted or excluded by the majority, holding hope and truth for future generations, provoking discomfort in wider society, acting as a sign, a mirror reflecting to society its actions and failings back to itself, refusing the hegemony of the present.

An example would be the Amish people, a remnant of the past but holding a truth for all of society regarding the future. Their symbolic sign is that there will be no future without rediscovering the importance of community over rampant individualism, without values that reach beyond greed, wealth and market capitalism, and the need for more simple and sustainable living (Western, 2000). The green movement is catching up on their truth of centuries past.

Quakers

The Quakers considered themselves a remnant people, a minority holding the truth in a fallen world. They were a "despised people" in the mid seventeenth century, radicals who challenged head on the hegemonic church and contemporary cultural standards. They felt called to act, to redeem a sinful world, a world of inequity, sin, and injustice. They fought enemies with their weapons based on their spiritual ethics that hold today: pacifism, equality, plainness (simple living), and truth.

Like our remnant group, the Quakers came into being both through their own acts but also through others naming them. "Quakers" was a derogatory term used to mock them because in their silent worship they would tremble before God. Quakers emerged from a vacuum caused by the failed attempts of radical groups, such as the Levellers, the Diggers, and the Ranters during the English Civil War, to bring about radical change. Let down, and put down, by Oliver Cromwell (himself once a radical), despondent radicals became "seekers", disparate groups of people who had fought and lost and were waiting for God to show them a sign. These were people in despair, waiting for salvation, and from these seekers emerged the Quakers. George Fox (founding Quaker) and other radical preachers had gone through personal despair, finding no relief from conventional religion, yet they discovered that through waiting and opening themselves to experience, God could speak to their personal condition directly. They discovered an experiential spirituality; they read the scriptures as words of liberation and experienced direct mystical spirituality that freed both men and women alike. They preached that no professional preacher was necessary, that God himself would teach his people directly, and they would rid themselves of legalistic and ritualistic forms of religion. Anyone could experience God and, furthermore, they believed in a universal deity, "that of God in everyone", overthrowing the Calvinistic belief that only a chosen few would be saved as "the elect". They claimed that even those (such as American indigenous Indians) who had never heard of Christ, had the seed of God within them.

This radical mystical teaching also contained the embryonic seeds of the more democratic and egalitarian society we have today. They believed all were equal under God, and women preached alongside men. (This was totally radical and threatening in 1650, before the idea of women's equality barely existed, and in contrast to the struggle for women's emancipation that continues in other churches today). What set Quakers apart was how they enacted the future in the present. They created an egalitarian structure for their own spiritual ordering, which has survived 350 years. The Religious Society of Friends (Quakers) is run without hierarchy, with all decisions taking place under spiritual consensus. There are no paid or professional clergy; anyone can come to meetings of worship and minister (speak to the congregants) if moved to do so. They have no written creeds, believing that words cannot capture the spiritual truth, only that you can experience it. Their meetings are of silent worship without any ritual. Sitting in silence, they wait to be moved by the spirit, and anyone can speak if thus moved.

The key findings from doctoral research on the Quakers were that their minority status as a remnant people helped them think independently. They were banned from public office and education, and they created a "Quaker Hedge", keeping them distant from wider society, which enabled them to find a space to think, away from social norms and conventions. This was supplemented by their contemplative worship form and their business method, both based on silent waiting and equality. Waiting in silence and giving everybody the space to think, to speak, and to receive wisdom from others (and the divine, if you believe in the transcendent) creates an excellent individual and collective thinking space.

From this emerged many social innovations. Famed for their honest trading, they became successful business people and used their influence to transform society. In 1673 they published the first anti-slavery pamphlet and campaigned to ban slavery everywhere, with John Woolman being a very influential figure. Elizabeth Fry was famed for prison reform, and the Cadbury and Rowntree families for improving urban working conditions. The first mental hospital in Britain (the Retreat) was founded by William Tuke, and more recently the British Quakers were the first church to accept gay marriage. In my doctoral research I described how Quakers' organising form and structure and deep values had enabled them to survive for so long when other "sects" of their time had all died out and how, as a remnant community founded on the idea of waiting in silence, they created maternal and paternal containers that allowed them to transform themselves internally as a religious movement and to innovate externally to save themselves from what seemed like certain destruction at different historical periods.

The Quaker experience offers a mirror to my Belgirate remnant experience in that to wait can be the most active and progressive thing to do. Both offer a template of a Remnant community that perhaps speaks to the wider group relations community, which I will explore in the conclusion.

Conclusion

A remnant then is not only a left-over, but it can also be an active cell, a social container, something that holds onto the spiritual or subjective truth when others follow fashion, modern trends, the normative path. In this spirit of inquiry, we should not dismiss religious fundamentalists quite so quickly, as they may hold opinions that are contrary to modern sympathies, yet beyond some perverse attributes they may also be a sign to modernity, warning it against its loss of community, of spiritual values, of runaway consumerism, rampant individualism, and sexual promiscuity, that reveals a pseudo-freedom and the instrumentalisation of life itself. Where love becomes reduced to a sexual commodity, friendship to a transaction, and the good life is lost.

The Quakers, and a theological perspective of remnant communities, offer a new view on our Belgirate experience. The experience of being a remnant group of sitting and waiting was informative and inspiring. It unleashed a truth effect in myself and others. Learning from this, I would suggest that the learning of group relations can no longer take place within the same co-ordinates, the same form. I would argue that the way forward for group relations is to rethink itself (and this is more than tinkering with redesigns, adding bits here and there) and to consider the metaphor of becoming a remnant, resisting becoming a conformist movement. A remnant stands outside the social norm, it creates a social container for experiential learning and action; as a minority it holds on to a truth that is lost in the mania of everyday life. The group relations truth can only be released and have an effect through individual and collective experiential learning. A truth that requires generational upheaval and innovation that is dynamic and not static. A truth that looks to the past retains continuity alongside change and carries the hope for the future. A remnant community in exile from the hegemony of the market and capitalistic social norms, challenging the knowledge-based learning assumptions of university and consultancies, group relations, like the Quakers, refuses to depart from experiential learning, from individual interpretation of experience. A remnant people challenge the status quo; to act as a remnant means to have faith in a belief system or some core values. As I have been writing this conclusion I have wondered what these core values might be for group relations? I will not try to answer this but leave it to others.

Group relations without an ethical and radical agenda is an empty form. Group relations provides potential space. This can be taken up with repetition, safe learning, creating an experience of community, a self-satisfying place where members and staff leave glowing. Or it can be a potential space for innovation, for experimentation and struggle for ideas that might help promote individuals to act differently, to create more ethical and sustainable organisations and a better world. To be a remnant is to be a bridge from the past to the future. In group relations terms, it means to carry a history of experiential learning from the organisational dynamics of the 1950s, a modernist period, with structure, clear roles, and hierarchy, into the post-industrial/post-modern period of the twenty-first century embracing the network society (Castells, 2001) and new organisational forms, and engaging with the multitude (Hardt & Negri, 2001).

Žižek cites Lenin's claim that "We should begin from the beginning again":

> This is Lenin at his Beckettian best ... His conclusion—to begin from the beginning—makes it clear that he is not talking about merely slowing down and fortifying what has already been achieved, but about descending back to the starting point: one should begin *from the beginning*, not from the place that one succeeded in reaching in the previous effort. (Žižek, 2009)

Perhaps this is what I am speaking about when I talk of a remnant group relations. Group relations explores organisational dynamics through the study of human experience. To "begin again at the beginning" means to wait with hope, to glimpse a vision of the future, and then to begin to create it. Leaving behind modernist notions of studying experience using scientific methods, we can then find "post-modern" ways to study human experience.

Our remnant group sat, and we were surprised at what we quietly discovered. We stayed *in situ* and let "the truth rise up within us", to paraphrase the early Quakers. Moving from a task focus to non-task, and from movement to stillness, we found ourselves transported from "dependency to autonomy" (Miller, 1993).

References

Balint, M. (1968). *The Basic Fault: Therapeutic Aspects of Regression*. London: Tavistock.

Berardi, F. (2009). *The Soul at Work: From Alienation to Automony*. Los Angeles: Semiotext.

Bion, W. R. (1961). *Experiences in Groups*. London: Tavistock.

Bollas, C. (1987). *The Shadow of the Object: Psychoanalysis of the Unthought Known*. London: FAB.

Castells, M. (2001). *The Rise of the Network Society*. Oxford: Wiley- Blackwell.

Hardt, M. & Negri, A. (2001). *Empire*. Massachusetts: Harvard University Press.

Lacan, J. (1964). *Seminar XI: The Four Fundamental Concepts of Psychoanalysis* (Alan Sheridan, Trans.) (1978). New York: W. W. Norton.

Latour, B. (2004). *Politics of Nature: How to Bring the Sciences into Democracy*. Cambridge, MA: Harvard University Press.

Law, J. (1993). *Organizing Modernity: Social Ordering and Social Theory*. Oxford: Wiley-Blackwell.

Lenin, V. I. (1966). Notes of a publicist (published posthumously in Pravda, 16 April 1924). In: *V. I. Lenin Collected Works* (Vol. 33) 4th English Edition, Moscow: Progress Publishers.

Miller, E. J. (1989). *The "Leicester" Model*. TIHR Occasional Paper No. 10. London: Tavistock Publications.

Miller, E. J. (1993). *From Dependency to Autonomy*. London: Free Association Books. Porter, J. R. (1993). Remnants. In: B. Metzger & M. Coogan (Eds.), *The Oxford Companion to the Bible* (pp. 645–646). New York & Oxford: Oxford University Press.

Rose, N. (1991). Power and subjectivity: Critical history and Psychology. http://www.academyanalyticarts.org/rose1.htm (last accessed 25 March, 2011)

Rose, N. & Miller, M. (1994). On therapeutic authority: Psychoanalytic expertise under advanced liberalism. *History of the Human Sciences, 7*: 29–64.

Western, S. (2000). Plain living—Provocative thoughts. *The Friend* (Quaker Journal). 8 September 2000.

Western, S. (2005). A critical analysis of leadership: Overcoming fundamentalist tendencies. PhD Thesis, Lancaster University Management School, UK.

Western, S. (2008). *Leadership: A Critical Text*. Sage: London.

Žižek, S. (2003). *The Puppet and the Dwarf: The Perverse Core of Christianity*. Cambridge, MA: MIT Press.

Žižek, S. (2009). How to begin from the beginning. *New Left Review, 57*.

Note

1. The Quaker experience of sitting in a silent group, and understanding individuals' ministry (speaking to the group) as a group-as-a-whole process. They waited collectively for "the seed within to rise up" before speaking (in secular terms the seed would be the unconscious—in spiritual terms the divine). Quakers also have an institutional relationship—local groups feed into regional groups who feed into a whole. The final authority for Quakers is Yearly Meeting whereby all members are invited and a large group forms (of up to 1,000), waiting in silence to discern business and strategic decisions that are made through spiritual consensus. This truly is a large group dynamic; as in a group relations event, anybody is invited to speak and the whole meeting reaches agreement after a period of silent reflection. See, in particular, John Rickman's work on Northfield and psychoanalytic groups and his Quaker influence on Bion (Western, 2005).

INDEX

For Product Safety Concerns and Information please contact our EU representative GPSR@taylorandfrancis.com Taylor & Francis Verlag GmbH, Kaufingerstraße 24, 80331 München, Germany

Batch number: 10726007

Printed by Printforce, the Netherlands